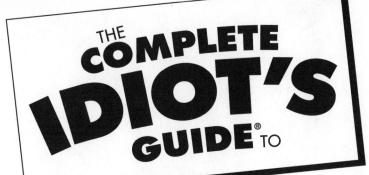

THE
COMPLETE IDIOT'S GUIDE® TO

Enhancing Your Social IQ

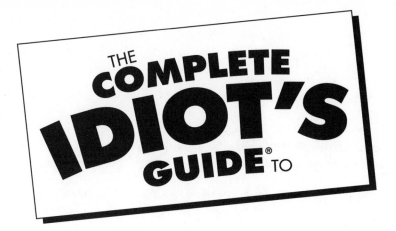

THE
COMPLETE
IDIOT'S
GUIDE® TO

Enhancing Your Social IQ

by Gregory P. Korgeski, Ph.D.

ALPHA

A member of Penguin Group (USA) Inc.

ALPHA BOOKS

Published by the Penguin Group

Penguin Group (USA) Inc., 375 Hudson Street, New York, New York 10014, USA

Penguin Group (Canada), 90 Eglinton Avenue East, Suite 700, Toronto, Ontario M4P 2Y3, Canada (a division of Pearson Penguin Canada Inc.)

Penguin Books Ltd., 80 Strand, London WC2R 0RL, England

Penguin Ireland, 25 St. Stephen's Green, Dublin 2, Ireland (a division of Penguin Books Ltd.)

Penguin Group (Australia), 250 Camberwell Road, Camberwell, Victoria 3124, Australia (a division of Pearson Australia Group Pty. Ltd.)

Penguin Books India Pvt. Ltd., 11 Community Centre, Panchsheel Park, New Delhi—110 017, India

Penguin Group (NZ), 67 Apollo Drive, Rosedale, North Shore, Auckland 1311, New Zealand (a division of Pearson New Zealand Ltd.)

Penguin Books (South Africa) (Pty.) Ltd., 24 Sturdee Avenue, Rosebank, Johannesburg 2196, South Africa

Penguin Books Ltd., Registered Offices: 80 Strand, London WC2R 0RL, England

Publisher: *Marie Butler-Knight*
Editorial Director: *Mike Sanders*
Senior Managing Editor: *Billy Fields*
Senior Acquisitions Editor: *Paul Dinas*
Development Editor: *Jennifer Moore*
Senior Production Editor: *Janette Lynn*
Copy Editor: *Jennifer Connolly*

Cartoonist: *Shannon Wheeler*
Cover Designer: *Bill Thomas*
Book Designer: *Trina Wurst*
Indexer: *Tonya Heard*
Layout: *Brian Massey*
Proofreader: *John Etchison*

Contents at a Glance

Contents

Introduction

There's a stereotype that says people become shrinks because they are trying to solve their own problems. Speaking for myself, I'd have to say "guilty as charged." Especially if by "my own problems," I mean my adolescent questions about how to function in the social world.

When I was a kid, there were not many shrinks around, especially compared to the glutted market of today. Nor were there many places a kid could go to learn about that really complicated, and really important topic of dealing with people. It wasn't taught in any of my courses in high school or junior high (God knows, it should have been!), and I think all of us kids kind of fumbled along trying to figure out the biggies in life: making friends, dating, sex, or just not getting laughed at in the gym or beat up by the goons after school. And I know I wasn't alone when I say I fretted a lot about how to manage all those things!

My saving moment came when I discovered some book (it's title now long forgotten) on psychology. It was a pretty Freudian book, which was fascinating and new to me. But mainly, it seemed to have at least some of the answers I'd been seeking about how and why people acted as they did. That launched a lifetime of reading—from old self-help books like Dale Carnegie's *How to Win Friends and Influence People* (which is still a gem) to the very first American "self-help" book, by my adolescent hero: Benjamin Franklin's *Autobiography*. (I say more about Ben's ideas later.) Eventually this fascination with finding the answers to the challenges of the social world led to a career as a psychologist, and to many years of trying to help other people, whether in the therapy office or consulting in schools, seminars, or the corporate world, to master the many challenges of dealing with others.

Along the way there have been more books, more theories. But recently, our understanding of how people function together has been growing dramatically with new discoveries in the field that is being called "social intelligence." It's that topic that is the subject of this *Complete Idiot's Guide*. (And I know you're not an idiot—especially if you recognize that this topic is one of the most important you can ever master.)

So what is social intelligence? In a nutshell, it's that combination of skills, attitudes, and insights that help people interact effectively with others. Whether it's playing with other children in preschool, making friends in high school, flirting and launching a romance, enriching your marriage, or dealing with the office politics and leadership challenges of a corporate job, you rely on your social intelligence (or "SI" in this book). And it turns out that in many ways, social intelligence can make all the difference between social, and even career, success and a lifetime of frustration and disappointment.

This book is designed as a practical introduction to social intelligence. After discussing what SI is and how it develops and can be enhanced, we'll explore ways you can nurture and enhance your SI skills (for much of SI is really a set of skills that you can sharpen) in a variety of life settings. More specifically:

Part 1, "Social Intelligence 101," explores the new science of social intelligence. We'll talk about what social intelligence is and how it differs from IQ. We'll also explore the four main dimensions of SI that will be the organizing core of this book: knowing yourself (tuning in to your emotions and managing them), tuning in to others, making contact with people, and the caring and compassionate attitudes that are really an essential part of SI. Then we'll talk about how social intelligence develops in people, plus we devote a chapter to the best ways to actively increase your social intelligence skills.

In **Part 2, "Enhance Your Socially Intelligent Self!"** we explore some key dimensions to social functioning and how you can make the most of the raw material that's you. So we talk about extraversion/introversion (how outgoing or "wallflower-y" you are—and why both are okay!), assertiveness, and managing shyness and social anxiety. Then we explore the benefits of effective social functioning. We discuss developing your empathy for others and how to increase your capacity for intimacy, and discuss managing the "dark side" of human relationships in our chapter on coping with toxic connections.

Then it's time to get into specific types of relationships. In **Part 3, "Personal Relationships and Social Intelligence,"** we explore friendships, romance, sex, marriage and committed relationships, and children. In each chapter, we'll discuss some of the most recent and cutting-edge findings on what makes relationships work, gleaned from psychology, brain research, and wherever else I could find good stuff to share with you.

Finally, in **Part 4, "Social Intelligence in the Workplace,"** we'll explore the ways social intelligence skills can help you survive and thrive in your career. Whether you're wondering how to connect with peers in the next cubicle (or the guy who's shackled to you while you bust rocks for the Highway Department), managing a single employee or a corporation, or dealing with clients, office politics, or conflicts in the boardroom, social intelligence skills will be your key to success.

Quizzes

This Idiot's Guide is designed to be a practical workbook, not just a book you read then put on the shelf. In addition to lots of practical tips, I've included a quiz in each chapter (except in Part 1) that was designed to help you think about your own strengths and weaknesses in the social intelligence arena. I do need to say something about the limitations of these: they're not formal psychological tests, and so have not been extensively researched, field-tested on thousands of subjects, or demonstrated to be scientific. What they are, are the kinds of "for example" questions that you and I might use if we were having a consultation to explore your concerns about a work or relationship situation. Say you wanted to know how introverted you are. I might ask a few things, such as "Well, do you enjoy parties, or find that they tire you out?" We know from research that introverts do tend to feel worn out more quickly in highly stimulating social situations, which is why I'd ask that.

My advice: take the quizzes, add up your scores, and use the results as a rough guide to thinking about your own social functioning. I'd also jot down some notes, self-observations, or key incidents that might help you make sense of the patterns you have noticed in yourself. And of course, if you really feel the need for some official psych tests and professional input, you ought to consult with a local expert such as a psychologist or life coach, who will be able to do a more formal assessment. (See Appendix B for info on how to find a coach or psychologist.)

Extras

Supplementing the main narrative of *The Complete Idiot's Guide to Enhancing Your Social Intelligence* are two appendixes with further info (readings and web resources), as well as four kinds of "extras" that appear in each chapter and that will give you additional information or insight into our topics. These are:

Caution!

Things you really, really, really want not to do, say, or blunder into while navigating the tricky waters of social life.

SI Tip

Handy ideas, suggestions, or things to try that will enhance your SI or solve little social problems.

Social Science

Cool factoids or additional points, often from the world of psychological or social research, or from history.

def•i•ni•tion

Short explanations of (possibly) unfamiliar terms used in the book.

Acknowledgments

We are the sum of our connections with others. In completing this book—heck, in even starting it—I owe a lot to several people.

First, warm thanks to Dr. Jennifer Lawler for inviting me to co-write this book in the first place. I was sorry that Jennifer, a great writer, editor, and teacher, was not able to co-author this with me, but I owe her a karmic cupcake for much help and support. Thanks, sensei.

Linda Formichelli, freelancer, author, speaker, and teacher extraordinaire, was my next stop in co-author-land. Alas, we also didn't get to continue the project together, but she helped me understand much about CIG books.

I'd also like to thank Marilyn Allen, my accidental agent, for her help and most especially for her support in getting started—and for much moral support and advice along the way.

Paul Dinas has been a great first editor in both senses of the word, and I appreciated his input and flexibility. Thanks are also due to Jennifer Moore for doing a spectacular job of cleaning up my unclarities and errors—a task that is probably akin to trying to rake tiny bits of adjectival and adverbial glass out of a vat of tapioca pudding.

Two colleagues deserve special mention: thanks to Dr. John Fennig for his help finding some resources for readers, and for encouraging comments about the project. And thanks to Dr. Lynn Grodzki, author and personal coach, most recently for resources and links on coaching, but really for flagging and supporting my enthusiasm for writing as a career that it's high time I get around to pursuing full-time.

Special thanks to Stephanie Whitney Payne and Dr. Donald Payne, for support, affection, and much more, including the use of the "writing barn" where some of this was writ. (Thanks also to Steph for helping me understand the quizzes, and to Don for valuable insights that were useful in some of the workplace chapters.)

And most of all, for everything else in life including support, encouragement, and life partnership (and for great expert advice on the childhood chapter), thanks to my wife, Skye.

Trademarks

All terms mentioned in this book that are known to be or are suspected of being trademarks or service marks have been appropriately capitalized. Alpha Books and Penguin Group (USA) Inc. cannot attest to the accuracy of this information. Use of a term in this book should not be regarded as affecting the validity of any trademark or service mark.

Part 1

Social Intelligence 101

The new science of "social intelligence" is giving us a clearer picture of ourselves than we've had in all of recorded history. Everything from the way our brains operate, connecting us with others, processing our feelings and thoughts about each other, to the way we make friends, influence each other, and find happiness in our lives … these are all becoming better understood. In Part 1, we'll explore all these exciting new discoveries, and how you can begin to apply them to your life. Your image of yourself and of others is guaranteed to be dramatically and forever changed by what you're about to read!

What Is Social Intelligence?

In This Chapter

- ◆ A new kind of psychology
- ◆ The elements of SI
- ◆ SI and intelligence
- ◆ SI in action

This is a book about a new field of psychology called "social intelligence," and how it can change your life. In this chapter, you'll find out what social intelligence is, how it's different than IQ, and how social intelligence can help you be a genius where it counts the most—in your relationships in school, at work, and in your personal affairs.

A New Kind of Psychology!

Suppose that one day you opened your newspaper and saw an article about a newly discovered life form. The article said that these creatures looked and acted nearly like humans, except for some odd differences in their behavior and in the way their brains worked. In fact, the article said that they were almost like something from a sci-fi novel—with a new kind of "intelligence."

Instead of being independent individuals, the minds of these creatures could link together in some mysterious way. When placed in brain-scanning machines, each of their brains would respond to things happening to others of their kind. For instance, if one of them threw a rock, the neurons in the other one's brain that controlled "rock throwing" would fire in an *identical way*, even though that one didn't actually throw any rocks!

Further research showed that these creatures were wired from birth to be sensitive to each other's emotions. In fact, they were almost telepathic in their ability to sense what others like them were feeling. From early in life, they built highly accurate working models of others in their minds. They could then use these models like virtual substitutes for the companions they had known, relying on these inner replicas for guidance and as a source of emotional comfort.

The creatures were highly dependent on both physical and emotional contact with others of their kind. Scientists reported that attempts to raise the creatures in incubators from birth had failed: they would actually die if they didn't get enough contact from others of their species—even if they were given enough food, water, and physical comforts.

The creatures sometimes behaved like swarms of insects or schools of fish—they would all behave in exactly the same ways, go to the same places, think and behave alike—with no conscious awareness or control over the fact they were doing it!

Finally, they were programmed to respond automatically, and powerfully, to discomfort and pain in others of their species. So much so that they would sacrifice their lives to spare other members. If they tried to go it alone and only take care of themselves, they were more likely to get sick and die.

If you had just read this story in the paper over your morning coffee, you might want to see one of these creatures yourself, right? No problem. Just look in a mirror!

Social intelligence is what makes you one of those creatures I've been describing. So what in the world is social intelligence? And how is it different than any other intelligence?

Social Intelligence Defined

Social intelligence (which I'm going to sometimes abbreviate as SI) is a term that scientists have been using a lot recently, though the term has been around for nearly a century. It refers to the parts of our intelligence that help humans relate to other people. Several kinds of abilities are lumped together as being part of SI.

> **Social Science**
>
> The term "social intelligence" was first used in modern times by psychologist E. L. Thorndike in 1920. He argued that human intelligence has three main parts: the ability to "understand and manage" ideas, objects, and people. Social intelligence, said Thorndike, included knowing how to understand and deal with other people and to act wisely in relationships.

For instance, SI includes the ability to recognize feelings in yourself and other people, to understand what's going on in a social situation, and to connect with others. It includes knowing how to talk with people you know and don't, knowing how to interact both verbally and nonverbally, and to size up the best way to respond to a person in a new situation. It also includes attitudes that help people do well, such as empathy and compassion for others.

Since scientists learn more almost daily about the social part of human minds, researchers caution that our understanding of what makes up SI is still evolving. Different experts list different talents and ways of thinking and behaving as being part of social smarts. But roughly speaking, there are four main groups of skills, or skill sets, that capture most of the SI discoveries. They are ...

- Knowing yourself
- Being sensitive to others
- Making connections
- Caring

In this book, I focus on enhancing your social smarts in these four areas. For now, though, let's take a closer look at each of these social intelligence skills.

Knowing Yourself

Knowing yourself means more than being able to recite your address and Social Security number. If you want to really "get" what's going on with people, you have to start with yourself. What kind of person are you? What's your personal style—outgoing social butterfly or quiet, homebody hobbit? How comfortable are you in social situations? Are you good at friendships, and if so, what kind? Finally, are you able to tell when you're getting provoked or teed off by someone or excited (with those little palpitations) by a possible romantic partner? Do you know what your own feelings are? A key part of social intelligence is understanding the first person you encounter every morning—yourself!

SI Tip

It's hard to "get" someone's emotional state unless you know what that feeling is like! Develop the habit of asking yourself how, and what, you're feeling, and you'll be more in tune with others as well.

Being Sensitive to Others

Tuning in to others, and knowing how to read them emotionally, is the second skill of the socially intelligent. You tune in to people on many channels. You watch their actions, listen to their words, and read their facial expressions and the tones of their voices. The exciting finds of SI science show that most people are more tuned in than they consciously realize: without knowing you do it, you often match the emotions, and even the thoughts of others in your own brain and bodily states.

Social Science

Much information about social intelligence comes from studies of the brain in action, using techniques called "neuroimaging." Neuroimaging techniques include functional magnetic resonance imaging (fMRI) and positron emission tomography ("PET" scans), which show how the brain reacts to social interactions.

Connecting

Connecting involves communicating with, and actively influencing, other people. You may assume that you do most of your communicating with words, but that's only the top layer. Your tone of voice, the ways you move, your eye contact, even your appearance and hygiene and the undetectable scents your body gives off, are part of the mix. And just as there are a jillion ways to communicate with others to get the results you want, there are a jillion other ways that you can miscommunicate and mess things up! The wrong word, too intense eye contact, or an offhand remark in an e-mail can make a mess of a relationship, or even of your life.

> **Caution!**
>
> Don't confuse social intelligence with being good at manipulating people. While some people are, indeed, pretty good at using social skills to con or manipulate others, many of their wins are often short-lived. People respond most positively to genuinely caring and compassionate acts by others, and often figure out when you're really in it for yourself.

Caring

Caring about others, responding emotionally to their distress or their excitement, wanting the best for each other—why would all that fit into a definition of "intelligence"? It fits because people are actually hard-wired to care. Research has shown that humans have a deeply ingrained need both for connection and to respond to each other's distress.

This actually turns out to be highly intelligent of us, if you see intelligence as including skills that give a species a survival advantage. As a species, we have probably survived and thrived exactly because we are so driven to take care of each other: to share knowledge, food, shelter, and other resources; to share our blankets on cold nights and to make sure that even the kid in the back row got the handout. All this sharing and caring adds up to a powerful survival advantage for the caring species.

In other words, if knowing how to set the clock on your VCR counts as intelligence, why wouldn't you also count knowing how to make sure you care enough to keep your child alive in the wintertime?

The Science of "SI"

Scientific discoveries in *psychology* are changing how we understand what it means to be human. It is clearer than ever before that our "social" selves and our "intelligent" selves are in many ways the same thing. We are "socially intelligent" beings.

def•i•ni•tion

> **Psychology** is the scientific study of behavior. Psychologists do research on every facet of human and animal behavior, from how the brain and nervous system operate to studying how we feel, act, and think in every part of life, including work, play, relationships, and love. Psychologists also do "applied" work such as counseling, psychotherapy, consulting, and teaching.

Psychology is showing that we are in many ways different than how we have been taught, in most of our cultures, to view ourselves. For instance:

◆ Brain researchers say that the human nervous system is an open system, meaning that when two or more of us gather together, we literally link our minds together as we communicate feelings and thoughts back and forth—nonverbally, nonconsciously, and at a speed that rivals the fastest computers!

◆ We have mirror neurons in our brains that unconsciously respond to the actions or feelings of others around us by mirroring exactly what their brains are doing. If you perform an action or express a feeling and I watch you do it, my brain will fire the same neurons that it would if it were me doing those things. Some scientists think this is the basis not just for learning how to do things by observing, but for empathy with each other.

◆ Far from being born as rugged individuals, babies are tuned in at birth to make, and need, social contact. They communicate their feelings and needs, and mothers (and dads and others) are pre-programmed to respond. And if they are deprived of social contact, many babies will not survive—even if fed, watered, and changed regularly.

◆ Many of the most important practical problems of life turn out to be social functioning problems, not problems that depend on high IQs alone. High-SI people, even with less formal education or school smarts, may be more successful both in personal relationships and in career and creative pursuits than conventionally smart individuals.

> **Social Science**
>
> People raised in different cultures often have different notions of how independent or connected they should be. In the United States, for example, people are often raised to see themselves as rugged individuals who don't depend much on others. In many other cultures around the world, that would be considered weird, impolite, or even crazy!

The list of discoveries goes on and on. In a nutshell, our need to connect with others, to understand and sense what they are feeling, and to communicate with each other are all part of being human. Even if you see yourself as a grumpy loner, you are far more social than you realize. We are designed to be social beings.

And a big part of being so social is social intelligence. While we all need and rely on others, some of us are better at it than others. And it turns out, much of your happiness and success in life may depend on how well you develop and use your social smarts.

IQ? Or SI?

"He's a real Einstein! He should go far in life!"

Once upon a time, people assumed that the big key to success in life was to be super smart. A genius. A real Einstein. Good grades in school, and most of all, high scores on an *IQ* test, would be your guaranteed ticket to riches, fame, and love.

For much of the past century, psychologists focused on the importance of cognitive intelligence (which was generally just called "intelligence" or "IQ") to understand what made us successful in life. The idea of social smarts was mostly ignored until the last few years. Instead, we studied the parts of intelligence that help you succeed in schoolwork.

def•i•ni•tion

IQ stands for Intelligence Quotient. Originally, it was calculated by dividing a person's "mental age" by their "chronological age," times 100. So if your scores were as good as the average 12-year old's, and you were 10, your IQ would be … hmm … (12 ÷ 10 = 1.2) × 100, or 120 (which is pretty smart!)

This ignoring of SI by the experts may now seem like a big mistake. But looking back, this stress on cognitive IQ was understandable. For one thing, it solved some important problems amazingly well. In fact, IQ testing proved to be a lifesaver at a critical point in history, as you'll learn in the next section. For another, it does help manage and predict some pretty important things about a person.

The New Secret Weapon: IQ Testing!

It was one of the largest mass mobilizations in U.S. history. The country was about to enter the Great European War, which would later be called World War I. America needed an army, and needed it fast!

The problem was that not everybody in an army carries a rifle. An army needs people for a thousand different jobs—cooks, file clerks, strategic planners, truck repair experts, and so on. How do you know who will be able to do what kinds of work? And how do you slot a zillion guys and gals into the right jobs, and do it fast? That was one of the urgent problems the Army faced at the beginning of the war.

Just in the nick of time, science arrived with an answer: a newfangled notion called the Intelligence Test. New soldiers were given a quick, pencil and paper test of something called their IQ. These new IQs gave the military instant intel on how well recruits could handle different jobs. For the first time in history, it was possible to rapidly assign large numbers of people to jobs based on whether they could understand the job and do it well.

Caution!

Beware the "self-fulfilling prophecy!" Researchers found that telling teachers that some kids had lower IQs resulted in poorer test scores and school performance, even though the kids' *real* IQs weren't low! It showed how beliefs that disadvantaged students aren't bright can have a damaging effect on their progress.

The IQ test was a dazzling success, both in helping to win the Great War and back home, in the schools of America. Psychologists kept refining these tests, and teachers began to use the results in order to design the best ways to teach children. And IQs did prove to be pretty good at predicting a lot of things, mostly school and some job success.

IQ testing has also been criticized. For example, equally bright minority students might not do as well on tests designed for white, majority cultures, so the testing was thought to give some students an unfair advantage. Many people also feared that "slotting" someone based on one test score could be harmful—if all your teachers think you're "not as bright as the other kids," they might not give you the same chances to succeed.

But despite these concerns, many experts were sure that a person's IQ was still the best all-round predictor of success in life. After all, IQ scores were great at predicting success in school, and if you did well in school, you'd generally have a great chance of getting a great job, and that was supposedly the key to "making it."

From IQ to SI

In recent years, we are less confident that an IQ score is the be-all and end-all of predicting stuff about people. Scientists have begun to learn more about what your grandmother could have told them a long time ago: that many of the most happy, successful, and long-lived people have something in common that isn't the same thing as IQ. In fact, some "book smart" people are total dolts when it comes to some of the things that really matter in life. Other people, who are not so book smart or good at school-type tasks, may still do great in school, get fantastic jobs, get more promotions, start and succeed at their own businesses, get the best dates, and have happier lives than the Einsteins.

It turns out that if you're good at human relationships, you're likely to do pretty well in life. Because when you're high in *social intelligence*, doors will start to open for you!

Social Intelligence in Action

"Well," you may say, "'social intelligence' sounds nice. But does it really matter as much as you say? *Why* is it more important than a high IQ?"

Excellent question, grasshopper! (And hey, I'd agree that a super high IQ isn't bad to have either!) Let's consider where, and how, social smarts might be useful.

The Power of SI

Did you ever play a role-playing game, such as Dungeons and Dragons? In many such games, your first job is to pick the tools, talents, and helpers or allies you'll need on your big adventure. You might decide you'll need a sword, the ability to see through solid walls, a wand, or a bag of magic beans that could do ... oh, any number of things: blow something up, make a unicorn appear, or turn into nurturing soup if you add water and boil them.

This is also the way you start out in real life. You get some skills, like learning to speak and tie your shoes. You get some resources, like maybe a college fund, or useful words of wisdom from your dad, and maybe his old pocket knife or Zippo. Or you may go to a far-off country with a letter of reference from a boss that will open a few doors for you. And there's always that magical device that can do more things than even Harry Potter's wand: your Visa card!

But what if you could only pick one thing—one tool or talent or personal attribute—that would give you the greatest chance of long-term survival in a real-life adventure? What would it be?

Hmm ... It would have to be something that could help you feel good when you were discouraged or hurt. Something that could help you get the basics taken care of: food, shelter, safety, warmth. Something that might open doors, protect you from enemies, and help you gain friends and allies, especially when the going got rough. Finally, it should be something that you couldn't lose or have stolen from you, or drop overboard during a storm at sea.

When you look at this list, you realize: magic beans can only do so much! (How many unicorns do you really need?) Same for that spectacular laser blaster—once you dispatch one or two Cylons, or use it to accidentally demolish your last can of chili while trying to open it, it's not so useful! And even your Visa card is easy to lose ... and there is that annoying credit limit!

On the other hand, consider some of the powers that come with social intelligence. Running through the elements of SI that I listed previously, imagine all its uses on your great adventure:

Knowing thyself: Remember how Yoda told Luke Skywalker that it's what you "bring into the cave with you" that can do you in? He was right!

You have strong passions and desires and fears. In a tough spot, an "enemy" can use them against you, right? Get you to blow up at the wrong time. Get you to turn and run in terror. Get you to waste your energy on trifles, to wreck your key alliances out of impatience or selfishness. And on and on—most "great adventures" you read about (or see in the movies) hinge on whether the hero or heroine can master their own passions. (Think about it—from Homer's Odysseus through Harry Potter and his friends, self-mastery, especially of those unruly passions and fears, is one key to survival or destruction.)

Tuning in to others: Empaths on Star Trek. Mr. Spock's original mind meld. Spidey's spider sense. Need I say more? Understanding the other person—their feelings, their needs, the things they are trying to communicate—is a key survival skill. Want a real-life example? How about Sacagawea, the Native American woman who guided Lewis and Clark's expedition to safety with her translation skills and understanding of the tribes they encountered? How about that mentor in college or on your first job, who helped you learn the ropes, including who was who and what was going on with other people's agendas? How about that great doctor (or girlfriend or boyfriend) we all want, who knows exactly what's wrong from the look on our faces? Pretty powerful, right?

SI Tip

Most of the time, getting information, support, resources, and even just cut some slack (by someone to whom you owe money, or by that policeman who just caught you drifting through the stop sign) depends more on your ability to connect and communicate than on being smart, wealthy, or well-armed.

Making connections: When you're in the galaxy of Glaxxon and need permission to pass, when you are in the cubicles of Widget Corps and need permission to buy a costly new widget press, or when you're in Target and want a refund, what's the main skill you call on? Right—the ability to connect with someone, to communicate, to win them to your side! Same thing goes for your personal life: if you have that winning smile, that way of talking to someone that inspires confidence and liking, game's over and you (both) win!

Caring: In your role-playing game, it may not be so clear that compassion or caring are important weapons. But think about it: ever see a movie or read a book in which the least caring, or the snottiest and most insensitive person wins? Maybe in the short run, but we all generally prefer to hang with the people who seem really to care about us and others. Selfish, uncaring people lose allies and friends faster than a collie sheds hair in the summertime.

So, in conclusion … in the game of life, what magical power, skill, or tool should you pick? Magic beans? Or social smarts?

I know, I know … maybe social intelligence is more useful than beans in a role-playing game. But in real life, is it truly more useful than Einstein's brains and Paris Hilton's money? How is that possible?

SI in "Real Life"

Let's consider a few more real-life examples, then. (Yes. Cylons aren't really real. Sorry.)

When people are having big problems with many things in life, they may go see a therapist or coach, right? Well, most of the time, the problems that people bring to shrinks and coaches are really about social functioning. And a lot of the work we actually do with people involves helping them to build up their social intelligence.

For example, most therapists have caseloads of clients with problems like these:

- People who keep messing up one romantic relationship after another (and so get more and more lonely, anxious, and depressed).

- Parents who don't know how to talk with their kids (and kids who feel awkward talking to their parents), resulting in school problems, conduct problems, maybe even mood disorders, substance abuse, and deteriorating family functioning and health all around.

- A gifted physician whose work is affected because she seems to have no empathy for her patients (and so, her job is in jeopardy, she is more isolated, stress rises, she gets depressed, or starts abusing medications …).

- A junior-high student who gets teased and bullied by other kids, no matter what he tries (and so … you get the point).

And the list goes on. And on.

And every one of these is at least partially, at root, a social intelligence problem.

On the other hand, consider these folks:

◆ A janitor in a small town whom everyone knows and likes, whether he's visiting the restaurant on Main Street or stopping by to see if someone is feeling good after she hurt her ankle.

◆ A high school student who seems to have a ton of friends, even though she's neither athletic nor stupendously attractive—there's something about her that gets her elected class president every year, and a prom date, and into a great college.

◆ A journalist who has a knack for sitting down next to anyone at a lunch counter and asking them how it's going, and so gets perfect strangers to open up completely about their lives, their work, and their opinions.

◆ A nurse who is super-gifted at putting frightened children at ease before surgery—so much so that her former patients still send her holiday cards years later!

What's the difference? It's obvious, right? These folks have skills, style, something that helps people feel comfortable around them. So folks seek them out, rely on them … but also help them out in return.

In a nutshell, they are all experts in social intelligence!

Social Intelligence and Health

Good social intelligence is not just useful for work and romance. It even helps you live longer because it turns out that people who have the best relationships are probably best able to avoid serious illnesses, and to cope better if they do get sick.

For example, healthy relationships have been linked with …

◆ Reduced risk of cardiovascular problems, such as heart attacks and high blood pressure.

◆ Better immune system functioning, and greater immunity from minor infections, such as colds.

◆ Lower levels of stress hormones such as cortisol, which in turn affect overall bodily functioning (including cardiac risk, diabetes-proneness, and even cognitive or brain functioning).

◆ Fewer psychological problems such as depression, anxiety, and even post-traumatic stress disorder.

In short, both physically, mentally, emotionally, and in terms of life success, you're likely to be in far more excellent shape if you've got pretty good social intelligence going for you!

And the best news of all is that unlike conventional IQ, it's quite possible to enhance and develop your SI skills.

Which is what this book is all about.

The Least You Need to Know

♦ Your IQ may predict your school success and your ability to master intellectual subjects, but your social intelligence may be a better predictor of life success.

♦ Social intelligence includes knowing yourself, being good at reading others and making connections, and genuinely caring for others.

♦ Social intelligence skills work by helping you communicate, emotionally click with others, and work together to accomplish both your and their goals, whether these are social or work goals.

♦ Improved social functioning is likely to help you achieve better short- and long-term physical health and survival.

♦ Unlike traditional IQ, you can do things to increase your social intelligence abilities a great deal.

How We Learn to Be SI

In This Chapter

- ◆ SI takes a lifetime
- ◆ How babies get socially smart
- ◆ Relationships and your brain
- ◆ How to get wisdom

As I said in the previous chapter, the goal of this book is to help you understand and develop your social intelligence. But before I leap into suggestions for boosting your social smarts, it may help to review a few basics.

Think of it this way: If I were your coach, being paid to help you improve your athletic performance (you know, for that *Tour de France* thing you plan to win next year?), I'd start by making sure you understood some fundamentals: how your muscles function and change, the training process, good nutrition, mental training, and so on. Then, when I piled on the workouts, all that sweating and pain would make better sense to you, right? (So you'll be more likely to do those workouts and win that yellow jersey!)

Same goes here: to really maximize your SI training, it's best to understand how people develop (or fail to develop) into socially intelligent high performers.

Here we go.

Social Intelligence Is for Life

Most people used to think that all you'd need to know about dealing well with people sort of popped into your head pretty automatically during childhood.

def•i•ni•tion

Developmental psychology is the branch of psychology concerned with how people change mentally as they go through the life span. Developmental psychologists conduct research into the intellectual, emotional, and personality changes that people undergo through their lives.

But back then, we only had a limited understanding of social intelligence. It's only been in the past few decades that *developmental psychologists* have learned how important and complex social intelligence is. Not only does SI not just pop into your brain—developing it to the max is an active, lifelong process.

As you zoom from 0 to 100 (years, that is), you will continue to develop and deepen your understanding of yourself and other people. At a point where you've learned a great deal about yourself and others, folks will say you've acquired a lot of wisdom. (Which we'll get to shortly.)

But the process all starts with babyhood.

A Brief History of Babyhood

Would it surprise you to know that once upon a time, folks knew practically nothing accurate about babies? In fact, until very recently, we didn't "get" babies at all!

Some historians say that until a few hundred years ago, people were barely aware that there was much difference between children and adults (other than that children couldn't talk for a couple of years and were too small to carry really heavy rocks back to the hut.)

Not that there weren't children around, and it sure had to be obvious that they were teensier and knew fewer facts than grownups. But many things we now see as obvious about children—their vulnerability, what they don't know or don't understand, the differences in their mental processes, and the really complicated things they're actually doing in those cribs while they're looking up at us so cutely—all that was poorly understood until recently.

For example, people didn't know that children needed certain physical and psychological nurturance in order to thrive. People often believed that children needed "regular beatings," and that they should be "seen but not heard."

It took many years and political battles (and the work of many religious groups and of writers such as Charles Dickens) to make child labor illegal. For years, educators and businessmen argued that six- and seven-year-olds were certainly capable of doing hard, dangerous physical labor for 14 hours a day! They even asserted that this did the children good! (It's unlikely you'd allow your child to be exposed for even a minute to the kinds of conditions that kids grew up with in nineteenth-century factories, though remember that this kind of child labor is still practiced in some countries!)

Similarly, people didn't always recognize that consistently gentle responses, paying rapt attention to their cries and gurgles, and giving them regular care and proper nutrition were actually good for them!

> **Social Science**
>
> Historians such as Philippe Ariès have argued that before the seventeenth century, people did not recognize that children were not just small adults. They based this on the fact that in old paintings, children were portrayed as wearing adult clothing; they also studied how children were described or portrayed on gravestones, in school records, and even the sizes of furniture that children used.

In addition to food and shelter, emotionally nurturing bonds with others who listen to children and tune in to their feelings are among children's most important needs. We've only recently begun to understand just how social babies and little children are and how crucial social contact is to their development—and even their survival.

Hospitalism and the Lost Babies

As an example of how far we've come in understanding the social needs of babies in just a few decades, let me tell you about a tragic occurrence that happened not so long ago. (I'm not talking the sixteenth, or even the nineteenth century here!)

Back in the 1930s, doctors used to diagnose certain babies who wasted away in hospitals with the term *hospitalism*. Though these babies were well-fed, kept warm in incubators, and changed as needed, many of them died. The strange thing was that babies in poorer hospitals were less likely to be affected by the condition.

def•i•ni•tion

> **Hospitalism** is a medical diagnostic term that refers to infants wasting away and dying while they are in hospital nurseries, with no apparent physical cause, such as disease or hunger. It was discovered that babies with the condition die because of lack of human contact.

Doctors discovered that these babies were literally dying because they were not getting enough human contact—touching, holding, cuddling, and so on!

Back then, it never occurred to highly trained and caring medical professionals that you can't just leave a baby alone all day and all night in an incubator, even if they are fed and changed. If you do, they don't get sufficient stimulation, especially social stimulation. They aren't held, comforted, cuddled, talked to, looked at, told they're going to grow up to be rich and famous—the whole pampering package.

Doctors finally learned that not getting enough human contact is unbearably stressful for babies. It would be like you being locked in a sensory deprivation chamber, blindfolded, and with your ears stopped up and unable to move or feel anything for months at a time. You probably couldn't survive that, or at the very least you'd become psychotic. Well, the babies couldn't thrive or even survive in their sensory deprivation incubators.

Why did the babies in poorer hospitals do better? Well, it turned out that the poorer hospitals were forced to do something that was great for their babies. Because they couldn't afford those high-priced incubators for keeping babies warm, the staff of the poorer facilities had to *hold* the babies just to warm them. So the babies accidentally got more life-saving attention, touching, and human connection, and more of them survived.

To take a more recent example, when I was a child, mothers often left their babies alone to "cry it out" for hours at a time. They had little pillow-type things that you could slide a "bottle" into, and stick the nipple into the baby's mouth, so you could leave the baby alone to feed. Mothers believed, and their well-meaning doctors agreed, that they shouldn't "spoil" a young infant with too much attention.

> **Social Science**
>
> Before the mid-1970s, mothers (and doctors) were taught that it was better not to breastfeed babies. Now we know breast milk is generally healthier for babies, and that the social and emotional "bonding" that mothers and babies do during breastfeeding is psychologically important for both of them!

We now know that neither leaving babies alone in their cribs all day, nor bottle-feeding instead of breastfeeding, are as good for the babies as hours of warm contact, attention, and breastfeeding. And it's impossible to spoil a newborn with too much attention! (You're more likely to ensure that they grow up healthy if you're super-attentive for the first few months, at least.) But these discoveries are pretty recent.

The Social Baby

Your long trek to become a socially intelligent individual began during your late fetal period inside your mother's womb. It is believed from the research on developing fetuses that at some advanced stage of development, you became responsive to sounds and the mental/emotional state of your mother. It seems likely that some very basic learning, the development of a human personality, was already underway by the later periods of fetal development.

And you probably hit the ground running! Well, not exactly "running," but cooing! Newborns are almost immediately responsive to contact. In fact, they need it. Hearing sounds, being touched, and as vision develops, tuning into human faces, become highly important activities of babies.

For example, we know that an infant would rather look at the face of another person than at just about anything else. You came along already wired to tune in and to begin learning to read your mother's facial expressions (which makes you probably already smarter and better functioning than any right-out-of the box PC.)

Babies also develop a special awareness of, and fondness for, their own mothers. For example, babies will recognize and prefer the smell of their own mothers' clothing or breast pad, and will turn more often toward breast pads that smell of their own mothers than toward other objects. Mothers also recognize and can pick out the odor of their own babies after a day or two. Skin-to-skin contact and the familiar smells seem to be important in making those early connections between mothers and infants.

> **Social Science**
>
> Newborn infants can nurse at their mothers' breasts within about an hour. The "breast crawl," named by researchers at the Karolinska Institute in Sweden, starts with spontaneous rooting and sucking movements. Within about 45 minutes babies have moved from these movements to knowing how to feed.

I've Grown Attached to You!

About 50 years ago, if you asked a physician or psychoanalyst why they thought a child got attached to their mothers emotionally, they would have told you that it was because the mother was where the milk came from. The belief back then was that emotional attachment was not the main mover of human behavior, but that attachment developed because the people we got attached to gave us the goodies we needed.

def•i•ni•tion

Attachment theory says that infants need close, secure connections with caregivers to survive—and to develop into healthy adults.

Researcher John Bowlby began to challenge that notion. He and his followers, whose work continues to the present day, began to consider the possibility that the psychological need for *attachment* to others, which begins at infancy, is a core human need. In other words, we don't love mommy because she gives us milk. Rather, we love her because *we need a mommy to love*. Milk is secondary, though also a pretty darn good thing! (Especially if there are also cookies!)

Years and years of research have confirmed John Bowlby's theory. We have learned that a great deal of how a person fares in life depends on success at forming these early attachments. When people start out as babies who feel securely attached to a mother or other caregiver, they often bring a quiet confidence and competence into the rest of their lives. Good things flow from that.

So what is attachment?

Well, it's a lot like love but is more than a warm fuzzy feeling. Actually, it is more like a dance—a set of synchronized interactions between mother and baby that link the two of them. Secure attachment depends on a mother (caregiver, really, since dads and grandparents and siblings also count) who is available and responsive to the infant. That is, the caregiver is attuned to the infant's needs and current emotional state, so that food is offered to hungry babies and play is offered to bored babies, and not vice versa. As the baby becomes too excited, the attuned caregiver begins to soothe and calm the infant. This not only helps the baby to transition from one state to another, but also lays the foundation for reciprocal social interactions—for taking turns and being aware of others' emotions.

When children become attached to their mothers, much of their lives and sense of self revolves around that relationship. They want to be near her. They want to touch her, talk to her, hear her voice. Mothers become a kind of "secure base" (to use the term of John Bowlby) that children can use to feel safe in the world.

One of the important skills babies develop is "social referencing." When the baby is presented with something new, whether a toy or a person or a puppy, the baby who is securely attached will look at (reference) mother to see her reaction. If she seems okay with this new experience, then the baby is likely to relax and accept it. If mother seems tense or uncomfortable, then the baby will also likely reject it. This is the beginning of social thinking—being aware of another's reaction and using that to guide our own response.

Attachment is something that we never outgrow. We just get better able to carry around our "attachment objects" (images of the people we are attached to) inside our heads. Researchers have termed this "inner mother" a kind of "working model" of our attachment object" (mothers, fathers, others.) We hold on to attachments through life and develop new attachment figures as we go.

For example, newlyweds must go through the major psychological processes of becoming attached to each other. The millions of little interactions they have with each other tend to strengthen and reinforce this attachment bond. And if they have a baby or two, the attachment goes both ways—the babies get attached to them, but they get super attached to the babies, as well!

> **Social Science**
>
> If a child's early attachments don't go well, they're more likely to develop psychological difficulties throughout life. This can happen if their caregivers are not emotionally engaged with the child. Therapists often help people with problems that began with attachment difficulties.

Where's My Blankie?

Remember in the *Peanuts* comic strip how Linus was very attached to his blanket? Little Linus took a lot of ribbing for this and sometimes outright persecution from Lucy, who even went so far as to bury his blanket.

But Lucy (like many moms, then and now) needn't have worried about Linus's little blankie problem—because it wasn't a problem at all! It's normal for small children to cling to blankies, favorite bears, and other attachment objects. And believe it or not, this attachment to a nonhuman *thing* is actually a part of a child's *social* development.

> **Caution!**
>
> Don't burn that blankie! It's normal for toddlers to become attached to favorite blankets, teddy bears, or other objects. Not only does it not help them to take their blankets or bears away, it may actually be traumatic.

Blankies are thought to represent mommy, and/or the comforts that mommy brought. The blankie brings the same comfort and sense of safety that mommy does. So it's a kind of portable mommy.

But attachment objects like blankies also become comforting in themselves. Throughout our lives we don't so much "give up" our blankies as we begin to develop substitutes: a favorite bike, our fancy car, the boyfriend's shirt that you wear around your apartment, or your Smith & Wesson. Though comforting in themselves, those objects are also thought to be symbols of the original comforts we felt in the arms of our primary caregivers.

In short, even our stuff is linked to our social needs. And you thought it was just stuff.

The Social Brain

For a few decades, most of what was learned about how our people needs work came from observing children. Developmental psychologists studied children as they grew, often in research projects that followed the same children and their families from birth well into adulthood. (For instance, some psychologists have spent decades studying psychological resilience in children—those qualities that help even children in high-risk families stay healthy as they grow. And yep, a good social environment turns out to help kids a lot.)

But in the late twentieth century, our understanding of the social needs of people got even richer, as we began to be able to put folks into machines and actually watch their brains in motion. The results have been astonishing. It turns out that the brilliant early insights about our social wiring were just the tip of the iceberg.

Snapshots of Your Brain

Scientists began to put people in machines called fMRIs, which stands for functional magnetic resonance imaging. In a nutshell, it's like an x-ray machine on steroids. An fMRI is able to take real-time photographs of activities such as minute changes in blood flow in various parts of your brain while you're listening to a song or commercial, looking at a picture of a loved one, or hearing someone's voice.

When you have this kind of technology, you just have to tinker with it. And tinker, scientists did! They began to gather a huge amount of information on how the brain functions under certain conditions: in pain, when asleep, when thinking about sexy memories, or listening to politicians talk on the radio.

The studies show that much of your brain is organized to process social interactions and to make social contact. This includes not just what you think and do, but also what you feel and how you communicate—or don't communicate—those feelings.

Different parts of your brain respond to different things. Sometimes, for instance, when you seem to not be having an emotion, even if you think you aren't "feeling" anything, your brain's emotion-processing areas may be very active. How could this be? Well, there may not be links developed between your emotion-processing areas and the parts of your brain that deal with putting feelings into words, or being conscious or aware of the feelings. So you say, "I'm not upset, honey," but your wife says, "No, I can tell you're *very* upset." And the brain scan may show that they're right!

SI Tip

That loved one who never seems willing to share his feelings may not be holding back deliberately. Strong feelings that turn up on the brain scans aren't always linked to the verbal parts of a person's brain, which means that for some people, telling you what they're feeling may be literally impossible!

You may not know that the feeling is happening, but a huge amount of passion could be going on under the hood.

Taking Your Neurons out for a Spin

So you're born with this spectacular brain. When you drive it off the lot it's already programmed to develop and learn huge amounts of social things, such as the language that the people around you speak, the nonverbal behavior that is considered appropriate for children and adults in your culture, and the rules for being polite, like remembering to say "please" and "thank you." And while still in your crib, you started learning and filing away much of what you learned about others.

For instance, you tuned in immediately to the presence of your mother (or whoever took care of you). You had this pre-wired urge to want to look at faces, to watch facial expressions. If you were given a choice, you'd spend much more time watching your mother's face than looking at anything else.

Then you'd go to sleep and your brain would process the experiences. And so it would keep growing new connections, thereby changing and developing your social awareness.

SI Tip

You may find that you need to rest, or even to nap more often, when you are "immersed" in a complex learning task such as learning a new foreign language. Sleep may allow your brain to process and store the new information.

As you got a bit older, what you could focus on got more complicated. For instance, that language thing. Remember learning to understand and speak your native language?

You don't? Well, you got "fluent" in it at a pretty young age. At one point you were able to learn new words and how to understand things at a rate that would boggle the mind of the average college French student who thinks it's great if they learn five new vocabulary words a day!

You were also learning a great deal about the mechanics of everyday interaction. For example, you've heard mothers and fathers ask that famous question, "What do you say?" after you give their child something. You went through it, too—though you probably don't remember hearing the question.

Of course, this was teaching you to say "thank you." But it was also much more: it taught you to tune in to the gift-giver as a separate person. When children are given presents, they tend to focus on the present, not the gift-giver. Not socially cool!

> ### Social Science
>
> Are we wired to be altruistic? In one study of 24 toddlers as young as 18 months, a researcher pretended to need help, by letting a book fall or dropping a marker. Twenty-two of the children eagerly offered help with no expectation of a reward.

What your parent was actually saying to you was, "Did you notice that there is someone interacting with you?" This was part of your basic SI training, in the art of tuning in to other human beings.

Throughout life, you've continued to learn and refine these lessons in the best way to interact with others. You started by being taught the rules by your parents, such as "share with your brother or sister," or "do not fart at the dinner table." It was all about noticing other people's feelings.

When you got into preschool or early school grades, the socialization process ramped up considerably. Children are schooled for hours a day in social behavior, which is really a bigger part of the school curriculum than the academic instruction. Many of the future successful presidents, corporation executives, and used car salesmen get their start at mastering the many social skills they'll need during those first school days.

Feedback Loops and Mothers' Frowns

The basic way people learn social intelligence, making full use of all the things their brains are built to learn, is through a feedback loop. A feedback loop is a process in which things you do trigger responses from others, which your brain processes, the results of which lead you to change your behavior. Everything you do gives your brain more data, which affects everything else you do after that. All this feedback and forth is a kind of "loop" that continuously changes your brain, your awareness patterns, and who you are as a social being.

Here's how it works: you do or say something, like "urp!" at the table. Mother glances at you and frowns. Instantly your brain processes her frown look on many levels. One level is the emotional level you're not even aware of: you take in the sight of mother's frown and that visual information—the sight of her frown—is processed in a region of your brain called the amygdala, a small, almond-shaped organ (two of them, actually) buried in the depths of your brain.

The amygdala helps in the processing of emotional information. It sends signals to two different places: one area is the cognitive processes toward the front of the top of your brain. This is where you consciously think about what mother's frown might mean. But the energy for this thinking comes from a different place in the brain.

The amygdala also sends information about the frown to a part of your brain that triggers strong emotions, such as fear. Fear is triggered because by prior experience, your brain has come to associate mother's frowns with "bad news!" So whenever mother frowns at you, it's a bad thing, and these fear circuits get triggered. The fear provides the emotional energy that motivates all that thinking that the other part of your brain is doing. Somewhere in that mix of firing neural circuits in your brain, your brain is learning that there was a connection between her frown and your "urp!" You learn that you'd better not "urp" in front of mother at the table! The whole experience feels icky to you, and so your urps are silenced.

Since you are no longer urping, your mother is not frowning. This teaches your brain something important: "I was right. It was the urping that caused the problem." So you stop "urping" at the table. Mother now smiles at you, her lovely urp-free child. Your brain processes the smile the same way, and the loop goes on and on.

All day long, every time we are with people, the brain is doing this same kind of processing, filing away the results, and developing new connections as a result. It starts with simple things like eye contact, but moves on to really big things such as learning the best way to connect on a very deep, intimate level with a lover as an adult.

SI Tip

You can learn a lot about how your social intelligence developed by identifying some of the unspoken rules in your family. Every family has them, and these rules influence our behavior and attitudes. You can identify many of these unspoken rules by talking them over with family members.

Wisdom and Social Intelligence

People have often revered and admired wisdom. Many have even said that wisdom is the highest form of human knowledge. From King Solomon's choosing wisdom above all other things he might have had, to people going off on long journeys to ask the wise man or woman on the mountaintop for advice and counsel, we have seen wisdom as one of life's major accomplishments.

But what, exactly, is wisdom? Actually, there are so many definitions of the mysterious quality that it would take a very wise woman or man to sort them all out. But maybe a really wise person wouldn't spend much time on the task, because fine-tuning definitions is not really all that important in life for most people.

Most agree that wisdom is something that develops over time. A child can be wise in some ways, but generally we assume that real wisdom is the result of a lot of experience in life, and thinking about and learning from that experience.

Most also agree that the main ingredients of wisdom, of all that experience, are pretty close to what we are calling "social intelligence." Wouldn't you consider these abilities to be key parts of wisdom?

◆ Understanding, and being able to manage, your own emotional life, your passions and impulses and urges, when it's really important to do so

◆ Being good at tuning in to, understanding, and "reading" others

◆ Knowing how to make contact, communicate with, persuade, influence, and make an emotional, intimate connection with others

◆ Having compassion, empathy, and genuine caring for the well-being of other people

These are satisfying and worthwhile things to achieve in your own right. But they also tend to bring people success at many of life's important challenges, from work to marriage to parenting and friendships. Even your physical and mental health will generally be better if you can manage these socially intelligent achievements.

In a sense, then, to seek to develop your social intelligence is to develop your wisdom!

The Least You Need to Know

◆ Developing your social intelligence to the max is an active, lifelong process.

◆ It's only in recent decades that we have learned how important social connecting is to the healthy growth of infants and children.

◆ Emotional attachment is one of the most important developmental processes of childhood.

◆ Recent brain research shows that we are wired to connect with others.

◆ Much of what we call "wisdom" is really well-developed social intelligence abilities.

Chapter 3

Raise Your Social Intelligence

In This Chapter

- When "smart" isn't "socially smart"
- Learning from Ben Franklin
- Nobody's perfect—at first!

We've been talking about how your brain is organized to help you develop your social intelligence. When you were born, you had a lot of potential in terms of the SI you could develop in life. But it takes more than "potential" to be a success! If you've got the "natural body and reflexes" of an Olympic skater, but don't practice on the ice every day, you'll never win the gold. The same goes with social intelligence.

In this chapter, you'll find out how you can improve your social intelligence. Because success in life often depends on social skills, any time you invest in developing these skills may repay you a zillion times over.

A Smart Guy with Poor Social Skills

The young man was prodigiously smart. In fact, he was one of the brightest guys that had ever lived in his town, and he was establishing himself as a successful businessman and community leader. But all was not well in his social life. At some point, his awareness that he was the brightest guy on the block seems to have "gone to his head." Finally, he confessed, a friend "informed me that I was generally thought proud; that my pride showed itself frequently in conversation; that I was not content with being in the right when discussing any point, but was overbearing and rather insolent; of which he convinced me by mentioning several instances."

Clearly, all this showing off, letting people know how smart he was, and making sure he trounced them in every argument, must have felt good to this young man. But it was starting to undermine his success, both socially, and probably in his business as well. Frankly, the guy sounds like a pain! Who would want to deal with him?

Caution!

Showing off your talents can backfire! You may be the best speller, juggler, or hacker on earth, but people will resent it if you let them know that you're—ahem!—"too aware" of the fact. We admire competence, but would rather see it in action than hear someone brag about it.

But all was not lost. The young man decided to apply himself to presenting a more humble side to others, and practiced this for a very long period of his life. Ultimately, his ability to deal with other people became one of the great sources of his success.

Recognize the dude? You're right if you guessed that this was Benjamin Franklin. As a young man, he took on the task of changing how he interacted with others. Through hard work and a system for self-improvement, Franklin became more socially intelligent.

In fact, due in part to his matured social intelligence, Franklin became one of the most successful leaders of early America. His charm, wit, and grasp of very complicated social situations led to great success during his years as a diplomat to France during the American Revolution. He "won the hearts and minds" of the French people and the very "socially astute" French court. Franklin was thus able to persuade the court to offer financial and military help to the young United States. Historians agree that if it weren't for Franklin's highly developed social intelligence, our country might never have won its independence!

Ben Franklin's Surefire SI Improvers

When he decided to improve his social skills, Ben Franklin went about the job in a systematic way. He made a list of the most important "virtues" that he wanted to improve in himself, and listed them on a weekly calendar. Not all of his virtues had to do with social functioning, because he also added things like Frugality and Industry. However, a number of his 13 virtues did have a great deal to do with social functioning, such as Sincerity, Silence, and Humility.

Franklin's method was simple, and one which you can certainly copy. (He wanted you to copy it, in fact!) He wrote his "virtues" down the left margin of a sheet of paper, and across the top put a column for each of the seven days of the week. Each week, he would concentrate on one particular virtue. Franklin would think about that virtue, and devote special attention to improving on it. At the end of the day he would put a mark for each time he violated that virtue.

Over a year, he would cycle through each of his 13 virtues four times (e.g., spending four weeks of the year on each virtue.) The result was that he was more aware of, and constantly working to improve on, the areas that were important to him.

You wouldn't need to adopt Ben's list of virtues to adopt his method. In fact, the best approach is to decide what SI areas you need to develop or improve, and to begin to track a few key things that you would like to change in yourself.

> ### Social Science
>
> Ben Franklin's self-improvement efforts are recounted in his *Autobiography*. The legend of his self-improvement success inspired many people, from the early 1800s to the present. Modern psychologists would agree with the soundness of Franklin's ideas for making changes in your behavior.

What Skills Do I Need?

"Hmmmm …! So many flaws—so little time!"

If you're thinking that about yourself, you're not alone. Most of us have a great many "flaws" in our social functioning. We mess up at parties, we hurt the feelings of our friends, we miss the clues we should get from others. A gaffe a day is probably par for the course for most of us.

But don't flood yourself with guilt! Making changes in your social performance doesn't have to be overwhelming. In fact, there's a simple rule that you can follow before setting out on any self-change project, which might raise your odds of success while lowering your stress level. I mean the *80-20 rule*.

The 80-20 rule refers to the fact that in most situations in life, we get 80 percent of the benefit from 20 percent of the work we

> ## def•i•ni•tion
>
> The **80-20 rule** is also called the "Pareto principle," named after an Italian economist. It says that 80 percent of the "effects" usually flow from 20 percent of the causes. The trick is identifying the "20 percent" place to put your effort! Brushing? Flossing? Avoiding sweets?

put in. Another way of putting this is that 80 percent of the problems we have in life come from 20 percent of the causes.

If you've ever managed a group of people, or taught a large class full of students, you would recognize that about two out of ten students or people you manage take up 80 percent of your "being hassled" time. They are the ones who bring most of the prob-lems into your life, and so you spend a great deal of your time working with them. Another example is that if you have to cope with a huge to-do list, you can often pick out the 20 percent of your tasks that will give you the really essential results you need. And sure enough, if you tossed out the other 80 per-cent of your to-do items, but got that key 20 percent accomplished, things would work out pretty well, right? (Try it!)

> **Caution!**
>
> Don't overwhelm yourself with lists of your social intel-ligence flaws! Nobody is perfect, and most of us manage to be pretty likable despite the occa-sional social goof-ups.

It's the same with your own SI limitations. Eighty percent of the social difficulties in your life probably flow directly from twenty percent of your behavior or attitudes. If you can just find those few problem items (like, say, Franklin's "small problem" with showing off his high IQ), you may find that your social performance improves dramatically.

Even if you're not troubled with any particular difficulties, focusing on your most important concerns or areas where you might need to improve your skills will give you the most gains.

So the question is, how do you identify the top 20 percent area—the areas of social intelligence functioning where you ought to put your greatest efforts?

Set Priorities!

If I were working with you as your counselor or coach, I'd start you off by having us do an assessment together of your main areas of strength and weakness. I'd ask you to list some of the "key areas" of social intelligence of concern to you. Then we'd review each area separately, and narrow down the list of your most important "growth areas."

Identifying key areas and narrowing them down to growth areas isn't as hard as it may sound. Remember that most of what makes up social intelligence can be divided into four categories: knowing yourself, tuning in to others, making connections, and showing compassion or caring. Just glancing over that broad list, where do you think you ought to focus?

Knowing yourself: Are you less clear of your own feelings, reactions, and desires? Are you able to "regulate" your moods or emotions when need be? If you're frustrated and irritated at your partner or friend, do you just blurt those feelings out, or do you take into consideration how they'll feel if you dump on them, and so calm yourself down? In short, do you take responsibility for your own emotional life?

SI Tip

Ask a close friend or relative what, if any, interpersonal behavior you might need to work on. Your moods and how you show them? Your listening skills? They'll know! And if they tell you, be grateful, not peevish! Think of that—how you respond to their feedback—as your first test!

Tuning in: Do you have trouble reading other people? Are you skilled at being aware of how other people are feeling? Do you pay attention to their emotional states? How much do you observe about other people?

Remembering others: Think of the last person you met on a superficial basis, such as a friend you ran into at a store or a waitress. Do you remember what their emotional state seemed to be? Were they smiling? Did they look tired? Would you be able to describe some of the main life concerns that are usually on the minds of some of your closest friends? Or do you think mainly about what they can do for you?

Making contact: Are you pretty good at clicking with the nonverbal behavior of another person? Do you smile in response to their smiles? Do you avoid eye contact and stare at your shoes, or do you look up and lock eyes for a second? How do you present yourself to others—as somebody who takes up the right amount of "space" in the room, who seems to look presentable and to fit into the situation? Or are you more like Pig Pen, the walking cloud of dust in *Peanuts* whom everyone avoids?

SI Tip

Get a small pocket counter, such as a plastic golf stroke counter, and carry it with you. Set a daily SI improvement goal such as making eye contact with people, or not talking about yourself too much. Each time you do it, click the counter.

Affecting others: How about knowing how to influence other people? Do you ever go into an encounter thinking through what effect you want the encounter to have on the other person? Do you imagine having some other kind of impact such as winning them over to your way of seeing a situation? Are you good at getting help on the phone from someone at your insurance company? Are you pretty confident that you could pick up the phone right now and have some kind of influence on someone, if you needed to?

Caring: How often do you think about the needs of others? Do you feel satisfied at the end of the day because you've done something to help someone or paid some attention to another person's needs? Have you taken the initiative to do some kind of favor or do something nice for someone today? Did you make anyone happy?

Grow Your Social Intelligence Skills

Back in Ben Franklin's day, there were no guidebooks to help a fellow decide how to make improvements in his social skills. He had to pretty much invent the method in order to use it. (Considering the many lists of his great inventions, it's surprising that people never give Franklin the well-deserved credit for having invented the self-help industry.)

SI Tip

It's been said that "the road to hell is paved with good intentions." Maybe so, or maybe not. But when it comes to making changes in your behavior, a systematic approach and clear behavioral goals is about a zillion times more effective than good intentions without a plan.

Franklin also deserves credit for an important insight: he recognized that he would get further with a systematic approach to changing his social behavior than by just trying to remind himself that he should be a "better person," and then flogging himself for failing to achieve that!

In fact, that is one of the most useful discoveries of both Franklin and (then again, later) psychology in our time: that you can make huge changes in many things about your behavior, but that you will do best with a systematic approach.

So rather than treating this book as just a list of good ideas that you really ought to get around to someday (which will pretty much doom you to failure), it's best to be systematic in developing your social intelligence skills.

Where to begin? Here are some suggestions:

Assess yourself: Start by identifying the most important areas where you need to develop your social intelligence. As mentioned previously, these may fall into one of the four broad areas of social intelligence, such as the ability to understand your own feelings and motives, your own reactions to others, and so on. Or it may mean focusing on your compassion and concern and attending more to the needs of others than you usually do, until it becomes second nature.

Another approach is to identify key situations in your life where you are particularly in need of some "rehab." For example, some people are naturally excellent at interacting with strangers in a business setting, such as dealing with clients or customers, but may have difficulties in the romantic sphere of life. Other people are spectacular romantic partners, dates and lovers, but choke when they have to deal with a client in a work setting. What's your list of strong suits? How about your weaker areas?

 **Caution!**

Don't announce to the whole world that you're making changes in your social behavior! It might just call attention to whatever mistakes you do make, instead of getting you the positive attention that you need. Let your new behavior do all the advertising!

If you've looked ahead in the book, you will have noticed that our chapters are designed to cover many of the most important life areas where social intelligence is important. It's fine to flip to the chapters where you need to devote the most attention and to start working on those. (In addition, each chapter has a "self-test," which will give you a rough idea of your strengths and weaknesses before you even begin.)

Focus: Focusing on one area to work on every day, and keeping track of that area, is also an excellent idea. Thanks to Dr. Franklin for that one! You may have an excellent memory for names, but you may notice that you butt in when other people are talking or commit other errors that you would like to change.

Start small: It's usually much easier to make a small change in your behavior than to transform your entire personality overnight. And not all of the changes have to be dramatic, or even visible to anyone else. For example, if you want to be more focused on caring about how other people are doing, you might simply review, at the end of the day, a mental list of the people you've met during the day and ask yourself how you think they were feeling, if you noticed any concerns, what they were feeling good about, and so on. Just getting into the habit of doing this, even if you did it only a few times, would probably create some changes in your social behavior.

Overlearn and overpractice: Say you've gotten this "make eye contact and smile to the other person" business down pretty well. Fine. Now is a good time to practice it even more. Maintaining gains when you change long-ingrained habits tends to require overpracticing. You could do like Franklin did: put the sheet away for a few weeks, but put it on your calendar that you're going to take it out and practice it again.

Get feedback: It can help to work on skills with another friend or classmate, and to exchange notes on how you're doing. If you feel shy about bringing this up with someone, shrinking that shyness might be a useful exercise!

Set specific goals: In order to know that you're being successful, you need to set *behavioral goals* to measure your progress against. For instance, if you need to develop some more skill at meeting new people, decide how many new people you should meet. Would you think, say, that meeting a new person a week is a pretty good rate? (Over a year, that would mean you've met more than 50 new people!)

def•i•ni•tion

Behavioral goals are goals that involve specific things you *do, say,* or even *think.* "Comb my hair" is a behavior goal, because it involves a particular action; "look neater" is not behavioral because it doesn't tell you what you actually have to *do* in order to achieve it.

Other examples of goals you might set:

◆ Once a day you will tune in, ask, or notice how your girlfriend, partner, or spouse seems to be feeling.

◆ At least once a week you will go to one new group event, class, or social outing, and say hello to one person.

◆ You will ask one close friend how you "come across" socially (or in terms of one specific concern, such as how well you express your feelings).

◆ You will make eye contact with each person you talk to at least once.

◆ You will apologize when you have injured someone or been tactless, and practice this the very next time you "blow it."

See? The idea is to be specific, to quantify each goal (e.g., ask *one* friend, attend *one* meeting, do something *once* a day), and to focus on simple, attainable tasks. It also means avoiding vague, mushy goals like "be a better person" (what, exactly does that mean to you? Whatever it means in terms of your actions, make the *action* the goal!).

Again, the particular goals you pick depend on your own situation and needs. As you read through this book, you'll be able to zero in on the main areas where you need to practice.

Nobody's Perfect—At First!

As you develop and enhance your social intelligence skills, expect to make mistakes. If you're not making mistakes, you're probably not really trying!

Dealing with social situations, with how we perceive others and how they see us, are fairly complex processes. If you are old enough to be reading a book like this, your life is probably already loaded with some pretty complicated situations, so there are many opportunities for mistakes.

Remind yourself (make it your "mantra" even!) that even small improvements that you can turn into habits will eventually change your life in big ways!

When You Gaffe!

The other day I sent an e-mail to someone, and realized only afterward that there were some lines in it that may have been read as "cranky." Because it went to an important friend and I didn't want her to get the wrong idea, I instantly tapped out a second e-mail clarifying my comments from the first and saying that I hoped she understood what I meant. She wrote back that all was well and she knew what I really meant.

It's very easy to make a *faux pas* like that, especially on e-mail. (We will discuss the special "social skills" needed to deal with e-mails in a later chapter of the book.) But this can happen in almost any kind of interaction with others. In fact, sometimes the fact that you did not interact becomes the way that you've given offense, depending on the situation. (Ever have someone later ask, "Why didn't you stop and say hello?")

Fortunately, in most cases the best way to cope with such mistakes is easy: just apologize. If you even *suspect* you gave offense, but aren't sure, you can say that! (e.g., "I was concerned that my e-mail might have sounded more cranky than I meant it to. Hope it didn't come across that way, but if so, I'm sorry.") Doing this can also give you a chance to clarify what you intended to say or didn't say.

Actually, making mistakes is a great way to learn! Especially if you do go to the trouble of reconnecting, apologizing, clarifying what you meant, hearing what the other person really meant to say, and so on. This process will help you remember how important it is to get the signals straight, and you're less likely to make the same mistake again.

def•i•ni•tion

A **faux pas** is a social blunder or blooper, or a tactless error you commit in a social situation. It is actually a French phrase meaning a "false step."

Social Science

If the words "I'm sorry" get stuck in your throat, you're not alone! For many years, doctors were taught that apologizing for gaffes with patients was a "bad idea." Only in recent years have they been taught that it's often therapeutic to apologize to patients if they mess up!

"Damage repair" is a very effective way to improve your social intelligence abilities. In fact, it may be *the* most powerful, since we have a tendency to vividly recall the "awkward" encounters we've had, and our apologies to others. And, as Ben Franklin might have told you, when you are known as the kind of guy or gal who does apologize when they mess up, people actually like you better! (It's the people who would rather die than say "I'm sorry" who look like jerks!)

Track Your Progress

Just as Ben Franklin did, it's useful to create some kind of log book to track your progress. You could use a spreadsheet on your computer for this, or just keep a card in your pocket where you make a check mark each time you do, or stop yourself from doing, whatever it is you are trying to change.

When professional coaches or counselors work with clients on behavior change, they often set "target goals" and create systems for monitoring the client's progress. For instance, if you were working in a corporate setting to increase your assertiveness and ability to manage some people skillfully, you might set goals, such as being able to approach an employee or colleague and ask him to do something without becoming too anxious.

One great way to track your progress is to have a clear definition of success. For example: do you wish you had more success making friends? What would "having enough good friends" mean for you? Knowing someone to do something with every weekend? Having three people you could invite to dinner for your birthday? The clearer your goals, the easier it'll be to know when you've made it!

Surviving Feedback from Others

Many of the examples I have been listing are things you can do on your own. However, as I mentioned before, there is no substitute for feedback from another live human being if you really want to surge forward in developing your social smarts! But getting feedback is not always easy, for several reasons.

For one thing, you first have to find someone to give you the feedback. This requires being able to approach someone, talking about the concerns or reasons you want feedback in the first place, and enlisting her aid.

Of course, enlisting someone's aid might just involve asking her a simple question over pizza and beer, like "Do I annoy you?" But at times you might want more specific or in-depth feedback from others. There will also be times when the feedback will be thrust upon you, by a friend or a co-worker. (So the art of receiving feedback is another social skill that you need!)

Ideally, a socially intelligent person receiving helpful feedback on his behavior or attitudes will receive it with minimal defensiveness. Like the way Ben Franklin did. Maybe it wasn't easy to hear, but he was able to get the message his friend had for him! It's nice if you can be grateful and learn from the feedback. It might even be a pleasant win-win situation for all concerned.

SI Tip

A simple way to ask someone for feedback is with one of these openers: "Can I ask you something?" "Would you mind if I asked you for some honest feedback?" Or the popular, "Can we talk?" These openers work because they automatically trigger a caring response from the other person.

Of course, as a practical matter, it doesn't always work that way. Hearing from a friend that "You just don't cut it at parties, Sue," can feel incredibly painful. It seems that it can be very natural to convert a little bit of negative feedback into a sweeping feeling of shame about our worth as human beings. This, however, can be unfortunate, and can undermine your ability to learn from the experience.

In truth, accepting feedback is universally difficult. Here are some suggestions for helping it go down a little more easily.

For one thing, it helps a great deal if you get the feedback from someone you trust. Someone who "has your back," who you know would never willingly hurt you. Many people who are in a committed relationship find that their partner or spouse is the best source of honest feedback. If you are younger you may have a parent, sibling, or teacher who can give you feedback that doesn't sting too much. If you want specific information about how you're doing, you will want to approach someone you trust first.

SI Tip

Learn from observing others! Pick out some people who are especially skilled at dealing with others, and watch them in action! Keep some notes—what do they do differently than everyone else that gives them that special *"je ne sais quoi"*?

It also helps if feedback is presented at the right time and place. Look for a chance to sit in a private location with a friend, and ask them the questions or get the feedback then. Remember, this may be one of those times that you will remember for the rest of your life. As such, making it a time that feels safe, quiet, and basically positive is very important. It also helps to be sure you have time to *"process"* the feedback

def•i•ni•tion

Counselors use the word **process** to mean the way you absorb, think about, and talk through the feelings you have about something. Processing someone's feedback is how you make sure you remember it, can tolerate thinking about it without being upset, and use it to help yourself grow.

you get—time to talk it over with that person, to ask questions and clarify, and finally, to "put it all in perspective" by being reminded that even if you make some mistakes, there are also good things about you.

It's important to avoid being too defensive when you get that feedback. Explaining how they're wrong, how they don't understand you, how they aren't seeing all your fine qualities, may not be very helpful, and may cause them to shut down any further input. Better to assume that if this person cares about you, the feedback is well meant and is, for her at least, a valid perception of you. You have to be willing to take your medicine if you want to get better.

Ask the person for some kind of support if you feel you need it. If you are upset at the feedback, no need to kid yourself or him about that, but that's different from being defensive. Being honest about saying, for instance, "It upsets me to hear you say that," can go a long way toward helping both of you talk it through. Besides, talking about what he is telling you, asking questions, and clarifying are important just to be sure that you understand what he's saying.

Finally, it helps to write down the feedback, so you can get a bit of "distance" from it. Seeing the feedback in black and white but then writing down many of your fine qualities can help keep things in perspective. Remember: nobody who gives you feedback is perfect either! (But don't remind anyone of that just now!)

Using This Book

This book is designed to help you learn about social intelligence, with a special focus on developing your SI skills in a wide range of life situations. The topics are divided into "personal" and "work" areas. You can read the book cover to cover, or pick out the areas of greatest interest or importance to you. It may be helpful to skim everything before focusing on one or two areas.

Are there some pressing areas of your life where your social intelligence needs sharpening? Have you gotten some feedback from a coach, boss, or loved one that there are some things you need to work on? These would be the areas to pick out first.

As I mentioned earlier, each chapter begins with a self-test, which is designed to help you think about your own social smarts in various life situations. Although these are not "official" psychological tests, they cover similar topics as those used by psychologists.

The tests are designed to cover the kinds of things that a psychologist or coach such as myself might ask you if we were to work together to help improve your SI skills. So they're not the "final assessment" of your functioning, but can help you kick-start your thinking on these topics. More help by way of formal testing can be obtained by contacting a local psychologist for a consultation.

A good way to use the chapters in this book would be to skim the chapter, take the self-test, make some notes for yourself about your results and any questions or concerns you have. Then read through the chapter, and mark the things you think would be most useful to you in developing your own skills. Next, identify the two or three things that would be most useful for you to work on or change.

Good luck! Have fun!

The Least You Need to Know

- ◆ Social intelligence isn't something you just have, it's something you can develop.
- ◆ Like Ben Franklin, you'll have the best results developing your skills if you use a systematic approach.
- ◆ Start by picking a few areas where you most need improvement.
- ◆ Make small changes and keep at them, and you'll see big results over time.
- ◆ You don't have to be "perfect" or socially flawless. Nobody is!

Part 2

Enhance Your Socially Intelligent Self!

In Part 2, we begin to explore some of the practical uses of social intelligence. The first part of being SI (socially intelligent) is to understand some things about yourself, so we'll leap into exploring a core building block of your social life: knowing whether you're naturally inclined to be an outgoing, extraverted sort, or a more quiet, inward-looking introvert. Both are cool—but it's really helpful to know where you're at. Next we'll talk about shyness and related challenges, and suggest some tricks for overcoming it if it's an issue for you. Then it's on to discussions of empathy—understanding the feelings of others, and intimacy—sharing yourself. Finally, we'll talk about toxic relationships and how to keep yourself poison-free!

4

Outgoing or Soloist?

In This Chapter

- ◆ Who are introverts and extraverts?
- ◆ Pros and cons of your style
- ◆ Tips for soloists and "social-ists"

Social intelligence skills are useful for everyone. But how you actually *apply* those skills will depend on a lot of other things, such as the situation you're in, the relationship you have with someone, or the other parts of your personality. And one of the main qualities of your personality is how outgoing you are.

Some of us are inclined to be pretty social. We may be the life-of-the-party type, or we may just like schmoozing and interacting with other people most days. Others of us tend to be soloists. We'd rather read a book or take a walk by ourselves, or with one close friend, than spend any time at a party or noisy bar.

Psychologists call these two types of personalities extroverted and introverted. Being comfortable with your personality type can take you a long way toward developing the social intelligence skills that work best for you.

Which leads us to our first self-test. Ready?

Check Yourself Out

Choose a time when you're feeling calm and not stressed, and can take this test without rushing.

Read the questions and circle the answer to each question that is generally the truest for you. Don't worry if an answer doesn't fit you 100 percent of the time. And don't choose the answer that you *wish* were true! Mark the one that fits you the best.

1. When I'm invited to a party with people I don't know, my reaction is to:

    A. Look forward to it with pleasure.

    B. Go through my list of excuses, or back out at the last minute.

    C. Sometimes I'll go and hope to enjoy it, depending on what else I know about the party and the people.

2. I like to:

    A. Talk.

    B. Listen and talk—an even balance.

    C. I'm really better at listening, thanks.

3. When I'm on my own for several hours, I:

    A. Feel great! Time to settle in with that best-seller I've been meaning to read.

    B. Feel anxious and on edge, or I start to get tired and look for stimulation.

    C. How do you expect me to answer that? It depends on so many things!

4. When I move to a new town or get a new job, I make friends:

    A. If I meet someone I click with, I can make friends fast; otherwise maybe it takes longer.

    B. Not so easily; it takes me a while to feel comfortable with people.

    C. Easily. In a week my new address book is full!

5. When I have something to say, I:

    A. Blurt it out.

    B. I'm a wild card—equally likely to blurt or think it to death first!

    C. Think, then speak.

6. After a party, I feel:

   A. Drained and ready to get home for some "me" time.

   B. Some parties tire me out, but other times I tell myself I left too soon.

   C. Ready for more. Why did it end so soon?

7. On the job, I prefer to:

   A. Work in groups. Exchanging ideas and getting it done together feels best.

   B. Work on my own; I'm a self-directed and independent worker.

   C. I don't get concerned about whether I work with others or alone.

8. I met Ralph just a few weeks ago.

   A. Depending on Ralph, we might be friends by now.

   B. I'm likely to call him my friend.

   C. I'm unlikely to call him my friend; he's still a casual acquaintance.

9. True or false (or maybe): People tend to think I'm self-involved, mysterious, uninterested, or aloof.

   A. True. It takes people a while to feel like they know me.

   B. False. I'm an open book.

   C. Maybe—some people get to see my "real self" pretty easily, though with others, if we don't click, I may keep a bit closed up.

10. When I need to make a phone call, I:

    A. Usually just grab the phone, but if it's important I may want to think it through before I dial.

    B. Rehearse what I'm going to say, or even write it down first.

    C. Grab the phone and make the call. What's the big deal?

Scoring: Circle which answer you chose here, then add up the number of circles within each column.

Item	Introvert	Ambivert	Extrovert
1. (Party)	B	C	A
2. (Talk/listen)	C	A	B
3. (Own)	A	C	B
4. (Move)	B	A	C
5. (Say)	C	B	A
6. (Post-party)	A	B	C
7. (Job)	B	C	A
8. (Ralph)	C	A	B
9. (Aloof)	A	C	B
10. (Phone)	B	A	C
Totals			

Interpreting your results:

If most (five or more) answers fall in the "introvert" column, you're probably pretty introverted. Likewise, most answers in "extrovert" means … you guessed it. And if your answers are all over the map or fall mostly in the middle *ambivert* column, you've probably got qualities of both introverts and extroverts.

def•i•ni•tion

An **ambivert** is someone who is more in the middle of the extroversion/introversion continuum—he has qualities of both introverts and extraverts. If you're not sure "what you are," maybe it's because you're kind of ambiverted!

What Are Extroverts and Introverts?

There's an old joke that goes, "There are two kinds of people in the world: those who think there are two kinds of people in the world, and those who don't." Noticing that people are different from each other, and making categories of the most common differences, seems to be a pretty human thing to do.

In fact, our sorting habit goes back to ancient times. Ancient philosophers put people in categories based on theories of what caused the differences in human personality. For instance, there was the humour theory of Hippocrates and other ancient Greeks (we get the word "humor" from that). That theory said there were four personality types, depending on how much of the four main bodily fluids, or humours, were sloshing around inside someone. (Those are blood, black bile, yellow bile, and phlegm, if you really wanted to know! Ick.)

And then, of course, there's astrology (I'm a Taurus—you know what *they're* like!), or the Chinese system that uses the year of your birth to tell what you're like (I'm a "horse," according to the placemats at my local Chinese restaurant).

Research on the differences in human *personality* took off in a big way during the last century, helped by new scientific approaches to the study of psychology. Modern theories evolved as the research findings accumulated.

def•i•ni•tion

Psychologists define **personality** as the enduring patterns of behavior, thinking, and feeling that you show over time. Those things about your style that a friend would use to describe you (stuff that's typical of you), and that might be very different than someone else, make up your personality.

People's tendency toward extroversion/introversion is one of the most well-studied personality dimensions. These terms have been defined in slightly different ways by different theorists.

Carl Jung, a twentieth-century Swiss psychiatrist and the founder of Analytical Psychology, thought that an extrovert's "energy" (roughly meaning where they direct most of their attention) normally flows outward, while an introvert's "energy" flows inward. Extroverts gain energy from being with large groups of people and feel drained when left alone; introverts are the opposite.

Hans Eysenck, a twentieth-century German-born psychologist, defined extroversion and introversion as the amount of social activity a person seeks out: extroverts look for a good amount of social activity, and introverts tend to avoid it.

Social Science

Psychologists sometimes disagree as to whether traits like introversion/extroversion fall on a continuum or are clearly different categories. Gender is an example of a category variable—most people are pretty clearly male or female. Introversion/extroversion is generally thought to be more of a continuum than a category dimension of personality.

Most modern psychologists currently hold to the Five Factor Theory of personality. Based on a great many statistical personality studies, researchers have identified five qualities or factors in human personality that seem to come up time and time again as the most central, the most important, and as the most distinctive. The five traits that make up who we are include openness to experience, conscientiousness, extroversion, agreeableness, and neuroticism (the first letters of which spell OCEAN).

> **Social Science**
>
> Psychologists study personality different ways. Sometimes they collect information on individuals in clinical settings (like Sigmund Freud did, studying his patients), but other times their research is done by looking for statistical patterns in the responses of large numbers of people on psychological tests.

According to the Five Factor theory, extroverts and introverts differ based on the kind and amount of stimulation they prefer. Extroverts need and enjoy outside stimulation. They prefer to be around lots of people in order to feel comfortable.

Introverts get more easily flooded or worn out by a lot of social stimulation. A busy party may actually *overstimulate* introverts—it tires them out! On the other hand, they are good at providing a lot of inner stimulation for themselves. They enjoy working with ideas, thoughts, fantasies, and have rich inner worlds.

From these definitions, you may be wondering what happened to the "shyness" that people often associate with "introverts." Introversion and shyness are actually entirely different things. Shy people are anxious about social interaction; introverts aren't necessarily anxious at all, but may just prefer to avoid crowds or lots of social interaction, so they can focus on their interests, thoughts, or inner lives. (I'm a pretty un-shy but very introverted person.) We'll talk more about shyness in Chapter 6.

Pros and Cons of Introversion

Introverts often tend to feel insecure because they live in an "extrovert's world." Their perception is accurate, but their conclusions aren't! Yes, there are more extroverts out there, but consider this: extroverts sometimes feel they should be more like you! That's because introverts often seem deep and smart.

> **Social Science**
>
> Extroverts tend to outnumber introverts, roughly three to one.

Extroverts tend to be more focused on the outside world—the stimulation is what they relate to. So they may not be very tuned in to their own inner lives, their ideas and conclusions about things. If you're an introvert, you look so much more on top of that stuff to your friendly local extrovert!

More Good News for Introverts

If that's not enough to help you relax and appreciate yourself, consider these things. If you're an introvert, you are more likely to be:

♦ Studious

♦ Creative

♦ Good in one-on-one relationships

♦ Thoughtful—introverts often have the ability to create rich "inner lives"

♦ Often gifted in music, art, science, or math

♦ Likely to have strong relationships

♦ Problem-solvers

♦ Blessed with good concentration

♦ Sensitive

Creative, studious, gifted … you've got a lot going for you, innie!

The Flip Side of Introverts

No one is perfect—and wouldn't life be boring if no one had any flaws? And for an introvert, those imperfections can include coming off as uninterested, awkward, or self-centered; having lower self-esteem than extroverts; and being easily drained by too much activity or social interaction.

Introverts sometimes keep their best selves to themselves: they don't show what they know or what they feel. They may hold back their contributions either out of shyness or because they don't realize that the other people in the room don't see what seems so obvious to the innie.

It's a vicious circle. Introverts:

May underachieve because they're reluctant to share their talents ….

… They therefore get too little reinforcement, feedback, and confidence-building praise ….

… So they put out even less over time than extroverts ….

… Then, they may resent it when other people, whose ideas seem so much less developed or rich, get all the praise.

Don't fret: in a bit, we'll talk about how introverts can maximize their good qualities and minimize their less-than-good ones.

You're an Extrovert: Pros and Cons

First we'll thrill you with details on the magnificence that is you—but then we'll have to temper that with a look at the negatives of extroversion.

Extra Good

They like you; they really like you! In Western culture, extroversion is where it's at. We're drawn to gregarious, active risk-takers. In addition, research has shown that extroverts tend to be happier than introverts, though researchers don't know if this is because being extroverted makes you happy, happier people tend to be extroverted, or something in between. Finally, extroverts tend to be ambitious; when they want something, they go after it.

The Darker Side of Extroverts

The bad news: extroverts tend not to be as scholarly as introverts—they can tend to get bored and antsy in academic settings. Extroverted children are also more likely to demonstrate delinquent behavior. It makes sense: who's more likely to get into trouble, the quiet kid reading a book in his room or the active kid outside playing chicken on his bike? And while Western culture sees extroverts as the perfect personality type, some (introverts, maybe?) also view extroverts as shallow and insincere (which we know is not true!).

Making the Most of Your Type

As I've mentioned, the first principle of social intelligence is "know thyself." In terms of introversion and extroversion, the best step you can take is to adopt Popeye's motto: "I yam what I yam!"

Introversion and extroversion are mostly about your brain's way of processing external and internal stimulation—extroverts thrive on lots of input, introverts get flooded. On the other hand, introverts are amazing at providing their own, internal stimulation, whether it's a good head for fiction or a love of music or pretty sunsets on quiet beaches. (You can probably tell if someone's an introvert or extrovert by the kind of beach resort they prefer! The one with the bustling nightclubs and hot social scene? Extrovert heaven! The one where there's nothing to do but read and take walks on long, empty stretches of sand? Paradise for innies!)

The real trick is to know enough about yourself that you can tailor-make the most comfortable world for yourself. Like with the beach example, it just makes more sense for extroverts to make sure that the resort they pick has lots of social stuff to jump into; introverts might prefer the quieter beach town, the one with a few good bookstores and nature walks.

> **SI Tip**
>
> Do you have an introverted child? Let her stay on the sidelines to check out the scene and get used to the amount of sights and sounds before getting involved in an activity.

Let's look at some other tips.

If You're an Introvert

Being an introvert means you probably have all sorts of inner resources to draw on when you have to solve a problem. Intuitions, insights, and creative ideas are all your forte! Which may mean you hardly need a list of coping tips—once, that is, you got over any guilt about "not being like all those extroverts" that was tangling you up! But here's a starter set of suggestions, just in case:

- Don't try to be an extrovert; appreciate what you have. You'll do better if you feel good about yourself and your vast inner resources.

- Maintain your energy. Don't try to "make yourself" enjoy nonstop partying in the dorms if you don't, and don't feel the need to apologize if you want to pop out for a break during a shindig, or to keep some free time for yourself. You may also find that you thrive on less noise than you're used to; try some time with the music off, or listen to recordings of seashores or quiet rainy days or birds instead of bass-thumping rock 'n' roll.

- Shop, drive, and run errands when things are less busy and the crowds are smaller, such as early in the morning—you'll find it less stressful.

- Nurture that inner life: enjoy your books, movies, Internet time, and time to write novels or paint.

◆ At big social events you'll probably enjoy yourself more if you focus on making contact with one or two people, instead of feeling like you should be talking with everyone or addressing the whole group. You may or may not find it easier to talk to other introverts; if they are choking up, too, it can be easier to chat with extroverts! But a few "What do you think about … " questions will often tickle introverts—they're often not used to people really caring about what they think!

◆ When you do need or want to get out there in the wide world, pace yourself, start small, and make a few connections at a time. Just smiling and asking people how their day is going is often a great opening.

◆ Go out for group activities and classes where you'll find people with shared interests. You can find classes for just about everything, from painting to financial planning. For group activities near you, such as writing groups and board game nights, check out www.meetup.com and www.craigslist.com.

◆ Plan social activities that fit your style: a book club or a date to see a romantic comedy or foreign film may fit you better than a large, unstructured party.

◆ When you're tired at a party or event, "check out" for a few minutes to recharge: go to a quiet hallway or part of the building and stare out the window. Pretend you're a smoker even if you're not (but don't start if you're not!)—go stand outside in the cool air and just enjoy the quiet for five minutes. Then rejoin the party.

If You're an Extrovert

Just like introverts, you have a lot going for you. Here's how to boost the benefits and nullify the not-so-good:

◆ Don't feel like you have to get all "quiet and deep" like introverts—your style is different, and that's just fine.

◆ Plan for the "right" amount of stimulation for you: you may go nuts if you can't get up and move around, be physical, and talk to people. Seek out situations where you'll be energized by groups of people and lots of activity, like parties, bowling teams, and karaoke (whether or not you can actually sing is beside the point).

◆ You may tend to "drive over" other people sometimes, especially if they're quieter than you. Work on noticing if you edge other people out of the conversation too much.

- Trying to draw others out, and especially trying to be sure you *mean* it, is important. (If your attitude is "But enough about what I think—what do *you* think about what I think?" it will show.)

- Build in some time to practice listening to your inner life. (Yeah—it's there!) Meditate, spend time reading (not playing video games), and write in a journal to help your brain develop some of those "innie" tendencies.

- Try out some introverts: sometimes that quiet guy in the corner can be a great complement to your more "out there" style. (There are a lot of very happy introvert/extrovert couples!)

The Least You Need to Know

- Introversion/extroversion is a continuum; everyone has some qualities of each type.

- Extroverts are more tuned to outside stimuli, while introverts are interested in their inner world.

- Neither type is better than the other; each has its strengths and weaknesses.

- You can make the most of your type while minimizing its weaknesses.

Chapter **5**

Assert Yourself!

In This Chapter

- ◆ Defining assertiveness
- ◆ Assertiveness the SI way
- ◆ Four elements of socially intelligent assertiveness
- ◆ Enhancing your assertiveness

The life of a doormat is not an easy one. People walk all over you. They leave their muddy shoes on your head. Worst of all, nobody ever asks a doormat what they want or like, or even if they mind being walked on.

Has anyone ever called you a "doormat"? Have you ever felt like one? Does it sometimes seem like other people walk all over you or ignore what you feel or want?

Or has the opposite happened? Have people accused you of treating *them* like doormats? Do friends or family say you ignore other people, push them around, or intimidate them?

No one really wants the personality of a doormat. Neither do most people relish a reputation for being a bully. The ability to find the middle ground—neither too passive nor too aggressive—is important in a healthy and successful life.

Making your presence known, asking for what you want in an effective way, is the essence of assertiveness. In this chapter, we'll help you assess and hone your assertiveness, using the science of social intelligence.

Check Yourself Out

This self-quiz is designed to give you a rough idea of how you handle assertiveness challenges. Circle the option that describes what *you would be most likely to do* in these situations. (Don't try to guess the "best" or "perfect" answer—the point is to learn about your current style, not to get a grade!)

1. Your teacher gives your class an assignment for a paper, but you're not clear on what he wants you to do. You are *most likely* to:

    A. Go home and struggle with it on your own, doing the best you can.

    B. Decide to give the teacher a negative course evaluation at the end of the term.

    C. Raise your hand and say you don't understand the assignment—can he please explain it again?

2. Your bank account was just overdrawn because your bank didn't credit a deposit the day you made it, though they did withdraw funds the instant you charged something. You:

    A. Call the bank and complain that they deliberately "set you up" to have an overdraft, and should repay you the money.

    B. Call the bank and ask if you can get help figuring out whether the mistake is theirs or yours, and hang on until it's clear to both of you what happened.

    C. Eat the cost, say nothing, and tell yourself there's no use fighting with them because they'll only say they're right.

3. In the library while you're trying to study, a couple of people in a nearby "study room" are having a meeting that keeps distracting you. So you:

    A. Go to the door of the study room and say "Excuse me, but you probably don't realize your conversation is being overheard—mind if I close the door?"

   B. Walk over to the room and, without saying anything to them, shut the door to the room—just a little bit loudly.

   C. Move your stuff to a different table across the library.

4. Your boss is a few months overdue with your performance review, which you need to get that important raise. You are most likely to:

   A. Keep waiting, because you know how busy she is and you don't want to add to her stress.

   B. Cut back on your work a bit, thinking "Why should I put out for her when she won't come through for me?"

   C. Ask her if there's a convenient time when she can get together with you and go over your review.

5. After you left your new doctor's office, you realized he didn't take time to answer your questions, and spent more time entering your "data" in his computer system than relating to you. You decide to:

   A. Write him a letter saying you weren't happy with his care, and that you're going to find a different physician.

   B. Come to the next appointment with a list of questions and concerns about how he interacted, then ask him if he has time to go over the list with you.

   C. Go on the Internet with all your medical questions from now on.

6. At a party, your best friend or date has clearly had too much to drink but says she is going to drive you home. You are most likely to:

   A. Get into the passenger seat and tell yourself she will probably make it home all right, just like every other time.

   B. Say she shouldn't drive, but when she gets angry and grabs the keys, refuse to go with her and think maybe a DUI will teach her a lesson.

   C. Gently as you can, but persistently, get her to let you drive, getting others to help, or even calling the police if she continues to insist on driving.

7. A boss or co-worker makes occasional sexually tinged comments that you find uncomfortable. So you:

   A. Start by privately and politely telling him that you're uncomfortable with that kind of comment, and ask him to please stop it.

   B. Immediately start secretly writing down all of his offensive comments and report him to HR.

   C. Say nothing and shrug off your discomfort.

8. Your spouse's temper has gotten more intense due to some recent stresses and health concerns. After she "loses it" and throws a dish at the wall, you are likely to:

   A. Sit quietly while she calms down, then not mention it again.

   B. Try to be supportive to de-escalate things, then later talk about how you can both manage the stress together.

   C. Say nothing and lapse into your own funk, acting hurt and withdrawn even when she is feeling better and apologizes.

9. In meetings, a co-worker tends to dominate discussions, to "take over" projects, and to ignore your ideas and contributions. Your most likely response:

   A. Decide you don't agree with his directions and go off and do your parts of the project the way you privately feel are best.

   B. During the meetings, you bring up and firmly confront his controlling behavior, even though it creates some discomfort in the room.

   C. Take the co-worker aside and talk about the project and how things are going, and when you have some rapport together, gently bring up your discomfort with his "taking-over" style.

10. Your roommate "borrows" a lot of your drinks and food without replacing or paying for any of it. Most of the time you are likely to:

    A. Stop buying the snacks she likes, and hide the rest in your private spots where she won't find them.

    B. Tell yourself you don't mind sharing, even though you really can't afford to pay for the food for both of you.

    C. Tell her you'd like her to chip in for the food, and suggest the two of you draw up a shopping plan and budget together.

Scoring: Circle which answer you chose here, then add up the number of circles in each column:

Item	Assertive	Passive	Aggressive	Passive-Aggressive
1. (Teacher)	C	A		B
2. (Bank)	B	C	A	
3. (Library)	A	C	B	
4. (Boss)	C	A		B
5. (Doctor)	B	C	A	
6. (Drinking)	C	A		B
7. (Sexual)	A	C	B	
8. (Spouse)	B	A		C
9. (Co-worker)	C	A	B	
10. (Roommate)	C	B		A
Totals				

Interpreting your results:

Assertive   6–10: If most of your answers are in the "Assertive" column, you probably tend to function with a fairly high level of both assertiveness and social intelligence. Your responses tend to balance your needs and legitimate concerns with an awareness of your impact on others and how they will feel when you ask for something.

Passive   6–10: Having many responses in this column might mean that you are too passive. You may have learned that the safe way to behave is to let others get their way, to be a people pleaser, to avoid conflicts even if you lose out. You may seem invisible to others.

Aggressive   2 or more: More than a few answers in this column may mean you tilt toward being too aggressive. You may come across to others as pushy or bossy—even though you may not get that feedback from them. (They may be too scared of you to tell you!) Sometimes being aggressive is a good thing, but more often it leads to frustration and uncomfortable relationships.

Passive-Aggressive   3–5: If you circled three or more answers in this column, you may tend to be passive-aggressive. Passive-aggressive people are actually pretty aggressive, but they conceal their aggressive and hostile behavior from others (and often, from themselves). They fight back by withdrawing, not coming through, pretending to be pleasing, but actually their behavior frustrates and annoys others.

Most people have a "mix" of styles, depending on the situation and the relationship they're dealing with. And that may be fine. But if you think your style of assertiveness doesn't work so well for you, this chapter may help!

What Is Assertiveness?

Assertiveness means being able to ask for what you want, to express your opinions (even if others disagree), to stand up for your rights, and to make your presence known to others. It includes knowing how to influence people, to tell people what they don't want—but need—to hear, to express your feelings (including negative feelings), and to manage *boundaries* that you may not want someone to cross.

def•i•ni•tion

Boundaries, in psychological parlance, means the limits of what is acceptable in how someone behaves toward us. For example, reading someone's private diary, making sexually inappropriate comments in a workplace, or asking someone intrusive and personal questions, may cross that person's boundary.

The opposite of assertiveness can include behaviors such as being too passive, deferring to others' opinions or wants, or being too self-effacing. It can also include being too aggressive. It may mean you back down on something you want or need, such as the salary you deserve or a car without that extra $500 seal-coating treatment the dealer wants to foist on you. Or it may mean that you give in all the time, but then walk around resenting everyone for taking advantage of you.

Things That Aren't Assertiveness

If you have trouble getting the kinds of responses you want from others, it may signal that you're either too passive, too aggressive, or too passive-aggressive. Most of us have a blend of passive, aggressive, and passive-aggressive behaviors—that's not "wishy-washy" but normal. It means you adapt your style to the situation. But if you tend to rely too much on just one of these styles for dealing with people, life can get pretty frustrating.

Passive behavior: Remember the Charles Dickens story *Oliver Twist?* The starving orphan who dared to ask for more gruel, only to be severely punished and thrown out of the children's workhouse? How dare he ask for more! After all, "children should be seen and not heard!"—especially starving orphans!

Unfortunately, many people grow into adulthood having learned that lesson too well. Back in the murky pasts of their childhoods, they learned that the best, safest way to live is to never ask for anything, never make a fuss, never make a demand. Being invisible, accepting what they're given and not asking for more, shrugging it off when bullies kick sand in their faces—these behaviors seem to passive people to be the keys to success (or at least, to being allowed to spend another night in the orphanage!). They may even learn to rationalize this passivity as a kind of virtue, mistaking a passive personality for being loving and kind.

While this may actually be a safe course of action in some situations (such as if you're a child in an abusive orphanage), over the long haul it leads to frustration, and even to a kind of empty, bland, and lonely existence. Not good.

Aggressive behavior: Aggressive people turn requests into demands. They tell people what to do, instead of asking. They come into a group and take over, ignoring other people's irritations. If passive people are socially invisible, aggressive people make other people socially invisible, by implying that only *their* needs matter!

Passive-aggressive behavior: "Who, me? Be aggressive? I'm not like that at all! I'm only trying to make you happy!"

Ever know somebody who had a tendency to infuriate people, but when called on their behavior, they always had an excuse? They don't speak up and say they want Italian, and then pout through the meal in the Chinese restaurant. They don't disagree with someone's suggestions to their face, but then forget to follow through with their side of the agreement.

People who solve interpersonal problems passive-aggressively generally have angry or aggressive feelings that they don't think are safe to express directly. In fact, they may not even want to admit to themselves that they have such feelings! Instead, they find indirect, deniable ways of fighting back or expressing these feelings. So they smile and politely agree with you to your face, then find other ways to express their displeasure.

Sometimes their main approach is to quietly not cooperate, but other times they

SI Tip

The best way to deal with passive-aggressive people is often to confront them directly, though not too harshly, on their behavior. "If you don't like this restaurant, I'd appreciate it if you would say so instead of sulking and not talking to anyone," for instance.

may even turn their aggressive feelings on themselves, in an "I'll hold my breath till I turn blue!" sort of way. As a character in a Woody Allen movie once put it, "I don't get angry. I grow a tumor!"

How We Learn to Assert Ourselves

If you're lucky, you grew up in a family or other environment where you were taught how to be assertive. This means you had a few things going for you: your opinions (like, "I *hate* spinach!") and requests were not punished or discouraged so much that you got afraid to express yourself; you had good role models in your parents, siblings, or other people, who could show you how to be assertive in balanced ways; and you were helped to understand what kinds of situations call for what sorts of assertiveness. (For instance, your mom told you it's okay to ask the teacher when you need help understanding an assignment.)

> **Social Science**
>
> Assertiveness training was first described in 1958 by psychologist Joseph Wolpe. He saw it as a way to help people express themselves and their feelings freely, without letting anxiety interfere. In the 1970s the focus of assertiveness training changed to teaching people to stand up for their rights.

Many of us weren't so lucky, though. Perhaps our parents weren't available very much, or were so stressed that any little demand we made (like Oliver Twist asking for more!) was stressful for them. Instead of getting what we wanted, we were sent to bed without any gruel at all! Or else our parents and siblings were themselves habitually self-effacing people who didn't know how to show us the way to assertiveness.

If you were super lucky in your childhood assertiveness training—great! Skip the rest of this chapter! But if you were like most people, there were a few gaps in your training which you can still work on.

Why Assertiveness Matters

In a perfect world, you might not need to be very assertive. Everything you wanted or needed would just magically be there, or would fall into your lap as soon as you wanted it. Want a juicy peach? *Voilà!* You got it! Want someone to do you a favor? Want your opinion listened to? *Voilà!* People appear to help, or to hang on your every word.

Of course, the world you live in isn't usually like that. Or, rather, it hasn't been like that since you were a delightful, lovable baby, hovered over by adults who spent much of their day scrutinizing your every coo and gurgle to see what you needed. (And even babies can be more, or less, assertive than other babies! Ask any mom who's had more than one!)

The world of adults is more hurly-burly, and sometimes dog-eat-dog. People stopped paying eager attention to your needs a long time ago, so if you're going to have any chance of having them met, you'll have to let someone know. And gurgling and crying won't work anymore—as a grownup, your best results will require some assertiveness.

Besides getting refills at a restaurant, what good are assertiveness skills? There are a bunch of good things that come from being assertive.

Payoffs from Asserting Yourself

The list is endless, but here is a short sampler of benefits you may see if you develop your assertive skills.

Feeling better about yourself. Skulking in the shadows while other people get all the attention and favors isn't fun, but it can also reinforce your self-image as unimportant, unlovable, and practically invisible. Being more in control of how people respond to you has the tasty side-benefit of making you feel more self-confident, valued, and loved by others.

Having your opinions heard. Nonassertive people with bright ideas and real solutions typically go unheard. If you want to contribute to solving problems, or let your creative light shine, you have to know how to turn up your personal dimmer switch.

Greater immunity to depression. Research shows that believing "nothing I say or do will matter" can lead to severe depression. This is more likely to be a problem if you're chronically under-assertive: how can you feel in charge of your life if you don't know how to get the things you need?

> **Social Science**
>
> Psychologists have found that one surefire way to make someone depressed is to put them in a situation where nothing they do makes any difference. The technical term for this is learned helplessness.

More fun in life. Asking for your turn on the water skis, speaking up when they ask "does anybody here want to take a spin on my mountain bike?", speaking up about the movie *you* want to see (instead of always letting your boyfriend pick)—these are all assertive actions. As a general rule, assertive people create more opportunities to enjoy themselves because they don't hang back all the time.

Career success. Assertive people are generally more successful in their careers. Not only are they better at asking for things for themselves (like raises, or that nicer cubicle near the window), but they tend to inspire more trust in co-workers and to demonstrate the kinds of leadership skills that lead to promotions and important assignments.

Effective parenting. If you have kids, they probably watch how you behave all the time. When kids see their parents being assertive and effective in the world, it helps them learn those critical skills.

Assertiveness and Social Intelligence

Although therapists, teachers, social science researchers, and even corporate trainers and coaches have taught the principles of assertiveness for decades, the new science of social intelligence sheds new light on the topic. Once we switch from thinking of ourselves as fully independent, unconnected beings, to thinking of ourselves as interconnected selves, asserting ourselves takes on a different quality. Assertiveness is less something you do to manage others, and more like something we do with each other.

Classic Assertiveness Training

Most approaches to assertiveness training were invented several decades ago, long before the field of SI developed. Back then, psychologists were trying to find ways to help people cope with problems of power and its abuse in human relationships. Therapists were uncovering massive amounts of abuse and trauma in their clients' lives, and were also addressing the concerns of feminists and minorities who felt that white males held most of the power in society. Assertiveness training became an important weapon in the fight to protect people with less power, to help people to learn to demand their fair share in life.

The science of SI is expanding the way we view even simple interactions. As we learn more about how interconnected people are, how the "emotion-processing" areas of one person's brain links up with and affects others, it will change how we view skills like assertiveness.

An SI Approach

Socially intelligent assertiveness may look and feel like traditional assertiveness skills, but there are some subtle differences. In traditional assertiveness training, the main attitude you learned was that it was somehow your job to manage how other people treated you. In contrast, the SI approach steers clear of people management. Instead, you take a more collaborative approach, focusing on the feelings and connections with others instead of just expressing your own needs. Mainly, this is a difference in attitude. But as the researchers are showing, when it comes to human relationships, attitudes matter—probably more than anything else!

Not tuning in to other people's subjective reality, to their individuality and feelings, can distort your connections. You start to approach them with an attitude that your job is to somehow demand, *manipulate*, or trick them into doing your bidding. Of course, you tell yourself (and old-fashioned assertiveness training always stressed) not to be too aggressive. But if you're ignoring their concerns and failing to make a solid connection before you assert yourself, it's actually pretty aggressive anyway!

def•i•ni•tion

To **manipulate** people means to try to steer, control, or influence them in indirect, unfair, slick, or dishonest ways. Some people tend to be manipulative, meaning that they often try to do this instead of being more honest or upfront about their agendas and what they want.

Steps to Assertiveness

In socially intelligent assertiveness, the four key SI principles all apply. Knowing yourself, tuning in to others, connecting, and being compassionate and ethical, are the hallmarks of an effective assertiveness style.

Know Thyself

Here are some questions you can ask yourself to get a better understanding of your assertiveness style. Spend some time on them—write them down in your journal or in a document on your laptop. Discuss them, if you can, with close friends or family members. What do you learn that can help you understand and, if need be, change your approach?

Family background: What were the ways your family members expressed their needs? How did they demonstrate assertive, or aggressive/passive, behaviors? Were you encouraged to say what you felt, to ask for what you needed? When you did, did your parents, siblings, and others tune in? How did your family manage conflicts?

Strengths/weaknesses: What kinds of assertiveness challenges have you managed well? Not so well? Horribly? (Hint: think about situations at work, school, in relationships, dealing with people like clerks, business acquaintances, and so on.) Make a list of things that went well, and events you wish you could do over.

Gender issues: If you are female, has this affected how you express your needs and opinions? Do you find yourself being talked over in class or at work by males? Do you think being female poses some extra challenges for you?

If you are male, do you choke or clam up around women, or perhaps do you feel more relaxed dealing with females, but intimidated by males? (Yes, that's not uncommon!) And to be fair, do you talk over women sometimes, or maybe let your aggressive side out a bit more freely with females than with males? How do you feel about it?

Tune In to Others

When you need to assert yourself, it will work best if you can tune in and pick up all the cues you can about the other person. What cues are you picking up? How do they appear to feel—what's their emotional state? What do you know about their situation, the pressures they are dealing with?

Make a Connection!

If you can do it, orient yourself to the other person nonverbally: Are you making eye contact? Is your body language "in sync" as much as possible? Does your posture signal openness, safety, and a "glad to see you!" attitude or does it show tightness, closed-in-ness, fear, or anger? How about your voice: Are you speaking at about the same volume? Is your tone and tempo similar to theirs? Are you feeling like you're in sync?

Verbal skills count—can you express yourself and your concerns clearly? Are you letting them know that you are asking for something (if you are)?

SI Tip

Practice being assertive with a friend, not just by discussing your concerns but actually role-playing the situations you are concerned about. You may also find it helpful to hire a professional life or business coach or therapist. These people often work with clients to develop their assertiveness skills.

Feel—and Show—Concern!

Do you really have some concern for the people you're "asserting on"? Are you mindful of the fact that you're asking for their time, their attention, and their energy? You may not be asking them to care about you, but if you're really tuned in to them, and want to find a way you can both get what you want from the interaction, they're more likely to care about your needs!

Enhance Your Assertiveness!

Okay! Now it's time to put all this insight into action, to build up your assertive skills. Remember, we are talking about skills here, so practice really will make a difference.

Basic Steps

The best way to build your assertiveness skills is to focus on three things: reducing your anxiety, practicing new assertive behaviors, and changing some of your thinking habits.

Anxiety management: That thumping heart, the dry mouth, the clammy skin—all telltale signs that you're anxious. If it's hard for you to assert yourself, anxiety may be the cause.

How do you get the anxious feelings under control? Fortunately, there are lots of things you can do to shrink your anxiety down to size. Simplest is to deal with the physical parts of anxiety: the muscle tension, the pounding heart, the surging fight-or-flight hormones like adrenaline.

Light exercise usually helps (walking or running is good). So do relaxation exercises, yoga, and meditation. Just good self-care—like getting enough sleep and cutting back on the jitter-causing caffeine—helps, too.

Change your behavior: Make a list of situations (work, in class) or relationships (your boss, your mom) where more assertiveness is called for. What can you do differently in those situations?

SI Tip

When making changes in your behavior, start with one small change that you practice until it's second nature, then make another, then another. In time, you'll have transformed yourself in major ways, and the changes will stick!

For example, let's say you realize that you tend to drop everything you're doing whenever someone comes to your desk with a new request. By the end of the day you feel frazzled and exhausted, and your important tasks never get done. Can you see what you need to change? You might practice saying, "I'll get to that, but I can't do it right now. Can I call you when it's taken care of?"

Rethink your thinking: Thinking matters! Your assumptions about whether it's okay to assert yourself may hold you back. Worse still, they may be all wrong!

Many people assume that there are rules about what they're allowed to say or ask, when in fact that may not be true at all. Who says you can't express your opinions, or disagree with a friend or teacher? Where is it written that you can't express an opinion to your co-worker, disagree with your instructor's views, or tell your boyfriend that you should get to pick the movie half the time?

The fact is, most of these rules probably exist only in your mind. Particularly if you tend to be under-assertive, you probably live in a world full of imaginary rules that the people around you don't even know you're following! This can be a great time to re-examine your assumptions about whether it's really okay not to assert yourself! Even rules you don't know you tend to follow, like always asking the other person where they want to go for dinner before mentioning your craving for Mexican.

If you can change your thinking about some of these rules, you'll be more likely to change your behavior as well. And little by little, you'll see your assertiveness quotient rise.

> **Caution!**
>
> It's rare, but real: sometimes people really *are* dangerous. Use common sense when practicing your assertiveness skills. "Defending your rights" when a mugger demands your wallet might have tragic consequences. But subtler dangers also exist: co-workers might sabotage you after your outburst of honesty and attempts to "clear the air around here" about some tensions between people. Angrily mentioning to a co-worker that she really blew a committee assignment may result in her resentfully starting a gossip campaign about you, or result in three years' worth of discussions at your annual performance review about "your progress on that temper issue."

Seven Ways to Boost Your Assertiveness

There's no end to the ways you can behave assertively—it's really an art form. But some of the most common techniques follow. Even mastering one or two of these might help you improve your assertiveness skills a great deal! Here's a list to get you started:

- **Practice some "request starter phrases."** Most people who are good at asking for things have just a few ways of starting out, such as:

  "Could I trouble you to … ?"

  or

  "Would you mind … ?"

  For example, "Would you mind not smoking in the house? The smoke bothers me."

- **Let them know you care.** Start off by signaling to the other person that you're aware of his situation, and not just your own. For instance, saying "I see that you're busy, but when you have a minute could you help me …?" is much more effective than just saying, "Hey, you! Help me with this …."

- **Check your tone of voice.** Do you sound loud and intimidating? Or are you barely squeaking out your request, or whispering it so they can't really hear you? A confident, quiet, caring tone usually works best.

- **Make eye contact.** Eye contact, especially the kind that conveys interest and attention to the other person, can help you create that sense of "connection" that will help the other person "decide to want to help you."

- **Smile.** No, not a silly grin, but a warm, nice smile can open doors, get a person's interest, and ensure that the other person tunes in to you.

 SI Tip _____

Three good times to get some eye-gazing in are when you first greet someone (be conscious of looking them in the eye for a second or two while you smile—hold that gaze till they gaze back and return your warm smile); when they're saying something to you, when a moment of eye-gaze and an "I get you" nod is good; and when you say something to them and want to check that they "got it." (Their eyes will say more than their words. An "uh, okay, I understand" while they look away dazed and confused is a clue that they didn't understand.) If you find eye contact hard, start with short, quick glances, or look at the bridge of their nose and fake it. (An old acting trick is to look back and forth from their left to their right eye a few times; it conveys a more "searching" and attentive gaze, and can be quite charismatic. If you're not sure how to do it, watch some soap opera actors and look for the "probing gaze" look.)

◆ **Relax.** Do whatever you can to keep your anxiety level down. We can tense up when faced with assertiveness opportunities, and tension is both unhealthy and works against us when we interact with others. (See the "anxiety management" tips earlier in the chapter for suggestions.)

◆ **Visualize outcomes.** Before you walk into a tension-causing situation, try to imagine everything going very well. Seeing things work out in your mental movie theatre may help you find the calm courage you need to bring up that touchy subject. Likewise, some failure rehearsal can help. Ask yourself, "If this doesn't work, what's Plan B?" Just knowing you have another plan can reduce your anxiety.

Caution!

Psychologists have confirmed that if you predict failure for yourself, you're more likely to fail. You may even be "programming" yourself to fail and "rehearsing" your disasters. Be careful, then, if you notice yourself imagining the worst possible response to your assertive behavior.

Practice Makes Perfect!

We've talked about what assertiveness is, how it works, and how to build your skills. Are you feeling ready for your complete Do-It-Yourself Assertiveness Makeover? Ready to rock—and maybe even change—your world? Great—time to get started! The best way to start is with some practice sessions.

Here's what you can do:

Make a brainstorm list of all the aspects of your life that would benefit from improved assertiveness.

Then list some situations that come up in your most important assertiveness target areas. For instance, if you've decided that you need to make some changes at work, make a list of three or four situations where you wish you could be more assertive.

Pick one of these situations, and go out and practice. It's usually good to start with the easiest ones. For example, you may find it less daunting to ask a waiter to warm up your coffee than to ask your boss to let you make changes in your job. (But after a few go-rounds with waiters, talking to your boss may be a little less terrifying!)

Whether or not you're successful, make a note of what happened; how you felt; how the other person reacted. And, most importantly, what you learned that you can use the next time.

The Least You Need to Know

◆ Becoming more assertive may help you feel better about yourself, prevent depression, help your career, and even make you a better parent.

◆ Asserting yourself with skill and sensitivity is generally more effective than being passive, aggressive, or passive-aggressive.

◆ Socially intelligent assertiveness focuses on the feelings and needs of the other person, not just on your own needs.

◆ Treat assertiveness like any other skill: start small, practice, and get feedback and you will improve.

Chapter 6

Don't Be Shy!

In This Chapter

- ◆ All about shyness
- ◆ Shyness and social intelligence
- ◆ How to shrink the shys

You've probably felt it at some time or other. Most of us have. You know—that wallflower tendency? Shyness can be something that you feel only occasionally, like when you have to give a speech, or it can dominate—and shrink—your life.

In this chapter, we'll talk about shyness and all its varieties, and suggest ways to battle it that may help you morph from a wallflower to a social butterfly in the garden of life.

But first, time to do some self-assessment.

Check Yourself Out

This self-quiz is designed to give you a rough idea of how shy you are. Mark the option that describes what you would be most likely to do in these situations, or that best describes you.

1. Your mother used to refer to you as "shy" or "the shy one":

    A. Never—she said just the opposite!

    B. She was always saying "Don't be so shy!"

    C. Mostly when I was very young.

2. Say you were to spend 24 hours in a small town on vacation. How many people would you probably talk to while you were there?

    A. I'd talk to one or two, if I found myself in a comfortable situation where it was easy to talk.

    B. Probably more than five, and I'd have to stop by and say goodbye on my way out of town!

    C. Just people I "had to," like the motel clerk.

3. Which animal's behavior might best describe your personality?

    A. I'm like the cautious cat who hides under the bed until any strangers have gone.

    B. I'm like a big, friendly dog who runs up to everyone with his tail wagging.

    C. I'm like a friendly cat who watches a new person for a few minutes, then passes by and lets him pet me.

4. How would you react if you got a call from a favorite charity or politician's campaign, asking if you'd come down and make phone calls for a fund-raiser?

    A. If coaxed, and they really needed me, and there was a script I could follow, I might do it for an hour or two.

    B. No way, no how! I'll send in a check instead, okay?

    C. I'd be happy to! And I'll bring treats for the other workers!

5. Which would you rather do—have a minor, pretty safe, hour-long surgical procedure, or give a talk in front of a group of strangers for that hour?

    A. I'd love to talk! What's the topic, or does it matter?

    B. I'd have to think about that one.

    C. Will I be having anesthesia with that surgery?

6. On a bet, to win five bucks, can you go to a grocery store and say hello to five people?

   A. You couldn't pay me enough.

   B. Make it ten and you're on.

   C. I'd be stealing your money—I do it all the time for free.

7. Say you learned that there was a group of people forming in your neighborhood who share an interest in your favorite hobby. Most likely, you would:

   A. Call someone to get the meeting times, and invite another of my friends to become part of the group with me.

   B. Doesn't matter—no way am I going to ever get to that!

   C. Go to a meeting eventually, but it would make me a bit nervous.

8. You experience physical sensations of anxiety, such as pounding heart, sweaty palms, dry mouth, and so on, in social situations:

   A. Sometimes, depending on the situation.

   B. Never had 'em and don't know what that would be like.

   C. Often, or even every time I have to meet new people or interact in a social situation.

9. When you think of going to a social gathering where there will be new people, you imagine that you will:

   A. Be ignored, silently critiqued, or even humiliated.

   B. Be welcomed and make new friends, and have a nice time.

   C. It depends—it might be okay, or it might not be a very pleasant time.

10. Have you ever worried about your shyness? How much?

    A. Sometimes, but I generally manage.

    B. I always worry about it.

    C. Never. I don't consider myself shy at all.

Scoring: Circle which answer you chose for each question, then add up the number of circles within each column.

Item	Wallflower	Depends	Fearless
1. (Mother)	B	C	A
2. (24 hours)	C	A	B
3. (Animal)	A	C	B
4. (Charity)	B	A	C
5. (Surgery)	C	B	A
6. (Bet)	A	B	C
7. (Hobby)	B	C	A
8. (Physical)	C	A	B
9. (Gathering)	A	C	B
10. (Worry)	B	A	C
Totals			

Interpreting your results:

Wallflower   6–10: Shyness may be a significant concern that may have a strong negative impact on your life. If most or all of your answers are here, it may be serious enough that you need to talk to a pro—just to make sure you don't have social anxiety or a similar condition (more on this later in the chapter).

Depends   6–10: Shyness may be a concern for you at times, depending on the situation and how you're feeling. Or you may just be a bit of an introvert—read on!

Fearless   6–10: Congratulations, you social butterfly! You don't have a shy bone in your body.

That Wallflower Tendency

The really odd thing about shyness is that nearly everyone has experienced it, but when you're feeling shy it may seem as though you're all alone with it. It can be as though you're out in deep space, cut off from all human contact. You can be among friends, in the middle of a party, or surrounded by classmates or co-workers who all know you and even like you. Yet when you're feeling shy, you may feel as though nobody knows you, nobody would really like you if you made a peep, and you may even feel too paralyzed to reach out to anyone.

What is shyness, and why is it so powerful?

Shyness can affect you in many ways. You may feel only a few of them, or all of them. For example:

Behavior: You may be passive, act nervous, or be inhibited. You may avoid situations, places, events, or people (such as your advisor or boss) that make you uncomfortable. You may choke when you try to talk, your voice dropping to a whisper, or you may even start to stammer.

Thinking: You might get obsessed about how you're being evaluated, or with making sure your comments are super-well thought out and perfect before you raise your hand to speak in a group. It may seem that there must be a "right way" to approach that comely stranger, so you hold back until you've checked a few more websites for advice on "how to say hello." You over-prepare until you under-perform.

Physical: Your body goes through all the fight-or-flight panic syndrome thingies: heart races, mouth feels full of sand, sweating, shaking.

Emotions: Everything feels bad: shame, embarrassment, stinging self-consciousness, sadness, anxiety, even depression.

Sound familiar? You're not alone. In fact, you're surrounded by people who know what you're going through! Because they've been there, too!

Normal, healthy children are often shy because so many life situations are new experiences for them. They often feel anxious, afraid of strangers or of what's going on in new places. They don't know the rules and so they hold back, hide their eyes in Mommy's skirt, and don't say "hello" to the nice lady like they were told.

Gradually this childhood shyness usually gives way to mastery and confidence—or so one would think! But not always. Researchers now say that as many as half of adults in the United States report that they are shy on an ongoing basis. That's right. *Half!* And the number seems to be going up, not down!

> **Social Science**
>
> The ancient Greek physician Hippocrates (who lived from about 460–370 B.C.) described a patient with severe social anxiety symptoms: "He dare not come in company for fear he should be misused, disgraced, overshoot himself in gesture or speeches, or be sick; he thinks every man observes him!"

> **Caution!**
>
> Don't ever try to scold or shame a shy child into not being shy. That's more likely to make them feel worse about themselves, which will only increase the shyness. Better to be supportive and help them find some places where they feel more relaxed and able to be themselves.

When "Shy" Becomes "Phobic"

Shyness can range from 0 to 100 in severity. It can last a moment or a lifetime. If it becomes very severe, you may actually have a diagnosable mental health condition.

The main conditions that are shyness-related (you might say, shyness on steroids) include social phobias and avoidant personality disorders.

Social phobia. The American Psychiatric Association defines a social *phobia* (also called social anxiety disorder) as excessive anxiety in social situations that causes extreme distress and results in impaired functioning in at least some areas of life. In other words, to qualify for the diagnosis, you have to have both things: high anxiety, and some kind of limited functioning as a result of that anxiety. Also, the things you fear must have something to do with social situations. It can be fear that you'll be criticized or scrutinized, or that you'll do something embarrassing or foolish, and so on.

def•i•ni•tion

> **Phobias** come in many flavors. For instance, ever heard of glossophobia? It's fear of speaking in public. How about topophobia? Stage fright. Or opthalmophobia? Fear of being stared at. Of course, for you extroverts there's always monophobia, which is fear of solitude, or autophobia, which is the fear of being alone.

It's estimated that about 13 percent of adults in the United States will have a social phobia at some point in their lives. At any given moment (such as right now, as you read this sentence) between 2 and 8 percent of the population suffers from social phobias. That makes it the third most common psychiatric problem in the country, after depression and alcohol dependence!

Social phobias usually start between age 11 and 19; if you haven't "caught" a social phobia by age 25, the odds are slim that you will. If you're female, you're twice as likely to have the condition, though this is one mental health problem that men seek help for more often than women. (Usually women get help with mental health problems more often.)

> **Social Science**
>
> If your anxiety occurs in many situations or regardless of where you are, you might have generalized anxiety disorder. If it happens in only one type of situation, such as public speaking, it might better be diagnosed as a basic phobia (such as a fear of public speaking).

And if you've got it, odds go up that you'll have some other problems as well: the *comorbidity* of social phobia and conditions such as depression (which we will discuss) or alcohol or drug use is high.

How you get it: some of it may be genetics. You have a better chance of developing a social phobia if you've got close relatives with the problem. Also, bad experiences— social embarrassments, being bullied as a kid, being rejected or ignored, or even hearing about someone else's negative experience—can do it.

Panic disorders. One of the problems that can develop from social anxiety is panic disorders and/or agoraphobia. A panic attack is an episode of extreme anxiety, which can be so bad that you actually fear you're having a heart attack. The experience is almost unbearable: fear with physical sensations of extreme anxiety such as heart pounding, chest pains, dizziness, vomiting, headaches, and so on; it can also include the certainty that you are going to die. Many of the possible heart attack visits people make to emergency rooms are really panic attacks. (Though if you're ever, *ever* suspicious that you're having a heart attack: get to the ER anyway, or better still, dial 911! Let *them* tell *you* "it was only anxiety!")

Sometimes people become frightened that they will become frightened, and that can actually start to trigger these reactions. The fear of being humiliated or judged by others in a public setting can trigger the fear that you'll have an embarrassing anxiety reaction. After a while, even going into a public setting such as a mall can trigger this fear.

Avoidant Personality Disorder. If a person has an avoidant *personality disorder* they tend to be socially inhibited, to feel inadequate, and to be super-sensitive to negative responses or evaluations by others; they generally avoid social interaction and find it painful. This isn't just in one or two areas, and it doesn't last for just a short time; rather, much of the person's life is dominated by this condition.

The "loners" of society, people who feel disconnected from other people and not a part of society, may have avoidant personality

def•i•ni•tion

Comorbidity is a medical term referring to illnesses that occur together. Sometimes that happens because one of them causes the other, such as when alcoholism causes depression. Other times, something else causes both: a bad fall may give you both a broken arm and a concussion.

def•i•ni•tion

Personality disorders are persistent difficulties in functioning that go beyond a few symptoms in just a few parts of a person's life. Rather, they take up much of the person's life or personality, and it often seems as though these are more a matter of who the person is than a specific psychological problem they have.

disorder. This generally starts in early adulthood. People who develop this problem may have had lots of rejection by other kids, by parents, or others.

It's estimated that nearly 5 million people, or 2 to 4 percent of the U.S. population, have avoidant personality disorders.

It's Not Introversion

It's worth remembering that neither shyness nor mental health conditions such as social phobias are the same thing as introversion. Introversion and social phobia may look similar from the outside because both involve a tendency to stick to oneself. But there is a key difference: anxiety level.

People with social phobia (or various other social-related phobias), or who are crippled by garden-variety shyness are afflicted with uncomfortable levels of anxiety in social situations. With introversion, on the other hand, the defining "discomfort" in social situations—if discomfort is present at all—is merely fatigue. Introverts just feel worn out more quickly in social situations if there is a lot of noise or too much interaction.

So introversion is about enjoying your own company and less-crowded situations, while shyness and social anxiety are matters of experiencing anxiety and pain if you have to be involved in social situations (even though you might actually long to be at those parties, and hate being home alone). It is possible to be both introverted and shy, of course—but they don't *have* to go together! (I'm an introvert, for instance, but I'm not very shy most of the time.)

In this chapter, we mainly focus on helping you deal with shyness and fairly mild forms of social anxiety. But many of the basic principles for dealing with these also apply to the more severe, diagnosable anxiety conditions as well. It's all a matter of degree. And so if what we cover here helps you, great. If you need more help because your difficulties seem more severe, we'll talk about finding help later in the chapter.

The Shrunken Life of the Shrinking Violet

Shyness costs you. In fact, you may be surprised if you add up what it costs in lost opportunities, lost experiences, and general misery. You may not notice this day to day—we tend to get used to problems that we've had a long time—until they're gone and we realize how much of a burden we'd been carrying!

But consider these examples.

Relationships you don't have. Does holding back cost you friendships, romances, or other pleasant connections that you long to have?

Career opportunities you've missed. Have you avoided potentially exciting and well-paying jobs because they would require you to take a risk and deal with the public? Did you not pick a career you secretly might have loved, because of the "people" thing? Were you afraid to leave your small but familiar town and go off to the big college campus to get that degree?

SI Tip _____

Track your no shy zones—places where you don't feel shy. Most of us feel shy at least some places, but relaxed in others. How about libraries, movies, or the mall? The more no shy zones you visit, the less often your shyness will rear its head.

New experiences. Have you not gone places you wanted to see? Not talked to interesting looking people at school or work or when out shopping? Not taken that course in ballroom dancing because you would feel awkward tripping on your "two left feet" in front of others?

The cost of loneliness. How often do you feel lonely? What would you pay to make that go away?

Mental and physical health problems. Socially anxious people are more likely to develop other anxiety problems and depression, and to turn to the comforts of substance abuse, food abuse, TV and Internet abuse, and to owning dozens of cats. And as we've discussed before, social isolation places you at far greater risk for severe (including terminally severe) health problems.

That Shy "Vicious Cycle"

One of the worst parts of having a shyness problem is that it tends to be a vicious cycle. You avoid doing something or going somewhere because you'd feel anxiety. You may not even realize you're doing it at first, but after a while your avoidance becomes a pattern that's hard to change. How did that happen?

When you begged off from going to the party the first time, you experienced a small surge of relief. This relief changed your brain: the instant you "backed down" you flooded your brain with "pain is over" messages. As you settled into your easy chair and turned the tube back on, your brain was being heavily "rewarded" chemically as you felt a sudden drop in anxiety.

The result? Next time, you were even more likely to blow off an anxiety-causing event, further reinforcing your anxiety.

Social Science
Charles Darwin described a painfully shy man who tried to give a speech, but was so anxious that he couldn't get a word out. But he acted as though he was giving the speech, and his sympathetic audience applauded his "imaginary bursts of eloquence." Darwin wrote that the man later told a friend "with much satisfaction, that he thought he had succeeded uncommonly well."

If you were just an introvert, these actions might just be a process of finding yourself. In that case, you wouldn't really be avoiding the situation because you were getting anxious as you reached for your car keys, but would simply be getting clear that you really, truly, actually, deep down in your bones love sitting home watching HBO or reading Tolstoy, or taking that walk along the beach with one close friend instead of hanging out with 15 of them at the pub.

But if you opted out of an evening on the town because of mounting anxiety, the result was probably something different: you may have felt unhappy about staying home. You know you haven't found your real passion in long nights with your cat and Tolstoy. You know you have a problem.

Shyness and Social Intelligence

In a sense, shyness and social anxiety are like living in a medieval castle that is under siege: they keep you trapped inside your own castle walls. You're afraid to go out, or even sometimes to look out over the ramparts. Who might be out there? What might they be thinking about me? What awful things will happen if I step outside the gate and cross the moat?

Of course, this pretty much amounts to the exact opposite of socially intelligent behavior! Because remember: social intelligence is not just a matter of knowing facts about society. It's about doing stuff. And the "stuff" that you are doing involves taking the kinds of risks that shy people want to avoid.

For example, socially intelligent people don't just know about their emotional states—they also actively *manage* those states. If there is some anxiety, one of their skills is knowing how to reduce that unpleasant state: they take a walk, do deep breathing, or reframe in their minds whatever is triggering the anxiety.

The same applies to knowing how to tune in to others. If you're preoccupied with how they're going to view or judge you, you won't be paying attention to the sig-nals they're sending. (Such as, say, the fact that *they* feel shy, too!) Nor will you be very good at making contact: it's hard to say "hello!" when you're bolting for the exit in fear!

And it's certainly hard to tune in with a great deal of empathy and compassion to another human being when you are the one who practically needs to be carried out in a basket because of your social panic!

> **SI Tip**
>
> Your doctor or psychiatrist might be able to prescribe medications that can help with severe social anxiety. These might include various antidepressants, particularly selective serotonin reuptake inhibitors (SSRIs) such as Paxil.

Shed Your Shyness

The suggestions that follow may help you reduce your shyness from a rolling boil to a gentle simmer, or may even help it to evaporate completely. Before plunging in, a couple of quick suggestions:

◆ As I've mentioned before, it's best to use a systematic approach, just like Ben Franklin. Take time to think through and organize the most effective approach for you.

◆ Whittle away at the problem. Don't try to take on too much at once. You don't have to become the state ballroom dance champion and Miss Congeniality all at once!

◆ Start where it makes the most sense for you. There are physical, social, and mental or "cognitive" techniques you can use to shrink your shyness. As you go through my list of suggestions, choose the ones that look best to you.

◆ Confide in someone about your shyness. Just having one friend to discuss your shyness with can be incredibly helpful, even if you're just e-mailing them in some other state (or planet). Look for support groups on the Internet, and join up! (See Appendix B for suggestions.)

◆ If you feel your problems are too severe, seek professional help. We'll discuss getting help later, but there's no need to work on this alone.

Tips for Boldly Launching You

Start by knowing a bit more about thyself. Retake the quiz at the beginning of this chapter. Make a list of the reasons you think you have a problem with shyness. What would you like to change?

Caution!

Self-medicating your social anxiety with alcohol or drugs is a bad idea! While some people find temporary relief by loosening up with a drink, a serious anxiety problem will tend to get more severe over time if it's treated with alcohol.

Work on your bod. If you notice that you have obvious physical signs of anxiety, focus on controlling those, even if you just reduce them 1 percent at a time! Most therapists know that if you can reduce the physical aspects of anxiety, the mental ones will also improve or even disappear. A good way to do this is to make use of your body's natural anxiety-reducing mechanisms.

You may have noticed that you feel more mellow on the evenings of days when you've taken a hike, cleaned the house, or cut the grass, instead of sitting all day in your recliner worrying about your problems. This works for two reasons: your body goes through many hormonal and brain-chemistry changes when you're more active; and when you're focused on physical activity, you're giving your mind a rest from focusing on your troubles. Give it a try!

Other relaxation techniques include deep breathing, systematic muscle relaxation exercises, and yoga. (But with any of them, you have to *practice regularly* to get them to work! Same goes for just taking those stress-lowering strolls: they work best if done regularly.)

Mental homework. Write down some of your less helpful, more frightening thoughts, and try to "rewrite" them in your mind. For instance, make a list of the top five things you tell yourself about why nobody wants to talk to you at parties, or what it meant that you couldn't maintain a conversation with that attractive stranger. Did it mean that she thought you were unattractive? Did it mean he thought you were boring?

Now, write out some possible alternative explanations for their behavior: she was preoccupied with that boyfriend she's breaking up with because she is realizing there are "much nicer guys out there—like you!" He thought you were just as interesting as could be, but he was not sure you were available and interested because you kept looking away. In other words, these people might actually have enjoyed talking with you.

Social Science
Cognitive therapy is based on the idea that your thoughts don't "just happen" but are *behaviors* that you control. For instance, you can practice different attitudes by reminding yourself of five things that are going well in your life or visualizing a peaceful place. Such exercises will actually change your mental and physical state!

Try visualizing. Make a list of two or three situations where you think things haven't gone so well in your attempts to interact with others. Imagine more positive, alternative outcomes.

Sit back, relax, and imagine how the situation might have gone differently. Do you see it? How did it differ when things went well? Can you do it that way again, first in your mind, and maybe then for real? Imagine the event from start to finish, seeing it going well.

Don't just think it—feel it! Feel how great it will be to get this positive reaction— their smiles, nods, words of praise. Practice these visualizations, even though they seem strange or hard to believe, until you have gotten very comfortable imagining things going well. Until you actually start to *expect* them to!

Tune in to the other person. It's very difficult to notice what other people are signaling if you are preoccupied with your worries about them. But this also presents you with a great way to reduce your anxiety: resolving to be more attentive to their signals! If you spend more time being attuned to the other person, you may find that you have less time to worry about how they are viewing you.

Try this exercise: at least once a day, interact with someone and afterward make a list of five things you noticed about that person. They might be physical things, such as their eye color, or the fact that they have a slight accent that you never picked up on before. It may be that they move their hands a certain way, or that they seem to tune in to, or avoid, eye contact.

The better you are at observing others, the more interesting your world becomes— and the less you'll be worrying about yourself!

Make a connection. Take a walk in a public area, whether your workplace, a shopping mall, or just down the street in your neighborhood. Say "hello" to someone who passes, whom you'd ordinarily pass without saying anything. Do they say hello back? Whether or not they do, do it again (to someone else!). And again. Make it a personal goal to say hello to ten people in a day. If ten seems like too many, try three. After a week of three a day, go up to four.

See if any of these "hellos" turn into anything more, like a conversation, or even a new acquaintance.

Take up space. When you're near others, stop shrinking! You know what I'm talking about: making yourself "small" by hunching down in your chair, keeping your arms pressed to your sides, locking your eyes on the floor in front of the other person, mumbling. Even though it feels strange to do it, take up space! Pull your arms further from your body and make some gestures! If you're going into a meeting, spread a pad of paper and some files and your laptop on the table in front of you. Make physical gestures when you're talking, and nod when you're listening. Lock eyes with other people and smile. You don't even have to say anything to do this exercise, but if you do it, you may find that talking is actually easier than usual.

Smile! Not only is this likely to impress the other person, it's also likely to reduce your anxiety and to improve your mood, both of which will be contagious.

Look for opportunities to speak to groups of people, especially if public speaking is one of your main concerns. Join organizations such as Toastmasters where you can practice these skills.

Caring. One of the most powerful ways to reduce your own anxiety around others is to remember that they may be as anxious as you.

You're not in this alone. Other people are nervous, too! Other people are struggling with their own concerns, even while you are worrying about how you are being seen by them. Sometimes it can help a lot if you refocus your attention on their anxieties, and get the focus off your own. Many people have found that devoting more attention to someone else's suffering actually reduces, or eliminates, their own!

Getting Help

"Who? *Me?* Ask for help? No way! I'm too shy to do that!"

Ahem.

If you're shy, you may be too shy to call someone for help. But if you really *do* need help (and I'm talking about "need" at about a 5 on a 1 to 10 scale, okay? No cheating by saying you don't "need" it until you're a terminal case!), then why not reach out?

There are lots of options. As I mentioned previously, there are online resources. There are therapists in most communities (not to mention mental health centers) who will be happy to try to help you. Then there's that old reliable—your family doc. And of course, friends, relatives, and others who might help you out with support, encouragement, and so on.

If getting in touch with someone is daunting to you, pick the easiest method to make the very first step. Maybe it's an e-mail. (And yes, therapists can be contacted by e-mail. Again, see the appendix.) Set a goal that you will initiate contact and follow through by a certain date, and that if you do, you'll reward yourself somehow. Do whatever it takes.

Most of all, be persistent! You can do it!

The Least You Need to Know

- ◆ Almost everyone has been shy at some point in their lives.

- ◆ Half of the adults in the United States report that they are often shy to the point that it's a problem for them!

- ◆ More severe problems with social anxiety include social phobias and avoidant personality disorders.

- ◆ You can reduce your shyness via a systematic approach, setting small self-change goals, and managing your anxiety.

- ◆ If your shyness or anxiety are more severe, you might try therapy or getting some medications from your doctor to help manage the problem.

Chapter 7

I Hear You!—Empathy and SI

In This Chapter

- ◆ What is empathy?
- ◆ How empathy develops
- ◆ Nurture your empathy skills

As you go through your day, many signals flow through you: the electronic pulses from dozens of radio stations, police band radios, and a half-dozen TV channels are even now passing through your body. So may be the Wi-Fi signals from a nearby Starbucks, the intimate cell phone conversations of lovers, text messages from 100 teenagers, and the Bluetooth signals from your laptop to your own phone. All this "chatter" going on right under your nose (and through your nose, too!), and yet you don't notice or even think about it most of the time!

Like those electronic signals, you are also surrounded by another kind of undetected chatter. But this kind is far more personal and far, far older. It's the signals that people send to each other via a zillion little channels—eye contact, body posture, tone of voice, what they say, and what they don't say. If you had a "feeling receiver" that worked something like your cell phone, imagine all the rich information you could pick up from the dozens of people you pass in a day.

Well, you do have such a receiver! And if you know how to tune it, you can expand your awareness of those signals, those wordless communiqués from the souls of others. The receiver is your own nervous system—an empathic receiving system that is incredibly powerful.

In this chapter, we'll explore the nature of empathy and help you develop ways to be the most empathic, understanding person that you are capable of being.

But first, it's time for some self-assessment.

Check Yourself Out

This self-test helps you assess how empathic (or empathetic) you are. For each item, select the response that best describes you.

1. You cry at the movies:

    A. It happens regularly—that's why I go!

    B. Never happened; never will. I always wonder about those people who say they cry in movies.

    C. It's happened a few times—maybe once a year or so.

2. Your friends always say they can share personal things with you because you seem to listen well and to understand them.

    A. Come to think of it, I've never actually been told that.

    B. I have one or two friends who've told me some personal things now and then.

    C. Most of my friends feel that way.

3. When you hear about some politician or celebrity who got caught doing something scandalous or improper, you generally react:

    A. It depends on the person and situation.

    B. I always wonder what they were thinking, and feel bad for them—I'm more inclined to see it as a human mistake than something "bad" or "immoral" about them.

    C. I think about it in terms of good and bad people—and so they must be one of the bad ones!

4. If a child tries to tell you at length about some event that happened to them, you tend to:

    A. It's doubtful a child would talk to me, and I'm not comfortable if they do.

    B. I get "lost" or totally absorbed in their story and we have a good time together.

    C. Listen politely for a few moments and think they're cute.

5. Have you ever thought about how life looks from the perspective of your dog or cat?

    A. I watch them sometimes and have wondered about that—I pick up their moods and can tell when they're distressed.

    B. Only at suppertime or if they're "not themselves"—then I notice and may realize they're hungry or ill.

    C. I have no idea what that question even means.

6. How often would you say you ask someone "how's it going" or "how are you?"—and really listen to their reply?

    A. I ask close friends sometimes.

    B. Only if I'm trying to sell them something.

    C. I do it every day—it's one of the pleasures of my day.

7. Do you enjoy songs about relationship issues or problems?

    A. Love 'em—they're the only kind I care about.

    B. No—I'm not really interested.

    C. Occasionally.

8. Have you ever been told that you're such a good listener that you ought to be a therapist?

    A. I've heard the opposite—people don't bother me with that stuff.

    B. Maybe once, but I was on a date and so I was trying hard to listen good.

    C. Hear it often.

9. Right now, how many of your friends, relatives, and acquaintances can you think of who are having a tough time with some part of their lives—health, finances, relationship concerns, job issues, etc.

   A. I know of one or two—big emergency kinds of things.

   B. I could run down the list of all my friends and relatives and tell you what each one's major worry or concerns are right now.

   C. I'm not actually aware of any.

10. How often in the past few weeks have you stopped to think about, pray or visualize good things for, or make a call to check on some of those friends or relatives?

   A. It wouldn't occur to me to do that.

   B. I do it a few times a week.

   C. One or two—if there is something urgent.

Scoring: Circle the answers you chose in the following table, then add up the number of circles within each column.

Item	Closed off	Tuned in	Empath!
1. (Movies)	B	C	A
2. (Friends)	A	B	C
3. (Politics)	C	A	B
4. (Child)	A	C	B
5. (Cat)	C	B	A
6. (Asking)	B	A	C
7. (Songs)	B	C	A
8. (Listener)	A	B	C
9. (Tough)	C	A	B
10. (Pray)	A	C	B
Totals			

Interpreting your results:

Closed off   6–10: Your answers suggest that you aren't very interested in the inner lives of others. Odds are your friends don't think of you and "empathy" in the same paragraph. Lots of room for growth here!

Tuned in   6–10: You probably have an "average" level of empathy most of the time—nobody will call you super-sensitively psychic about people's moods, but you tune in to others when they're expressing loud and clear feelings. You can probably increase your "empathy quotient" and it might be useful to look over the answers you got your lower scores on, and keep them in mind.

Empath!   6–10: You appear to be an empathy champ! You probably have a sensitive nature and a deep understanding and "feel" for others' experiences.

Getting a Handle on Empathy

Fifty years ago the counseling biz was flooded with theories. Counselors and therapists had to spend a lot of time trying to figure out the complex dynamics of each case they treated—often starting out with a patient by spending weeks drawing up elaborate histories and diagnoses of their patients' problems and core conflicts.

One young psychotherapist became concerned about all this theory noise. He felt that the core experiences of his clients—what was really important to them—could get lost amid all these theories. Of course that was not anyone's intention, but he felt that there was definitely a problem.

This therapist wanted to develop a different way of seeing and understanding his clients. In the end, he concluded (and later research verified) that the main healing in psychotherapy happened because the client experienced the therapist as having empathy for them. Ultimately, the work of this therapist became a milestone in the history of psychotherapy. The therapist's name was Carl Rogers.

Rogers discovered that three qualities in a therapeutic encounter were powerful in helping a person heal. One was the experience of unconditional positive regard—therapists conveyed clearly that they felt positively about their clients, with no conditions attached. A second quality was called congruence, which meant that the therapists' actions matched their words, that they seemed honest and straightforward.

The third quality was most important. It was empathy. Rogers defined empathy as perceiving a person's feelings and his frame of reference as though you were him, while still remembering that this was his experience and not your own.

What was really amazing, and hard for many therapists to accept, was that empathy was so powerful that if a therapist was good at conveying that, and if the client felt that empathy, the shrink didn't really have to do much else in order to help the person. In an era when therapists agonized over proper analytic technique and had complicated notions of what to say and when during the therapy hour, this was understandably hard to swallow.

> **Social Science**
>
> Therapists in training spend a lot of time honing their empathy skills. For instance, they may listen to a tape recording of therapy sessions and supervisors will stop the tape occasionally to ask, "What was the person feeling there? How do you know?" Moral of the story: people can expand their empathic skills.

But years of research have supported Rogers's insight, and it totally fits with modern social intelligence science. Rogers's theory of the importance of empathy made it one of the most important concepts in every form of psychological treatment—and it still is, to this day. It is a powerful, life-changing and enriching process.

What Is Empathy?

Science fiction is packed with empaths. From *Star Trek* to *Marvel Comics*, the idea that there are rare beings who have the uncanny ability to read (and maybe influence) the thoughts and feelings of others has captured our collective imagination. Maybe the reason the idea is so important in sci-fi is because we all secretly crave more empathic ability. Maybe we are even a little afraid of the empathy of others, if it means they can see into our minds or even control our thinking.

> **Social Science**
>
> Empathy can be a military weapon. During the 1989 invasion of Panama, U.S. PsyOps (psychological operations) units broadcast messages to Panamanian soldiers to "cease hostilities." That phrase was chosen after research showed that the term "surrender" would be perceived by the troops as dishonorable and not compatible with their machismo.

Generally, though, "empathy" is neither mysterious nor dangerous. In fact, it is usually a very positive force for good. Especially in your personal and relationship life.

There are various definitions of empathy along with its sister traits such as sympathy, compassion, and pity. But empathy is the star of the show. It's the term we use with the richest meaning of all of these concepts.

Generally, empathy refers to the ability to "feel with" another human being. (Sometimes, we also use the term to refer to "feeling with" nonhumans, such as when a good veterinarian seems able to sense the pain of your pet.) It's broader than just feelings, and includes the ability to understand the desires, the state of mind, and the thoughts of that person.

One way of thinking about empathy is the ability emotionally to resonate with the other person, much the way a tuning fork might resonate with the vibrations of another, identically tuned instrument. You vibrate in sync, or have *rapport*. So if the person is sad and seems slowed down, you might experience some of that sadness and slowing down yourself when you talk to them.

def•i•ni•tion

Rapport means being in sync with another person. Rapport can be increased by tuning in to the person, trying to "get" what she's feeling and saying, and even by trying to match her body gestures, breathing, and other physical behaviors, such as voice tone.

In his book on social intelligence, psychologist Daniel Goleman suggests that empathy consists of three things: knowing what people are feeling, experiencing the feeling yourself, and then responding with compassion to their feelings.

Other writers have described empathy in similar terms. Psychoanalyst Heinz Kohut described it as the most important "tool" of psychoanalysts. He defined it as the ability to think and feel yourself into the inner life of another person. Other writers also stress the importance of "getting into the head" of other people.

Sometimes empathy also involves being clearer than the person herself about what she is feeling. We can't always put our tangled feelings into words, so if we're with someone who not only "gets" what we're feeling, but helps us articulate it, that can be a powerful experience. (Many therapists—and moms!—try to do exactly that.)

Empathy and Sympathy

Most people use the words *empathy* and *sympathy* interchangeably, and sometimes what one person calls "empathy," another calls "sympathy."

We usually use the term "sympathy" to mean understanding someone's feelings or thoughts without really "feeling" them yourself. It's like a well-meaning neighbor who says "sorry for your pain" but who doesn't really know you very well, and who feels it would be intrusive to ask you how you are really feeling about a loss.

Sympathy isn't necessarily insincere or an inferior form of caring. Rather, when we experience sympathy for someone, we have not gone further than a kind of general understanding of their concerns. There is nothing wrong with that. We sometimes need to reserve the deeper, emotional immersion in someone's inner experience and feelings for situations or relationships where it's most needed, or most important to us.

Empathy and Social Intelligence

The science of social intelligence is rich with studies of empathy in action. The really exciting news is that our brains appear to be wired for empathy. In fact, it's believed that empathy is one of the main survival skills that enabled human beings to thrive.

Why would that be? Because if we can tune in to each other's suffering, feel it as our own, we will naturally want to do things to reduce the suffering of our friends and family.

Remember that in primitive times, reducing suffering usually meant doing something that might help that other person survive. This might mean that more of the resources of your group or band would be intact. If you helped keep alive the only guy who knew how to build fires (by sensing and responding to his distress or pain), you could all stay toasty and warm through the coming winter. If cave moms didn't tune in to the frightened cries of their "cave babies," they might not have rescued them from a great many saber-toothed tigers, and our species might have gone extinct.

In terms that we've been using, empathy is really at the hub of all four key SI behaviors:

♦ **Knowing yourself:** To be aware of your own emotional life you need to have empathy for others. If you've sealed off your own ability to feel sadness, for instance, you might not be able to even recognize when a loved one is feeling sad. "I know what that feeling is like" is the key to being able to "feel with" someone else.

♦ **Tuning in:** Our minds are built to tune in to others. Remember those mirror neurons, for example? Or how our brains process facial expression data by sending signals to the parts of our own brains that trigger emotion, then matching the emotion that the other person is expressing on her face?

- ◆ **Connecting and making contact:** Empathy seems to trigger the desire to connect with the other person. It's not a spectator sport!

- ◆ **Compassion and caring:** If I do manage to "feel your pain," it's as though it's my own pain. I naturally want to help!

How Empathy Develops

There is evidence that by age two, toddlers are beginning to show the neurological processes that signal empathy. At about that age, they are also beginning to respond fairly clearly to the emotional experiences of others. For instance, they will attempt to comfort another toddler in distress—a sure sign of empathy!

But even younger babies are beginning to work like little artists in empathy. In fact, under normal child-rearing conditions, infants are already immersed in the world of empathy because of what they experience with their mothers and other caregivers. Research shows that from very early on the average skilled mother is constantly tuning in to the emotional experiences of her baby. She will mimic the facial expressions of her child as a way to tune in to the child's feelings. This can trigger a "matching" feeling in the mother so she can "read" what the baby is feeling. Her response is picked up by the child, who will then start to mirror back the emotional expressions of the mother. The two get in sync and function as a kind of single being many times each day. This is the beginning of the child's development of the capacity for emotional resonance with others.

Caution!

Moods are as contagious as measles! The distress of loved ones may get under your skin and start to affect you as well. Your nervous system will resonate with their gloom or despair and you'll start to feel it, too. Just remember: it doesn't help them if you "catch it" too!

Children who can read the feelings of others most adeptly are likely to be popular kids. They also tend to be successful academically and to be more emotionally stable than average. Kids with higher empathy tend to have higher grade-point averages, better reading comprehension, and better critical and creative thinking skills.

The development of empathy in children is becoming better understood. For example, researchers have shown that responsive mothers are more likely to have empathic children. Likewise, parents who are not punitive or authoritarian tend to increase their children's empathy levels. Parents also provide good models of empathy, and this helps develop pro-social attitudes in children, and helps them develop empathy as well.

A few things that are known to help children increase their empathy quotients:

Encouraging them to think about how their behavior affects others. This helps them learn to "step into the other kid's shoes," and provides them with valuable training in learning to imagine how another person might be feeling.

But probably the best empathy builder is their parents' empathy for them, and for other people. Children learn how to feel and talk with others by "absorbing" the personalities of their parents and others. While some children are probably genetically predisposed to be more or less sensitive to feelings, developing whatever empathic gifts they have to the max will require the best training that money can buy. And that, dear parent (or teacher), consists of you demonstrating empathy in your daily interactions with them and everyone else.

> **SI Tip**
>
> Scolding or punishing a child for hurting someone may actually interfere with their budding empathic skills. If your child injures another child, the best way to help them develop empathy is to explain how what they did hurt the other child, and to help them think of ways to make amends.

Surefire ways to wreck your child's ability to experience empathy include threatening them, physical punishment, or not being consistent in your care and availability. Children also have more trouble with empathy if they witness physical abuse of one parent by another. Finally, "bribing" or paying children to behave tends to reduce their empathy, since they become more focused on the reward than on the feelings of the other person.

Nurture Your Empathy Skills

The group of 12 men and women sat together, their chairs arranged in a circle, in total silence. It had been over 20 minutes and no one had spoken yet. Most had their eyes closed, some in prayer, others just sitting with a patient sense of calm waiting.

Feelings had been running high in the group, and everyone knew that they were facing possible fragmentation over the concerns people were having. At issue was deciding how they would respond to requests that they support homosexual unions in their religious community. While most felt inclined to support the unions of people with any sexual orientation, a few who saw themselves as traditional Christians felt that this would somehow be wrong, an endorsement of a "sinful" lifestyle.

Gradually, one after another began to speak, expressing their doubts, concerns, anger, and other strong feelings about the matter. When each one spoke, the others listened attentively, nodding, making eye contact, and holding back any impulse to reply or to argue. After each person had said all they needed to say, the group would again lapse into silence for a time.

Gradually, different perspectives and ways of developing some kind of consensus emerged from the group. Instead of anger, each person began to appreciate the viewpoints and emotions of the others, especially of those with whom they were inclined to disagree. It wasn't a matter of there being winners and losers. Rather, the key issue seemed to be finding a way to respect the deep feelings of each person in the group, instead of running roughshod over any minority opinions. The result was that this small Quaker meeting, attempting to be true to their traditions, managed to avoid a devastating split in what had been a very old and mature community.

This is a description of a group of people who have a long tradition of fairly skillful empathic listening. The example shows that empathy not only feels good, but turns out to be very practical as a way of keeping groups together, overcoming conflicts, and solving problems when many people's feelings are involved. A number of the things the Quaker group did might be useful to anyone wanting to develop their empathic abilities:

- Clearing the path: giving the other person a chance to speak, to express all of their thoughts and feelings about an issue without jumping in to correct or argue with them.

- An atmosphere of safety: nothing bad happens to someone because they say what they feel.

- Respect for opinions of others, even though they are not in agreement with your own: there is often much to recommend in anyone's opinion about anything.

Caution!

Be tactful! Someone may feel intruded on if you seem to have too much empathy, or to perceive too much information about them. People need a privacy zone—alertly noticing the "how to slim down" magazine in their bag and asking, "How's the weight problem going?" might not win friends!

Raising Your Empathy Quotient

While it's true that many of the fundamental empathic skills, the responses that experts like Daniel Goleman term *primal empathy*, are rapid, unconscious behaviors, the good news is that most of us are born with pretty good circuitry for developing these. This is especially true if we can remember not to do things that might artificially shut down our empathy.

def•i•ni•tion

Primal empathy is a term coined by Daniel Goleman that refers to the elements of empathy that happen rapidly and outside of our conscious awareness. Goleman and other scientists think that mirror neurons are involved in this kind of information processing.

SI Tip

If you want to know how someone is really feeling, pick a private moment to ask them. If you ask them where other people are going to overhear their response, they're likely to clam up—they'll be hyper-aware of all the other ears and eyes on them!

Remember, not only do children have to learn a great many empathy skills, but even adults (such as shrinks in training) often build up those empathic muscles!

Here are some suggestions for developing your EQ. Remember, practice and a systematic approach to developing your skills are recommended.

Just ask. Anything that helps you to "take the part" of another person can be a valuable empathy expander. One of the simplest ways to do that is to just learn to ask the person. Even with a stranger, a simple question, such as, "How's your day going?" can be a powerful way to open up an empathy channel with them. Practicing those kinds of questions can be a good beginning.

Clear the path. You are probably well wired to respond empathically to others, and to develop fairly acute sensitivity to their feelings. But first, you have to keep your channels open. Give yourself time, particularly in important relationships, to actually listen to the other person. Don't assume that you have to jump in with answers, advice, or questions. Listening, saying nothing, giving them time to express themselves can be very important.

Expand your horizons. Yogi Berra once quipped, "You can observe a lot just by watching." You can learn a lot about how people feel by watching good films, since so much of that is an exploration of people's inner lives and experiences. Talking your favorite books over with someone, taking a course or reading about these books, or even just asking yourself afterward what people were going through, can expand your empathic imagination.

Tag your feelings. Practice noticing your own feelings, and putting them into words. Finding a list of common "feeling words" such as happy, fatigue, fear, jealous, envy, excited, and so on can be useful. Many people have trouble identifying the feelings of others because they don't even know how to label their own! Start with understanding yourself, and you'll find it easier to understand others. (That's why many therapists consider their own therapy to be critical—it's the very best way to learn to understand their clients!)

See "me" in "thee." Focus on the similarities you have with others. You may be from a completely different world from another person, but might be able to relate to some of the things they are feeling.

Your empathic abilities can expand if you practice taking on the role of another person. This can be done in your imagination, or you might actually "switch lives" for a day. What does your spouse go through every day? Suppose you were in her shoes? Think it through, and talk it over.

> **Social Science**
>
> Many graduate programs for new therapists require them to go through psychotherapy themselves. One reason for this is to help the students learn more about their own emotional lives, because that can help them increase their empathy for others.

When you're listening to someone, notice their posture, tone of voice, and so on. Mirror these as you listen to them. If they're frowning and leaning forward, watching them carefully may lead to your moving your own body to match theirs. Let it happen! If they're rocking back and forth, you may find yourself rocking a bit also. If their foot seems twitchy, don't be surprised if yours twitches, too.

Don't interrupt. Control your attention deficit thing! Don't steer a person off onto other things when they're expressing themselves. Give them time to express their thoughts, and if they need to pause a second, don't jump in with a different topic or direction.

Don't be a "fixer." You may have a tendency to want to jump in with instant solutions for others. Budding therapists fall into this trap all the time. Their heads are chock-full of great ideas for fixing people's problems, so that they forget that the main task is to just listen to their clients.

The same thing often happens between spouses. When your partner needs some time to vent at the end of the day, don't keep pouncing on them with advice and suggestions. This can leave them feeling put down and demoralized, since what you're really saying is that you'd have solved the problem better than they did. This is not experienced as very empathic by most people.

Social Science
Psychotherapy researchers have found that when people reveal something personal and feel that their therapists accept them, they have a brief burst of energy. They become more expansive, share other feelings, and volunteer new facts or feelings.

What you communicate to the other person will help them open up with you. If they feel safer, they'll tell you more. So conveying that you're curious and attentive is more important than suggesting that you have all the answers. On the other hand, don't tell a person that you understand them if you really don't. They'll know—and you won't seem as reliable.

Remember that people might not always be able to put their feelings into words. You know the scenario: the strong, silent husband who never expresses his feelings to his wife, even though she talks freely about hers. The more stressful things get between them, the quieter and more distant he seems to be, even though he's not at all really ignoring or failing to hear her. It just looks that way.

Many people can't say what they feel. That doesn't mean you can't pick up on their emotions, but you do have to be more tuned in to their nonverbal statements.

Shrinking Empathy

There are several things that can dramatically decrease your empathic abilities. These are things to be aware of:

Stress. If you're worn out or distracted by your own problems, it's hard to tune in to another person's feelings.

Discomfort. It's hard to listen to someone if you're feeling intimidated by them, angry at them, or having other uncomfortable feelings about them. Give yourself time to sort those feelings out and to get clearer about what's going on.

Dismissing others. If you decide someone is just "evil" or "not human," it would obviously interfere with your empathy. In fact, those kinds of labels are the opposite of empathy, and can make it impossible.

Attitudes like those may mean you're limiting your ability to understand some people, and this may keep you from putting forth the effort. On the other hand, if you believe you can understand anyone eventually, and that virtually everyone is, in principle, understandable (and trying their best), you won't tune them out. Sooner or later, you'll be likely to make a connection. (Again, this doesn't mean you always have to agree with them.)

Being the "final authority." Avoid suggesting that there's just one way to see things. Even statements such as "You're right!" can suggest to the other person that you think you're the "decider" of "right" and "wrong" attitudes. This can be a conversation stopper, though you may never know it happened.

The Least You Need to Know

- Empathy means being able to understand and share the feelings of another person.

- We are "wired" for empathy; children begin showing signs of empathy by age two, or even earlier.

- You can increase your empathy skills by practicing and being aware of the emotional states of others.

- Tuning in to your own emotions is an essential skill for being able to tune in to others.

Intimate Connecting

In This Chapter

- ◆ Intimacy and SI
- ◆ Our need for closeness
- ◆ Bringing intimacy to your life

You may be an extrovert or an introvert, a party girl or a hermit. But you still need some kind of intimacy. Intimacy is about connecting with others on the deeper levels. It's about being known, and knowing others, at the most personal and emotionally meaningful levels of our existence. We're built to like and need intimacy. Our bodies and minds thrive on it, and we can wilt without it.

In this chapter, we'll explore the wonderful world of intimacy, and ways that you can develop and enhance your intimate self.

Check Yourself Out

This self-test is to help you assess how comfortable you are with and how skilled you are at intimate connections. For each item, select the response that best describes you.

1. When you're anxious about something, you prefer (or even need) to talk it over with someone ...

   A. Sometimes, if they already know about it, for instance.

   B. Never. I prefer to keep things like that to myself.

   C. I usually want to talk worries over with someone close.

2. Is there someone in your life you share "almost everything" with?

   A. Not really—I'm a pretty private person.

   B. I am close to at least one person and can, and do, share anything with them.

   C. I can share some things with some people.

3. The thought of spending an hour talking over something personal with a therapist or counselor makes you feel how?

   A. I'd avoid it. Prefer to have my taxes audited.

   B. It would be okay.

   C. I would like to do that—or I do talk with someone sometimes.

4. If you were suddenly paralyzed and couldn't speak and in the hospital, is there at least one person in the world who you would trust to know you well enough that he or she could "interpret" what you'd want to the nurses and doctors?

   A. There's someone who would know some things about me—I'd be hoping they got it right.

   B. There's someone who knows me so well I'd feel I was safe as long as they were around.

   C. I don't have anyone like that—they'd have to figure it out or do the best they could.

5. How do you imagine it would feel to be a "spy" who had to bury most of your personal life and pretend to be someone totally different for months or years at a time?

   A. It would be impossible for me to do that—I'd probably get ill because I'd miss having confidants.

B. I could handle that—it'd be the foreign food I'd hate.

C. I'd probably manage it for a while, but under stress I'd end up telling at least one person who I really was.

6. How long has it been since you shared something so personal that you at least got a tear in your eyes?

A. I can recall the last time—it's been less than a year, or even more recently.

B. Happens rarely, but has happened a few times in my life.

C. Not since childhood, probably. If then.

7. If today you got some really awful news, like that you were fired from your job or had cancer, whom would you call?

A. There's one person, like a spouse or partner, who would pry it out of me.

B. I don't really have anyone I'd tell.

C. There are several people I would contact—not that I'd "broadcast it" to the world, but I have a small support network.

8. Do you have anyone in your life with whom you've talked about the relationship between the two of you?

A. Not unless my cat counts.

B. I do have one or more such relationships (though we may not talk about "our relationship" too often—I know we can and have).

C. That has happened but it's a rare event in my life.

9. When's the last time you've said "I love you" to someone and really meant it?

A. Can't say's I remember that.

B. It's kind of a habit to say that to a partner/spouse.

C. I say it often to someone special, and hear it back, and we both mean it.

10. How would you rate the feelings of closeness or intimacy you've had in your best sexual relationship?

A. It's been … kinda nice, I guess.

B. I have felt/feel very emotionally close to a sexual partner or spouse—the sex deepens the feelings of closeness.

C. It's been fun but I haven't felt much "emotional" closeness in it, if that's what you mean.

Scoring: Circle which answer you chose here, then add up the number of circles within each column.

Item	Aloof	Flexible	Intimate
1. (Anxious)	B	A	C
2. (Share)	A	C	B
3. (Therapy)	A	B	C
4. (Hospital)	C	A	B
5. (Spy)	B	C	A
6. (Tears)	C	B	A
7. (News)	B	A	C
8. (Relation)	A	C	B
9. (Love)	A	B	C
10. (Sex)	C	A	B
Totals			

Interpreting your results:

Aloof   6–10: You may not have many intimate connections with others. If this is a recent or temporary change, it would be helpful to be aware of it, to make sure it doesn't signal some kind of depression or high-stress situation. And if you're not ill or depressed, and don't mind living with this much nonintimacy, that's fine—but many people with your score would want to explore why they don't seem all that connected to others.

Flexible   6–10: Most people fall in here. A score in this range suggests that you have some intimate or emotionally close connections with some people, though you might want more. Look over your answers and see if there are any particularly troublesome (or missing) parts of your "intimate life" you want to focus on.

Intimate   6–10: You're pretty comfortable with intimate connections with others. This probably enhances your health and works well for you.

No Man Is an Island

Pity the spies, and Superman, too. Despite their secret powers, and/or their cool decoder rings, spies and Superman share the same occupational hazard: they are absolutely forbidden to enjoy complete intimacy with anyone. At all costs, they must withhold information about who they really are from everyone in their lives, even their nearest and dearest. This is not only a source of incredible tension, but as many of the best spy novelists have explored, it can actually warp a human personality.

What is intimacy, and why is it so important to your well-being?

Intimacy means openness with another person about the most personal, or core, parts of who you are. It is being able to share your personal information or secrets, but it also includes sharing your emotions with someone. It's partly *what* you say, and partly that you allow someone else to experience your passions, your fears, your shyness—things that people typically prefer to keep to themselves.

From the perspective of social intelligence, intimacy includes the nonverbal communication links that we share with another person. To sit quietly with a friend and talk about a painful memory or a dream for our lives, and to let our voices crack a little, a tear well up in our eye, and to allow that other person to share in those powerful feelings, would be an example of this kind of a link with another. It goes beyond the mere content of our communication—it isn't just the secrets we exchange.

SI Tip

"Can we talk?" That famous question is actually a great way to start an intimate conversation with someone. Most people recognize that it's an invitation to get personal, and also recognize that you're really asking permission to leap into that personal stuff.

Something marvelous happens in an intimate moment. We experience a sense of trust, closeness, safety, and connection with another. There may be a sense that we are making ourselves vulnerable to the other person.

Caution!

You can damage a close relationship if you don't keep some "balance" in the amount of personal sharing that goes on. If someone feels they have "opened up" with you a few times but that you haven't reciprocated, they may start to resent or mistrust you, and pull back until they feel you're also being open with them.

This kind of closeness is not really an option, either. You may actually *need* to reveal yourself to another in this way, at least in some points in your life, or in some relationships as they begin to deepen. In fact, there are times when not letting yourself take this next step can harm a relationship, particularly if the other person feels that she or he has taken the risk of revealing herself to you and is waiting for you to reciprocate. Plus, that kind of isolation may actually do you physical damage.

Your Need for Intimacy

It started when you were a baby—that need to make a connection with someone, to communicate your emotional states to them, whether you were feeling hunger, loneliness, or delight. Over the past few decades researchers have learned much about the importance of these little dances of communication between infants and their caretakers. Attachment bonds from infancy become the "secure base," in John Bowlby's famous phrase, upon which a healthy adult personality is founded. No attachment, no healthy adult—that seems to be the rule in human development.

As we grow and mature, our need for intimacy, and the levels and complexity of the intimacy we need, continue to expand.

Psychoanalyst Erik Erikson, based on the earlier work of Freud, developed a theory of lifelong psychological development and growth. He felt that one of the most important stages of early adulthood was the stage during which a person had to work out the conflict between intimacy and isolation.

Social Science

Many therapists think that the real goal of most psychotherapy is not reducing symptoms, such as insomnia or tension. Rather, they see it as helping clients develop more ability to have intimacy in relationships. Reason? Most other mental health problems go away by themselves, or at least get much more tolerable, as people's intimacy quotient improves!

Not that you can't use some healthy isolation, some private inner spaces. But you need to balance that with the ability to reach out to others, to express yourself fully, and to connect with another. For most of us, this need includes the need for intimacy with a life partner as well. Thus, one has to go beyond trying to get all one's needs met through a bunch of superficial or more distant friends.

Most psychologically healthy, thriving people say that their close friendships are a form of "wealth" or "richness" or "blessings" in their lives. They often feel the same about having a life partner or spouse, and thriving family connections. These close connections include elements of giving as well as receiving, in a dance in which sharing something of ourselves, our secrets and feelings, becomes a form of gift to the other.

Intimacy and Health

The greatest scientific invention of Sigmund Freud may have been the medicalization of the phrase "uh huh."

Even before Freud did his work on the couches of Vienna, people surely understood that one of the most important things in life was having a confidant. Freud neither invented nor claimed to invent this fact—it was already in all the great novels of his day. But Freud's brilliant discovery was that there was a science to all this whispering of secrets.

Freud showed that opening up to another person not only felt good, it actually cured diseases. Many of the neurological conditions that Freud's patients complained of were actually *psychological* conditions. They often melted away if the patients spent enough time talking about themselves and their life and concerns with the good doctor.

Modern research confirms that intimate connections not only might cure some diseases and psychological ills, but they also prevent the development of new physical problems. As mentioned in Chapter 1, social isolation and the lack of intimacy is statistically as dangerous to your health has becoming a heavy smoker!

Psychologist Daniel Goleman, in reviewing the neurological research on brain functioning and intimacy, points out that intimate connections trigger the release of important pleasure-causing neurotransmitters in the brain. He notes that there are two pleasure-inducing substances that scientists have found to be released in the brain when people experience a positive back and forth "looping" connection with each other's brains, and these chemicals trigger the experiences of relaxation and pleasure.

Caution!

Unwanted intimacy can damage relationships. It's important to sense whether someone wants to exchange personal feelings or thoughts with you. If you're not sure, check it out before dumping your deep feelings on someone. "Mind if I tell you something personal?" is a good opener.

There are a great many scientific studies of the health effects of intimacy (and the health consequences of a lack of intimate connections!). It seems likely that virtually every body system is affected by the number and quality of your intimate connections. Herewith a bio-intimacy sampler:

- When married people have a tense relationship with their spouse, their wounds heal more slowly.

- When married couples experience conflict, the wife's immune system can be suppressed for several hours, which makes her more likely to get colds and other health woes. (The reason this happens to wives and not husbands may be that women consider emotional relationships extremely important, and they reflect more about conflict. Going over a tiff in your brain time and time again can't be good for your stress levels!)

- Your relationships can affect your ticker: how negative heart patients' marriages were predicted how well they recovered. Those who had more negative relationships were up to eight times as likely to die within four years as those who were less negative.

- What do you think is the second most significant factor in how long we live (after a history of cigarette smoking)? No, it's not diet. It's not exercise. And it's not a family history of disease. Give up? It's the absence of social support. People with wide circles of social support live longer than those with smaller groups of friends and family.

- In people with irritable bowel syndrome, symptoms are worse in those whose family relationships had a lot of conflict.

- Married men have a higher life expectancy than single men.

- During and after nerve-wracking interactions with others, levels of the stress hormones epinephrine and cortisol zoom up and stay elevated for more than 22 hours.

Happy relationships can boost our health, while unhappy relationships can actually make us unhealthy.

Intimacy and Sexuality

People sometimes use the word "intimacy" to mean "sex." While that is not the main meaning of the term as I'm using it here, sex is important, and often is linked with intimacy. But—and this is critical—not all sex is intimate sex.

While we often say that we have "intimate knowledge" of someone we sleep with, it's equally easy to become even more estranged from someone, and less connected emotionally to them, depending on how we make use of our sexual contact. Strangers who are sexual with each other, but who have not taken the time to develop a personal connection (or who even suspect they dislike each other except physically), may find the experience of physical "intimacy" to be anything from neutral to unpleasant. That "day after" feeling may not be a pleasant one.

But when things go well, sexual experiences can be tremendously powerful enhancers of a sense of knowing each other, connecting with each other, and strengthening a powerful bond.

Grow Your Intimacy Skills

In movies and novels, the critical moment often occurs when the secret agent or Superman finally reveals his true identity to his close friend or lover. Of course, for a spy or a super-powerful being from another world who has been concealing his true nature under a pair of thick glasses, this sudden burst of intimacy can often spell the beginning of great danger. And in fact, there certainly can be a powerful change, both in your relationship with the other person, and even in how you experience yourself, once you have taken the risk of opening up! It may literally change who you are to do this.

Fortunately, this is usually a good thing! As many people in the psychotherapy biz are well aware, sharing your deepest self with another is often a powerful, self-transforming act. Having another person acknowledge parts of us that we have kept to ourselves, putting into words—or hearing another put into words—things about ourselves that we had only dimly suspected before, can make those qualities in us seem more real. It can give us a stronger, more "grounded" sense of who we are.

Intimate exchanges are often experienced as the best parts of life. It follows, then, that the more skilled you are at having such exchanges, the richer your life may be. What are some of the secrets of the intimately skilled?

Get Comfy with Closeness!

The first hurdle to intimacy can be overcoming discomfort with it. That may seem paradoxical—if intimacy is so wonderful and even so healthy, why wouldn't everyone be totally cool with being intimate all the time?

Would that it were so! Alas, it's not so simple. But surely you knew that!

Make a quick list: what are *your* favorite reasons for not totally opening up with, say, each of the last three people with whom you've had a meal? A quick review might give you a few whoppers:

◆ You don't want to say what's really on your mind about that person because you might hurt their feelings.

◆ There are some things you want that person to say or do for you, but you don't want to take the risk of asking and being turned down.

◆ If you really shared some of your current fantasies or preoccupations, they'd disapprove and it would wreck your relationship.

◆ It would be considered "inappropriate" or "not cool" to open up with that particular person.

◆ People "just don't talk about that kind of thing" with each other!

And on and on!

There are a lot of practical-sounding reasons for keeping your own counsel, as they say. Relationships aren't all "personal" and in fact, some work and school relationships are actually pretty dangerous places to share! ("Yes, officer, there is a pound of weed in my trunk!")

In addition, some things that you might be thinking or feeling, ranging from feelings of repugnance to a throbbing case of sexual attraction to someone, would be big no-no's to share. In other cases, you're very clear that being open about your feelings would change, confuse, and muck up the relationship.

But there are usually even deeper, less conscious and less "practical" reasons that people avoid intimacy. Remember that when you open up with someone, you expose feelings. And often, that triggers mental and even physical discomfort. Particularly if you aren't one of the minority of people who had totally perfect (or at least, optimally healthy) relationships with parents and others when growing up, you may not have learned to do much intimate sharing simply because, well, nobody else did. Or because your parents were so uncomfortable themselves with that kind of emotional expression that their reactions (ranging from ignoring to scolding you—or worse!) scared you off the idea of "opening up."

At the deepest level, your brain may just not be all that well wired up yet for intimate disclosures. Researchers have shown, for instance, that the areas of our brains that surge when we have intense feelings aren't always accessible to "verbal self-description." An fMRI scan might show huge spikes in a person's emotion centers, but reveal nothing of note going on in her verbal processing areas; and if asked, she might not even "know" that her brain is showing that she is feeling, say, shame or embarrassment.

In other words, if you didn't grow up in a family where emotional sharing was a regular event, and you haven't had much practice at it recently (like the kind you get in a new romance sometimes, or in therapy), you may have a bit of an uphill slog in learning to share intimately with others.

Where to start, then? How about the way I'd ask you to start in a clinical consultation? Just tell me something about yourself.

Opening Up

Okay. I'll go first. Seems only fair.

I have a confession to make to you. This is my first book, and I'm worried.

As I write this chapter, I'm sitting in a chair looking out the window at a winter landscape. It's dusk. It's been a sunny day, and a rare warm day during what has been a long cold spell here in St. Paul. So I appreciate the cozy landscape and the chance to contemplate one of the best parts of being human with you.

But mainly, what's on my mind is fear. This chapter has to be written very quickly to meet a deadline, and here I am, tackling intimacy—one of the most complicated, emotionally rich topics in all of psychology, and in fact, in all of world literature.

It's daunting. And I'm worried that I won't have enough "new and valuable information" to share with you, whoever you are. I've even been losing a little bit of sleep about this. Not too much—it seems to be going generally well, but some.

I sometimes wish that I knew who you are—that I could get a clear picture in my mind of your face, your age, where you live, how what I'm writing here affects you. Will you find it helpful, or will you feel that it isn't very useful, that you've heard it all before? It would feel better to know more about you, so I could write this better.

There! I feel a little better! I feel better in part because I have just done some 100 percent accurate, absolutely truthful disclosing of my personal thoughts and feelings with you. It's not fake, and it's not just a demonstration. How does it feel for you, having just heard your author tell you how he feels about you? What does this trigger in you?

Social Science

Years ago, therapists were trained to reveal almost nothing about themselves to their clients. You could tell your shrink everything about yourself, but never hear them utter a peep about themselves. Over time they learned that a little bit of sharing by the shrink didn't really hurt. It made them seem more human and so more trustworthy.

Now it's your turn.

One of the most basic skills in developing intimate connections is the ability to let other people know what we're thinking and feeling. Of course, you can't always share everything! Whether you're a spy or just a person meeting someone from an online dating service or at a speed date for the first time, you will want to use judgment and common sense about what you share. But intimacy starts with self-disclosure.

Pace Your Sharing!

It usually works best to open up to another person gradually. From the standpoint of social intelligence, the sequence of understanding some things about ourselves, tracking our own feelings, being tuned in to the other person, and in this case, how receptive we are to hearing this, are the first important steps. I might want to share something with you to get closer to you. And here's a secret: *It might not matter what I share, as long as it's something slightly more personal than what we've shared before!*

SI Tip

When you begin to open up to another person, remember that you are not just disclosing personal facts to them. You're giving them the chance to be in your presence as you uncork your emotions. This is powerful stuff! That's why going slow is often best.

Here's an example of how the process works: I have a favorite restaurant nearby, and enjoy getting to know the many waitpersons who work there. I may just ask them how they're doing if they wander by my section of the counter and stop for a second.

Usually it takes one or two visits for us to learn a few basic facts about each other—the fact that they are going to school, working on a degree in something, and the fact that I am trying to sell my house, might be the things that come up right away. Or someone might ask what I'm reading, and it might lead to a conversation about the writing I'm doing, or something like that. None of these are deep personal secrets, but after a few such exchanges, we begin to feel we know each other a little better.

If you jot down 10 important facts about yourself, many of them are things that are semi-public information anyway. Where you work (unless you *are* a spy!), where you live, what you're studying in school, and where you grew up are all fairly innocuous things. But just telling these things to another person, if they're reasonably attentive, is giving them a pretty good grounding in your *public self.*

If you're like most people, you tend to move gradually from showing your public self to revealing your *private self* to others. After a person notes these basic facts about you, you may talk about some of your likes and dislikes. What are you reading? What do you like about mysteries?

def•i•ni•tion

> Your **public self** is the view of yourself that you may freely share with others. In contrast, your **private self** concerns your inner self and feelings. Your private self may not resemble your public self! You may present yourself as one kind of person (say, outgoing and intelligent) but privately feel that your "real" personality is more reserved and actually not all that bright.

From public information you may start to disclose things that have to do with feelings, but not feelings about your relationship with each other. Your "feelings" about the neighborhood, about a movie you just saw, or about your aching back, might all be more personal than a "fact of your life," but less so than, say, your religious beliefs or your reaction to you as a person.

As your connection deepens, you move into more deeply personal things. At some point, this can start to include your feelings about the other person. These may be positive, such as the kind of feelings that signal romance or friendship. They might just be admitting that you appreciate the other person's interest, or are grateful because they called you to check if you needed something when you had a cold.

These kind of exchanges, at this level, can become the most rewarding, because they are neither distant nor too intense. Intimacy doesn't always have to mean the most personal, emotionally intense thing you could possibly say. (In fact, that could get pretty burdensome.)

Over time, a relationship with someone that is truly rewarding is built on many, many such open expressions.

At its most intense level, intimate conversations may be more emotion, less clear descriptions of feelings. But these may be among the most powerful moments you have in our life.

Eye Contact and Quiet Moments

I watched my student's face and felt it was important to share with her and her classmates what I saw happening. She was doing a role-play, being the "therapist" while another student played a lonely, isolated man in a nursing home who seldom had many friendships or connections.

"That man," I told her, "will probably fall in love with you."

What my student was doing was simply good work—she was listening to the man intently, focusing all her attention on him. Her eyes were locked on his, and her face expressed empathy with the emotions he was struggling to describe. But her eye contact, the intensity of her focus, would probably have been more intense, more compassionate, than just about any encounter the man was apparently having—or had ever had—in many years.

> **SI Tip**
>
> Long, unbroken eye contact and a sympathetic, nodding, caring expression on your face while you listen to someone disclose personal things may be a great way to intensify a sense of connection between you. It's a great therapy technique, but it's also a swell way to make a friend (or to pick someone up at your local coffee shop or bar!).

Under those conditions, her responsiveness to him would often be expected to trigger, without either of them knowing it, some pretty intense longings for more connection with her. (Those feelings are what therapists call "*transference*.") So she would have to be prepared to help him sort through the feelings that her attention might stir up in this client.

def•i•ni•tion

> **Transference** means strong feelings (and sometimes, beliefs or fantasies) that clients in psychotherapy may develop about their therapists. The corresponding feelings that therapists might develop about clients are called countertransference.

New therapists are sometimes unprepared for the powerful feelings their work may stir up in their clients. Being trained to focus on the techniques they are sharing with clients, they can be surprised when it's not their great advice, but just their attentive listening and caring gaze, that seems to be the most powerful tool they bring to their therapy sessions. Because in making long, sustained eye contact with an often isolated person, they are indeed using heavy doses of a powerful, brain-changing substance.

An intimate connection with another person can stir more powerful feelings than anything you'd ever experience listening to the most beautiful music, or watching the most intense theatrical performance. Sometimes, sitting quietly with someone and just sighing can speak volumes.

If I wanted to get to know you well, and to feel known by you, I would not plan to do it in the middle of a busy party (that restaurant counter isn't so hot either!). I'd look for a time when we could sit together uninterrupted, the TV off (which should go without saying, but sometimes it doesn't!), and when we might have a little bit of time to talk. I would also prefer not to do it in a too dark, badly lit room where I couldn't see your face.

> **Social Science**
>
> When a man sees a pretty woman make eye contact and smile at him, his brain cells release a dose of pleasure-causing natural opiates. Seeing her smile is literally a mildly addicting drug fix!

A quiet walk, the back booth in a restaurant, or sitting in a car might be good places to share more personal things about ourselves. The point is, choosing your time and place is often important to developing the best connections with others.

From "I Talk" to "We Talk"

Most of the time, most intimate friendships involve exchanging information about each other as individuals. But even with many of your closest friends, you may not take the final step of discussing your relationship.

Moving from talk about "my life" and "your life" to discussing "we" topics is going to be interpreted as an escalation of the intimacy level. It works fine if we both want to do it, but if one person brings "we" talk up, it signals that they want a more committed relationship.

Boundaries

Boundaries are the guardrails in intimate (and other kinds of) relationships. With most relationships, there are points beyond which you don't want to go.

You may not want to reveal certain things to a close friend. For instance, you may feel that they're not doing something correct in how they're raising their child, or not behaving ethically in a business situation. Or you may have some private tensions or worries that are best kept to yourself and not shared even with your own children, parents, or spouse.

Or you and your dear, close friend may have an unspoken agreement that despite your attraction to each other, your relationship won't "cross the line" and become sexual.

Even married couples may need boundaries of different sorts: at the very least, a shared understanding that they won't physically abuse each other or discuss some painful and private topics.

Mostly, we live with the paradox that even our most open, intimate relationships have boundaries. This is not a bad thing. In developing your connections with others, it may be reassuring to remind yourself that you will always have some private space for yourself, as long as you want and need it.

The Least You Need to Know

- ◆ Intimacy is an open sharing of emotions as well as facts with another person.

- ◆ Your mental and physical health, as well as the quality of your life, depend on intimate connections with others.

- ◆ Intimacy isn't necessarily sexual, but sexual connections can greatly intensify and magnify intimacy between people.

- ◆ Intimate sharing isn't always easy. There may be practical concerns, such as a lack of practice stemming from family training, or even brain-wiring issues, that keep you from being able to share with others easily.

- ◆ The best way to become intimate is to start gradually and open up the safe things about yourself to others, and gradually share more.

Chapter 9

Toxic Connections

In This Chapter

- ♦ It's a jungle out there!
- ♦ Types of toxic relationships
- ♦ Defend yourself!

Our bods evolved for rugged terrain—we're the original all-terrain vehicles. In the event of a life-threatening emergency, our bodies mobilize complicated and highly effective mechanisms that enable us to stand our ground or head for the hills, all in the service of survival. But these emergency response systems can take their toll, especially if you find yourself having to deal with chronic, low-level social emergencies.

Ironically, it can be many of our highly evolved social intelligence abilities that make us most vulnerable to nonphysical threats. In turn, these social threats can actually threaten our physical survival!

In this chapter, we'll explore the dark world of toxic relationships. We'll discuss how these relationships affect us, and run through an A to Z compendium of toxic personalities and interactions that most of us encounter. Then we'll discuss the best ways to protect yourself and your loved ones.

But first, some self-assessment.

Check Yourself Out

This self-test is to help you assess the toxic people complications in your life. For each item, select the response that best describes you.

1. As a child you were bullied or teased a lot.

    A. I never seemed to have that problem.

    B. Yes—I hate remembering it.

    C. It happened maybe once or twice, but I managed to stop it.

2. How do you use "call screening" on your phone?

    A. There are some people who, if their name turns up, I never answer.

    B. Rarely, I have to "brace myself" before taking calls from certain people.

    C. It seldom or never bothers me to answer the phone, no matter who's calling.

3. People seem to seek you out to "dump" their problems on you.

    A. That's rare, but there is this one person ....

    B. I manage to keep that from happening, though of course if someone really needs some help or support, I'll respond.

    C. It happens fairly often.

4. You've been accused of "overkill" because you respond pretty aggressively to someone else's intrusive or obnoxious behavior:

    A. Happens regularly—OR—I *wish* I knew how to "overkill" some of the jokers who keep on bothering me!

    B. Never really happens—or if it did once, I outgrew it.

    C. From time to time, I admit I do maybe "go overboard" and end up having to do some relationship "damage repair."

5. Do people in your life seem to give off a lot of negativity—and does that get to you?

    A. Somehow I manage to steer clear of most of that.

    B. There are some, and when it happens, it can be annoying.

    C. Yeah—and it bothers me a lot!

6. There's someone in your life you're angry at ...

    A. Sometimes—one or two people who know how to push those buttons and do it occasionally.

    B. At least once a week!

    C. I don't think I've been all that angry at anyone in some time.

7. You have felt threatened or been made uncomfortable by a boss, co-worker, or teacher ...

    A. That rarely comes up, and if it does I can generally talk with the person about it and that takes care of it.

    B. It seems I'm a magnet for that kind of thing and it drives me crazy.

    C. It happens sometimes—it's part of life that I dislike.

8. You have been physically threatened or assaulted in your own home or primary relationship—and the situation is not yet resolved.

    A. That's true—it scares me (or, it's true but I try not to think about it).

    B. I'm not threatened, but we do seem to argue a lot or have a lot of tension.

    C. I would not tolerate either threats, abuse, or ongoing, unresolved high tension in an important relationship.

9. You feel stressed, and sometimes fear you'll get ill because of the tension or pressures of some of your relationships.

    A. Occasionally I find some of my relationships stressful enough that it "gets to me" for a while.

    B. Not really—my relationships are mainly a source of comfort or pleasure.

    C. That pretty much describes me.

10. It's hard for you to ask someone to stop doing or saying something that makes you uncomfortable.

    A. Yeah—I'd rather endure it silently than confront them about it.

    B. I don't really find that to be so hard. I am pretty comfortable telling people when they are bothering me.

    C. There are some situations or people in my life like that.

Scoring: Circle which answer you chose here, then add up the number of circles within each column.

Item	Toxic	Average	Detoxed!
1. (Bullies)	B	C	A
2. (Screening)	A	B	C
3. (Dump)	C	A	B
4. (Overkill)	A	C	B
5. (Negativity)	C	B	A
6. (Angry)	B	A	C
7. (Threat)	B	C	A
8. (Physical)	A	B	C
9. (Tension)	C	A	B
10. (Ask)	A	C	B
Totals			

Interpreting your results:

Toxic   6–10: You appear to have a lot of toxic relationship problems. Some of your relationships seem to be stressing you a great deal and/or you may need to improve your skills at taking care of yourself in the presence of toxic people. At worst, you may even have come to expect that people will typically be pretty unpleasant to you—which could set you up for some real stress problems!

Average   6–10: Your answers suggest that there are some situations that are causing you some higher stress levels, so identify what they are and focus your energy on them.

Detoxed   6–10: You seem to be pretty comfortable managing the toxic or unpleasant people situations that come your way. Congratulations!

It's a Jungle out There!

You may never actually be in combat, or be physically assaulted in a dark alley. Yet you may go through life battered and bruised, both emotionally and physically, by your everyday encounters with others. Not only can unhealthy relationships wear you down mentally, but they can actually impair your health and livelihood.

And the most socially sensitive among us may suffer the most. This seems unfair: shouldn't your core social intelligence abilities—your higher-than-average levels of empathy for others—give you a stronger measure of protection against the negative vibes of others? The answer is, it depends.

It depends on how skillful you are at using your *other* social intelligence abilities.

As you've already learned, your nervous system is hard-wired to be tuned in to other people's brains. But what if those other people are transmitting all sorts of unhealthy messages—aggression, fear, paranoia, or indifference—to you? It stands to reason that if you're walking around like a computer with a really good Wi-Fi antenna, tuning in to all those emotional signals, they're going to affect you.

And if some of those signals carry little "thought viruses" that might mess up your emotional software, you might be in some jeopardy!

But the answer isn't to climb into a lead-lined bomb shelter and avoid human contact! As you know by now (if you've been reading along!), that would be a sure way to limit your life as well! So what's a person to do?

First, how is it that people can affect us so powerfully? Let's start with some understanding of the process.

How They Get Under Your Skin

Emotional effects: Our nervous systems are wired to respond to others as though we had plugged ourselves together. So if you are interacting with someone who is anxious, fearful, or angry, their strong emotions will affect yours. Without your being aware of it, their emotions will literally activate parallel (or complementary) emotion centers in your brain! (It would be parallel if, say, their sadness left you feeling sad; it would be complementary if their aggression triggered your fear responses.) Either way, their intensity becomes yours!

When I was in graduate school, one of my teachers was a renowned researcher in the topic of clinical depression. One day, some of us students asked him why, given his excellent skills at working with patients, he decided to go into research instead of sticking to clinical work. He explained that he found himself getting too depressed around all those depressed patients! He decided it would be better for his own mental health to focus on doing research in the disorder instead.

Not every therapist has that strong a reaction, and many have great skills at taking care of themselves, but most therapists are well aware that it's not difficult to become *vicariously traumatized* by traumatized patients, or to be made depressed or anxious by depressed or anxious patients.

Physical effects: The emotional cues we absorb from others activate complex brain networks that include systems for processing emotion, as well as for processing your thoughts about the information you're picking up. When these brain areas get activated, it may affect you in many ways, including triggering your body's natural *fight-or-flight mechanism.*

def•i•ni•tion

> Vicarious traumatization is a traumatic reaction one gets from hearing about the traumatic experience of someone else. Therapists and first responders such as fire, police, and rescue personnel can develop the reactions after working with trauma victims.
>
> The fight-or-flight mechanism is your body's system for responding to a perceived threat. This includes brain changes that increase alertness, and shifts in other body systems including the endocrine, cardio, and digestive systems. These changes prepare you to run from danger, or to fight hard if need be.

Your brain's activity, in turn, begins to affect virtually every other organ system in your body: your endocrine system begins to make shifts in the amount of emergency stress hormones such as adrenaline and cortisol that it begins to put out. Your respiratory system reacts, with your breathing becoming faster or more shallow. Your cardiovascular and even your digestive system responds.

Behavioral effects: With all of these organ systems running wild, your behavior around toxic people may be less effective. You may get worn out, and have more difficulty regulating your moods. Your behavior around the other people may be less skillful or well managed. For example, their anxiety may increase your annoyance with them to the point that they pick that up and so become even more anxious in your presence! Or you finally snap at them, say something impatient or rude, and it creates more problems for the relationship.

Vicious cycles: As you respond less effectively to the other people, and your own mood is affected, they pick it up. This may in turn trigger a deterioration in their condition. They may not even be aware that they're sensing your shifts, but it may reinforce their feeling that everyone around them is "as depressed as I am." (That may be true, if they are indeed triggering some depression in everyone they meet!)

Social Science

Friends and relatives of depressed people who try to cheer them up are often met with a lot of "that isn't helpful" messages. In turn, they get worn down, exasperated, and even angry at the depressed individual, compounding the "sick one's" depression. But by now, the helpers are depressed, too!

The Damage They Do

Most of the damage inflicted by toxic people is insidious. In other words, it happens a little at a time, as though you were being slowly poisoned. A few drops of toxic inter-action doesn't seem like much at first, and indeed, if it were just that few drops—that brief interaction with the whiney co-worker one day—it wouldn't be so bad.

But it's the constant drip-drip-dripping of the poison into your system that gets to you. Effects start to build up, day after day, but you don't notice because, well, you've gotten used to it. Psychoanalysts call this kind of thing *strain trauma.*

You may be used to it, but it's taking its toll on you. It's urgently important to remember that being "used to" something unhealthy doesn't make it less unhealthy! After all, millions of heavy smokers spent years getting "used to" being short of breath, craving nicotine constantly, hacking up lungs every morning, and all the other "routine" effects of smoking—that eventually killed them!

def•i•ni•tion

Strain trauma is traumatic damage to your personality that results from exposure to constant stress. For instance, growing up in an abusive home or having an abusive workplace can result in the same symptoms as surviving a fire or assault.

Ever go on vacation and suddenly feel free, relaxed, and at peace, and realize that you haven't felt that way for a long time? You're away from all your daily worries and toxins, including all those toxic people you usually have to work around, right? And your body and mind feel great! Until the last day of the trip, that is. But that peaceful reaction is a good gauge of how stressed you usually are!

But hey, you're used to it, right? Uh-huh. (That was my skeptical-shrink-looking-over-his-glasses-at-you uh-huh, by the way.)

Your body is affected in various ways by chronic threats of this sort. For instance, your adrenal glands release hormones such as cortisol into your system when you feel a threat. Over the short term, this is an excellent preparation for emergencies. But if you're exposed to chronic stressors, the chronic high levels of stress hormones in your system can have major effects on your physical health: you're more susceptible to heart problems, hypertension, diabetes, immune system problems, and even damage to your memory. Gradually, your higher stress levels may even reduce your ability to regulate your own fear responses—a kind of vicious cycle in which your fear leads to more intense fear that you can't shake!

A Toxic Sampler

There are a number of well-known patterns of behavior that people can engage in that tend to have toxic effects on us. Often, people aren't aware that they are having these damaging effects on others. They may not see themselves as unpleasant or hard to live with at all. In fact, more often than not they see themselves as the true victim. But from your point of view, their difficulties can become your illness.

The first step in learning to protect yourself is to develop some awareness of the kinds of poisoned patterns that you may encounter. Circle the ones that fit the relationships that bug you the most:

Intrusive people   These are the people who ask you overly personal questions, volunteer advice that you neither need nor want, and have opinions about your life that seem nosy. They may be the person who just stops by with no notice and at awkward times—and they do it over and over. They camp in your life, or get into your affairs when they're not wanted.

Critics   These people always find a way to let you know that there's just some little flaw in you or what you're doing. They may couch it in very well-meaning terms. Of course, any of our friends might from time to time criticize something we say or do. But with these people, it's a regular event.

Drama Queens (or Kings)   Being around this person is like having a free subscription to HBO and The Movie Channel. Their lives and perceptions of reality are always portrayed in dramatic terms. Everything is very intense for these people, and they seem unsatisfied if you aren't mirroring and affirming their level of intensity. Some of these people have what psychologists call histrionic personalities.

Bullies   There are all sorts of bullies, from the standard schoolyard-issue types with their unsubtle physical threats, to the "bullying lite" types who are more about humiliating and criticizing you in front of others. There are even lovable bullies whose bullying only comes out if you disagree with them, which is when they get intimidating and spooky.

Children suffer more from bullying, both emotional and physical, than adults. Talk with your child occasionally and ask them if they're being bullied, and give them support and advice. Work with their teacher and other parents to organize no bullying systems. And remember—bullies need help, too!

Narcissists   It's all about them, all the time. They walk into the room and somehow get all the spotlights shining on them. When you're around them, you feel diminished and your ideas aren't important. Sometimes they're very charismatic, dominant individuals, and people's initial response is to give them the reins. They may regret it when they find that the narcissist's main talent is enhancing their own status, not necessarily doing a great job once they get all the power and control.

Social Science

Narcissistic personalities see themselves as superior and more deserving than anyone else. Since they invest tremendous energy into their success, they often ascend to top leadership positions. But they can be damaging to organizations, since protecting their inflated self-image takes priority over other goals.

Nonstop talkers   This person can't ever say enough! They can't slow down enough to notice that there are other people with thoughts. They may be very entertaining, but they can get exhausting as well.

Blamers   This is the kind of person who sees all the ills in the world as someone else's fault (like, say, yours), and who spends much time needing to expound about that.

Insecure and helpless   Everyone feels insecure and vulnerable at times, but when it becomes a major character trait and something that the person uses to get constant affirmation or support, you may become exhausted around them.

There are also some clinical conditions and more severe behaviors that are extremely toxic at times. Here are some of the most common:

Depression   Being around a depressed person can be draining. If it's a clinical emergency that clearly needs help, you may be in a position to get him assistance. But if it's a more subtle character issue, the kind of person who is generally depressed, who spends much of his life talking about how things are never going to go well for him or anyone else, it's mainly just a downer. He may not be able to change himself, but he can definitely change *you*. You won't enjoy it.

Anxiety   Some people's anxiety levels are chronically so high that it's painful to be near them. If there is a clear reason for the anxiety (such as a pending surgery), you can generally help a person get through it, and the feelings, though intense, will be less severe in time. But if it is a long-term problem, it may just be exhausting for you and you'll end up feeling like giving up, or blaming yourself for not being helpful enough.

SI Tip

Confronting a friend or relative about a problem with alcohol or drugs can backfire, causing wrecked relationships or even violence at times. You may need to arrange a professional intervention and get the help of trained professionals to help a loved one with their substance use problems.

Substance abuse   Friends or relatives who are struggling with addictions (or maybe not struggling as much as they ought to be!) are major sources of stress for loved ones and co-workers. There's a whole range of typical behaviors that tend to occur in addictions, and pretty much none of them are comfortable or healthy to be around. Whether it's more severe effects such as violence or car wrecks, or more subtle effects such as the "not really here with me" feeling of being with someone who's really "married to his bottle" instead of to you, you'll be pulled into their pathology.

Psychological violence   This can take place in either home or work situations. For example, consider a boss who makes long speeches about how people need to be more respectful to each other in the workplace, but who arbitrarily threatens people's jobs and blows up when talking to employees. While he may do nothing physically violent that merits a 911 call, there is a level of psychological violence coming from such a person that can damage you over time.

Domestic violence   Actual physical violence, and threats of violence, are extremely toxic for partners and children who are exposed to it in the home. The important thing to remember is that the threat of violence, even if it never actually turns physical, can be every bit as damaging as actual physical violence.

Survival Skills Training Camp

It might seem that the ideal solution to the problem of toxic people would be to eliminate them from your life. Sometimes this is true. But there is also much to be gained by developing the skills of working things out with many of these people.

For one thing, you can't eliminate all toxic influences. The very fact that life is sometimes hard for everyone means that at times, any one of us may be a bit toxic to others. Since compassion is an important part of being a healthy, socially intelligent person, some compassion for the pains and difficulties of many of these people is a valuable quality to nurture in yourself.

But there sometimes comes a time when you do have to respond proactively to the behavior of people who are affecting you. While every situation is unique, and calls for a different response, and while every socially intelligent person is also unique, and so has many of their skills and ideas to draw on, some of the following steps may prove useful in some of these situations.

Self-Defense Around Toxic People

Be aware of their impact on you: "Knowing thyself" is an essential part of emotional intelligence, and you can use this self-knowledge to defend yourself. It boils down to asking yourself how you feel around that person. Are you noticing that a particular acquaintance seems to trigger strong feelings in you? If they are a nurturing person, those will be good feelings; if they are toxic, the feelings won't be so good.

Make a list: Can you identify the people in your life who have a negative emotional impact on you? Try to describe what happens. For example, if you have a friend who constantly radiates depressive messages, picking that up and recognizing that pattern may be helpful.

Try to understand: It's not your job to fix or even necessarily to truly diagnose the problems of friends and acquaintances. But neither is it helpful to just dismiss their concerns, by labeling them as toxic or abusive or whatever other label is currently in vogue. That's not particularly socially intelligent or compassionate on your part, and sometimes that kind of labeling can become part of an abuse cycle of its own. If there are ways to understand what's happening with the other person, that can be the best course.

Once you have the clearest possible understanding of the other person's behavior and how it affects you, you have three options. You can do nothing, which sometimes is actually a very good response. Just knowing that "Bob is like that" is sometimes all the "work" you need to do to deal with the situation. This might be the case if the person is someone you don't see very often, or if their behavior doesn't really have that big an effect on you. If you think about it, most of us have lives filled with friends who all have their quirks, idiosyncrasies, and imperfections. (Just like we do.)

But there may be times when it is important to take things to the next level.

Confronting Toxic Behavior

When or how you confront a friend, co-worker, or acquaintance will vary a great deal. Most of the time, a brief word to someone should do the trick—no need to build every difficult person up in your mind into some kind of monster! (If you find that you do that, you may want to consider whether *you* have a bit of drama queen in you.)

Before confronting someone else, it's important to try to get a handle on your own feelings. The best time to talk to someone about your concerns is *not* when you are feeling angry or upset with her. Of course, sometimes that will be when it will happen, and sometimes that is actually a pretty good time.

Most of us would prefer not to be confronted by someone who is trembling with rage. If, in your urge to confront, you upset someone, they're less likely to hear you. Tact matters.

When you do decide you need to confront someone, choose the time and place carefully. A private setting is generally better, since embarrassing them in front of others will be avoided.

> **Caution!**
>
> There will always be colleagues who wait for you to say the wrong "off color" thing or even to compliment someone, so they can feel offended (or report you to HR!). Of course, you wouldn't make comments that a reasonable person would feel are inappropriate, but don't assume that everyone is reasonable.

It also helps to lay the groundwork. Let them know, as an opener, that you have something you need to say to them. This way, they will tune in and be a bit better emotionally ready for the shock that might follow. You know: "We need to talk, Phyllis."

You can also give them some guidance as to the sort of response that you would like. You might say that you "have something hard to tell you, and I hope you will think about it carefully before you respond." Most of the time, people will try to respond more thoughtfully when you have given them this kind of heads up.

One of the best ways to let people know a concern is to focus on their behavior and your reaction to it, avoiding blame words such as descriptions of their character. For example, telling someone that they are overbearing may trigger defensiveness. That won't help you get what you want from them. But saying, "When you come into my office and stand over me and tell me what you want me to do, without asking my thoughts on the matter…" you are describing what they do in very clear behavioral terms.

The next part of that sentence is: " ... I feel." Hence, "When you come into my office and stand over me ... I feel ... " (intimidated, frightened, annoyed, or whatever).

Telling them about your feelings may help the person to see that their behavior is having an impact on you that they don't wish it to have. Your emotion triggers a mirroring response in them, and so they become aware that you do get anxious or uncomfortable. In SI terms, letting them know that you feel discomfort may activate their emotional resonance to you, their empathy. This may make them less likely to feel judged or criticized (or diagnosed) and create a social intelligence loop between their feelings and yours.

SI Tip

There is a model sentence that counselors recommend for confronting someone: "When you (X), I feel (Y); so please (Z)." "X" is a clear, nonblaming description of their behavior. "Y" is how you react to what they do. "Z" is how you'd like them to behave differently.

Keep in mind that the type of relationship you have with the person matters. If this is someone who has a positive relationship with you, and who is inclined to respond to your concerns, they're likely to want to help you feel more comfortable. But if this is someone who actually dislikes you, who feels they're in competition with you (such as in a work setting), or who is just not very caring in general, things won't always go so smoothly.

At times, this initial confrontation may trigger a longer discussion with the person about other concerns you or they have. For that reason, it'll help to be clear in your own mind about any other concerns about the person, before you have this meeting with them.

Know When to Flee!

The world would be a nicer place if everyone always responded instantly and automatically when we confronted them with our concerns. Not likely! Some people aren't willing or capable of altering their behavior, and some will actually respond aggressively, or blow your feedback off.

In fact, in some cases it's downright dangerous to confront someone. It may expose you to physical assault, or to consequences in a work setting where a "crazy" boss is not amenable to reason.

It's helpful to know when you should not get too invested in someone's response to your concerns. In some cases, the best advice is to limit your exposure to the person and their toxic impact on you. In other cases, you may actually need to end the relationship, or to get help from a third party.

> **Caution!**
>
> Just because you're right doesn't mean it's smart to say so! When you're caught in a conflict with someone and the tensions are rising, it's often better to back off, concede that they have a point, or apologize than to risk a full-scale riot by sticking to your guns! Sometimes it's best to wait and make your point when heads are cooler.

Examples of problems that are potentially more than you can—or should—try to handle on your own include domestic violence or severe substance abuse problems in a close friend or relative (or both problems together!). In these cases, you may need to ensure your own (and your children's) safety, to leave the home, or to involve professionals who know how to organize safe and effective interventions with the individual.

The Least You Need to Know

- ◆ Your ability to tune in to others means you'll also absorb a fair amount of toxic psychological gunk from people, so self-defense skills are crucial.

- ◆ Negative or threatening behaviors of others affect us emotionally and physically, and undermine our own coping skills.

- ◆ There is a wide range of toxic behaviors, ranging from bullying to chronic self-pity.

- ◆ Coping with toxic people requires awareness, strategy, and skills at tactful confrontation.

- ◆ In some cases, it's better just to avoid a toxic threat than to try to fix it.

Part 3

Personal Relationships and Social Intelligence

Much of your personality is really made up of your human connections—the important relationships you carry around inside yourself. You think about these people, plan your life around them. What they say to you, think about you, how you and they get along—all of these things affect you deeply, both physically, emotionally, and spiritually.

The science of social intelligence can help you nurture the kinds of connections with important others that can make your life feel like heaven on earth ... instead of the "other place." In Part 3, we'll discuss the science of friendship, romance, committed relationships, and dealing with kids. There's the usual self-assessment quiz in each chapter to help you think more deeply about your relationships and the latest SI tips to help you build the relationship life you want.

Chapter **10**

Friendships of the Socially Intelligent

In This Chapter

- ◆ Your need for friends
- ◆ Friend-finding starter kit
- ◆ Making friendships deeper

A person high in social intelligence will almost always have thriving friendships. In this chapter, we'll explore the nature and benefits of vital friendships, and explore ways to enhance your friendship-growing ability.

But first, a brief self-assessment.

Check Yourself Out

This self-test is to help you assess your ability to develop and function well in friendships. For each item, select the response that best describes you.

1. How many people do you know that you could call to go out and do something fun with?

    A. I usually call one of several friends.

    B. There are one or two people I could call, but they might be surprised.

    C. I know five or more people who wouldn't be surprised if I were to call them—they'd be surprised if I didn't!

2. If a friend were doing something unkind or unethical or that might be harmful to them, I could talk to them about it.

    A. More likely, I'd assume they didn't want my input, so I'd just quietly hope they didn't do it.

    B. If it were a big enough issue, I might be able to bring it up with a very close friend.

    C. It might feel awkward, but I can certainly do that, and have at times.

3. When is the last time you got in touch with a friend whom you thought might need cheering up, or checking on?

    A. Most weeks I probably do that for at least one person.

    B. I think I probably do that a few times a year or so.

    C. Can't recall—my friends always seem fine.

4. How many people would you think would get in touch with you (or call your home, parents, or partner) if they heard you were ill and in the hospital?

    A. There would be at least one and maybe two people who'd do that.

    B. I think there'd be five or more people who'd check out how I was doing.

    C. Probably nobody—and I'm not saying that just because I'm feeling pessimistic.

5. How many of your friends' birthdays (or other important dates or anniversaries) are written on your calendar for the year?

    A. Five or ten, or more!

    B. I don't think my friends expect that.

    C. Two or three.

6. Do your close friends know each other, or are they strangers to each other?

    A. None of my friends know each other. It's all one-on-one connections.

    B. A number of my friends (e.g., five or more) are part of a "network" of people who all know each other.

    C. Some of my friends also have connections with each other, independent of our relationship.

7. When is the last time you met someone new, whom you imagined might become a friend?

    A. Probably within the past year or so.

    B. Almost never happens—I can't recall when it last occurred.

    C. Within the past few weeks I met someone or realized that a casual acquaintance might be nice as a friend.

8. Did you have a "best friend" during adolescence (or if you are young—under 18 or so, do you have a best friend now—or would you really like to find one?)

    A. Absolutely. We hung out and did a lot together (or, we still do.)

    B. Had a "casual friend" or two.

    C. Not really. No one special.

9. How well do you have to know someone, or how "close" do you have to feel to them, before you'll call them your "friend"?

    A. A "friend" is anybody whose first name I know—I use the word pretty all-inclusively.

    B. A "friend" to me is someone I really feel I know.

    C. If we know each other by our first names and have talked at a social gathering (like a church breakfast) or at work once or twice, I start to refer to them as a "friend."

10. If you met someone today you thought you might enjoy having as a friend, would you know what to do in order to develop that friendship?

    A. *Que sera, sera.* If it happens, it happens.

B. I have a vague idea but mostly it would depend on luck.

C. I can't "force" everyone to become my friend, but I'm a good enough judge of what "works" in developing friendships that I would probably be able to develop something with the person.

Scoring: Circle which answer you chose for each question, then add up the number of circles within each column.

Item	Few	Some	Lots
1. (Calls)	B	A	C
2. (Ethical)	A	B	C
3. (Cheer)	C	B	A
4. (Ill)	C	A	B
5. (Birthday)	B	C	A
6. (Close)	A	C	B
7. (New)	B	A	C
8. (Adolesc)	C	B	A
9. (Friend)	A	C	B
10. (Develop)	A	B	C
Totals			

Interpreting your results:

Few   6–10: You are describing yourself as someone who doesn't have many friends, and someone who isn't really sure how to go about developing them (or who isn't very interested in friends). Read on!

Some   6–10: You've got the raw material to develop some pretty good friendship patterns, but might benefit from some pointers.

Many   6–10: You seem to be blessed with some healthy and rewarding friendships, and have the skills you need to grow more.

We All Need Friends

The term *friendship* means different things to different people. Your age, the culture in which you live, and your life experience, how you view friendship—and whom you decide to consider a friend—all help determine what friendship means to you.

Friendships among kindergarteners may spring up after two children have just met. Three minutes after meeting another child, your kid may be ready to tell you about "my new friend." On the other hand, a mature adult may consider someone a good friend only after having known them and experienced much together over a period of decades.

People have defined different elements that are required in order to call a relationship a friendship. These can include:

♦ Knowing the other person

♦ Caring about the other person

♦ Feeling supported by, and supporting, them

♦ Loyalty

♦ Helping each other

♦ Understanding each other

♦ Identifying with each other—we are "alike"

♦ Sharing each other's values

♦ Participating in activities together.

> **Social Science**
>
> Friendship is by no means a modern invention. The ancient Greeks prized friendship highly, and in the Bible, the relationship between David and Jonathan, the son of King Saul, has long been praised as a tender and inspiring example of friendship. (That's in I Samuel 18–20, if you're curious.)

Perhaps the strongest indicator that someone is a friend is that we choose to call them one! If I consider you my friend, then you are, by golly!

As you recall from Chapter 1, we're wired to connect, and we're particularly wired to connect in the kinds of relationships that get called friendships. Most people find friendships both pleasant and important to their well-being. There are many emotional and health benefits of good friendships.

Emotional Benefits

People with friends generally seem to be emotionally healthier than those people with few or no friendships. Of course, it is obvious that the healthier someone is emotionally, the more able they are to attract and hold on to friendships. But friendships also provide valuable support during times of stress, confusion, or when faced with difficult life events. Research shows that people under stress tend to cope much better if they also rate themselves high in social support—a.k.a. friendships.

Health Benefits

Someone once said, "A good friend is cheaper than therapy." Many medical studies have shown that friendships are vital to our health. In fact, physicians now agree that lack of friendships and close supportive relationships is as dangerous to your health as being a chronic smoker!

It's not totally clear why friendships are so life preserving. Currently, researchers have identified several possible reasons:

◆ Friends may help each other manage intense physical and psychological arousal. This would reduce the damaging wear-and-tear effects of stress on your body.

◆ Friends support each other's healthy behavior. If you and your friend take regular exercise walks and exchange healthy recipes, you both keep off a pound or two. When your buddy shares racquetball tips or you play a few rounds of golf together instead of spending the day alone in front of the tube, your bod benefits as well as your emotional life.

◆ Friends motivate. Just hearing how your girlfriend is trying a yoga class can bolster your interest in checking it out, and now you have someone to go to the class with!

◆ Friends may share important resources with each other, such as referrals to doctors or to their favorite health food store.

◆ It may also be that friendships positively impact our immune systems and other body systems. There's a ton of research on how our bodies are directly affected by our social supports, beyond simply improving our health behaviors!

Benefits with Friends

Abraham Lincoln once said, "Am I not destroying my enemies when I make friends of them?" In addition to the health and personal benefits, many friendships also function as business partnerships or as other practical relationships. For example, you and your friends may be more successful getting through law school because of the study groups you organize. You share resources other than just health information with your friends.

Creating friendships *just* in order to advance your career may not feel comfortable or sincere to you, and it can backfire, particularly if someone senses that you are using them. It generally works okay if you go into it one of two ways: one is that you join organizations or groups because you mainly are interested in the group, but discover that you "click" with some individuals in the group and so develop friendships. The other way is to develop friendships first, just because you like someone, meet them as a neighbor, or whatever … but then discover that you are in positions to help each other.

Companionship

It's difficult to enjoy many things in life on your own. People get tremendous pleasure by having someone to go to the baseball game or concert with, or to share other activities with.

The pleasure of another person's company, if that person is a close friend, is ranked by many people as the best part of their lives.

And friendship can bring its own kind of love. Not sexual or erotic love, but something different, which many people call *agape.*

def•i•ni•tion

> **Agape** (pronounced "AH-ge-pay") is an ancient Greek term meaning "selfless love" or the kind of platonic love felt between friends (in contrast to erotic or sexual love.)

When your friendships include this love element, it changes both of you, and changes your sense of self as well. Your close friends become a part of yourself, and as social intelligence research shows, that's not just a figure of speech! Your relationship with close friends, especially if there are loving feelings involved, becomes deeply integrated into your sense of identity. You create internal representations or working models of these people. Often, our friendships are a big part of who we are in life.

A Friendship Starter Kit

If you had just arrived here from some faraway land (or perhaps some faraway planet!), one of the smartest first steps you could take would be to begin developing friendships. As a "newcomer" you would need not just practical resources and the health benefits of friendships, but the pleasure of new companions. In addition, you may enjoy being of help to them as well!

So how would you start? Or, since you probably aren't newly arrived from Mars, how might you enhance the friendships you already have?

To start, think about the main ways people locate potential friends.

Common Interests

Many friendships start because people share interests. This can include everything from enjoying *Star Trek* conventions or archery or horses. Having recently moved to a new part of the country, my wife has been delighted to have found a women's knitting group which she attends regularly. Though new to the group, she's already aware that the group includes many compatible people whom she's enjoyed meeting, and some of whom she expects may become long-term friends.

> **Social Science**
>
> Research shows that most people know a few hundred other people on a first-name basis. Almost anyone you know probably knows at least a few people who share your interests in something, from Charlie Chaplin films to knitting to bow-hunting. Ask around!

You could do worse than to make a list of your top five interests, especially things that you've been meaning to learn about for some time. Find some people who share those interests. In this day of nearly universal Internet connectivity, finding people who share your interests is easier to do than it ever was.

Common Connections

Some friends may arrive on your doorstep based on mutual connections. For example, one of my best adulthood friends was also a friend of a graduate school teacher of mine. When the teacher learned that I was beginning my private psychology practice, he introduced me to a psychologist who was starting up her new practice. In part due to our similar situations, we developed a very strong friendship.

Good Chemistry

Sometimes we just click with someone. It's as though we knew them before—we may even start to believe, even if briefly, in past life connections. All we know is that our energy (or personality style, or karma, or something) seems to match up very well. Even though we don't share strong interests or common networks, we may just find that there's something about that person—the intangible things that are part of their personality—that draw us toward them.

When this happens, rejoice! Enjoy that connection! Get to know the person better, and see if that initial impression, the result of some kind of magical, unconscious neurological synchrony (or some mystical past life relationship?) is strong enough to develop into a long-term friendship.

Friendly Networks

Friendship networks happen when some of your friends know each other as well you. This can include your weekly poker or knitting group, but it can also include complicated webs of connections between hundreds of people. Networks can have a couple of advantages: they work as social capital that helps people through life, and they are often more stable than un-networked friendships (where your friends don't know each other).

Social Capital. Friendship networks function as a powerful form of social capital for many people. In other words, both for professional and practical reasons, being part of a more connected network of friendships tends to carry other, more tangible benefits with it: you exchange more information with more people, you have more common experiences and understandings, and are more likely to share resources. Even if you are an introvert (see Chapter 4), it's probably worthwhile to look at networking potentials among your friendships.

Many people develop networks of friends who share common interests and exchange news that might be helpful. For example, would it surprise you to hear that I learned about the opportunity to do this book from one of my writer friends? And that another writer friend, who had introduced me to the *first* writer friend, helped me learn how to get started on the book?

> **Social Science**
>
> As a young man, Ben Franklin and his friends formed a little society that they named the "Junto." This group met regularly to exchange news, to support each other's work, and to think up ways to improve their community. It was the prototype for modern chambers of commerce, scientific societies, and similar groups.

Relationships that don't break. Some researchers have found that the most "resilient" relationships, the ones that are least likely to be disrupted if the going gets rough between people, are "networked" relationships. In studying the friendship patterns of people with various levels of psychological health, these researchers found that there were three different kinds of friendship networking.

There are people who are severely mentally ill—in their case, the major "network" that might form around them is of people taking care of them. People get to know each other in the course of trying to keep that one person afloat. (This might, for instance, include a few friends, a few family members, and the person's doctor and social worker.)

A second kind of pattern is the person who isn't severely ill, but who may have some psychological difficulties. People struggling with chronic, mild depression or anxiety might fall into this category. They're more likely to develop a few one-on-one relationships, making friends with people who don't know each other. (This may be because they are more likely to be anxious about groups and so on.) The disadvantage is that if such a person has a bit of a bad patch with any of those friends, there aren't other mutual friends who might help the two of them get reconnected. As a result, these friendships are more fragile—one small tiff and they may lose that connection.

The strongest connections are often those in which your friends also know each other. That way, if you are out of touch with a friend for a while, you may still hear news of them from the other friends you both know. In addition, if you do have a disagreement it's more likely that you'll be able to repair the breach and get back together. That's because when you have only a single connection to a friend, you're more likely to just stop talking to them and imagine they're upset with you, until you discover in ten years that you just "drifted away from each other." If you both share other friends, it's much harder to avoid each other because other people will be arranging events, parties, dinners, meetings, or whatever, and you'll both get invited. And so you'll have a much better chance of seeing their smiling face across the room and reconnecting. (Or else your other friends may just nag you to patch up the tears in your relationship.)

Deepen Your Friendships

Most likely, your friendship-building system doesn't involve a whole lot of planning, or even conscious awareness. Which works fine when you're still young and in your school years. Later on, maybe not so much!

When you're in school, there are always lots of people around—in a class, on the football team, in a club. In addition, though you may not have been consciously aware of it, you probably benefited as a child from the hard work of your parents or teachers, who made sure that you had chances to meet new friends. (The average three-year-old doesn't plan a "play date" so that they can meet other kids!)

As we get older, the natural opportunities that children have to develop friendships start to disappear. Once you leave high school or college, your well-stocked friendship pond may have evaporated. One day you realize that you aren't meeting new people in the same life situation anymore. At that point, your social life may start to shrink as your old friends move to other states, get married, or aren't free on Saturday nights.

It's never too early to develop the active skills of going out and rounding up your own friends!

Acquaintance to Friend

As a rule of thumb, you grow friends from casual acquaintances. Though there are exceptions to this rule, for the most part people start off as strangers and go through a series of normal developmental stages in the growth of a friendship. The point is, don't try to jump in and become instant bosom buddies. Sometimes it works, but usually it won't.

Here are some suggestions for developing acquaintances into friendships:

You gotta meet somebody. It seems obvious, but if you want to fill a "friend vacuum" you have to dig up some raw material—people who *could* become friends!

If you're satisfied with the crop that you've run into during the course of your day, such as if you're a student or work in a large company where you have the opportunity to meet many people, excellent! Other times, you gotta get out there and beat the bushes. You may need to join some kind of organizations, such as a church or community group, or go online and find some folks who also want to learn about the mating habits of the duckbilled platypus. Wherever you find them, look for people you might enjoy a conversation with.

> **Social Science**
>
> One of the most successful best-sellers ever written is Dale Carnegie's *How to Win Friends and Influence People*. Carnegie's guide to the art of making friends (which stresses thinking of them before yourself) has sold 16 million copies since it was first published in 1937; it's currently in its 42nd edition.

Talk with them. One of the best things you can do to develop a friendship is to spend time talking with an acquaintance. This may actually be *the* most important step in making friendships. If possible, seek some time to chat over coffee or a beer when you're not at the heavily scheduled meeting of the "Duckbilled Platypus Study Club."

Time spent one-on-one can be very useful. This can also include e-mail and telephone contacts, though when possible, nothing beats good old-fashioned eye contact. Remember, social intelligence research shows that those in-person contacts are the most powerful ways to develop some kind of a shared consciousness, which can make a friendship more powerful.

Create friend-building events. Look for opportunities to do something with this potential friend. Invite them to take a walk around a lake with you. Ask if they'd like to go see the latest duckbilled platypus exhibit at the museum, either together or with some other friends.

SI Tip

From a social intelligence standpoint, "quality" may count for more than "quantity" in friendships. Understanding, resonating emotionally, and caring for a friend—and them doing the same for you—is the healthiest combination.

Open up a bit. As you spend more time with someone, begin to disclose more information about yourself. Most of us start by talking about fairly "public" things: our jobs, where we live, and so on. We may also toss in a fair amount of chatter about things like the weather. But if you spend more time with someone, you may gradually reveal slightly more personal information. Don't go into the deep end of the pool too early! Talk about things that are slightly more personal, then wait to see if the other person reciprocates. If so, excellent!

Some people aren't very good at reciprocating, or talking about themselves. Most likely, they're not being snotty—they're just anxious! When you're with such a person, it can help to have a few questions that you can ask, that will help them talk with greater ease about themselves. These might include:

- "So what's new with you?"

- "Are you planning any interesting vacations?" (or something like that, depending on the season, like "Are you traveling anywhere over the holidays?")

- "How's school/work going?"

- Follow-up questions on whatever they *have* been talking about. If your friend is into playing guitar, ask how they learned about it, or what they like to play, or whether they practice much, or whatever else comes to mind.

Whatever you do, remember your lessons from SI-101: read the signals they're sending! If you ask, "How's your relationship with your dad lately?" for instance, and they look away and grow pale, you have received a strong nonverbal signal to back off! On the other hand, if they have a small energy burst and start going on about their dear or annoying (or dear but annoying) dad, you've hit pay dirt.

Don't be an intimacy addict. A psychologist friend of mine made the point that many of his patients who work in professions that require a fairly intense amount of rapid intimacy with their clients or patients (such as attorneys, physicians, or other therapists) sometimes make the mistake of leaping into casual relationships and immediately expecting to have conversations about very personal topics. Then they come to their own therapists saying they are having difficulties making friends. Any guesses as to why?

Pacing is important! Becoming addicted to nothing but extremely personal conversation may make it harder for you to relax and enjoy the early stages of casual friendships. Besides, you may freak some people out. It's like asking the waitress you just met to marry you—the odds are slim that she'll say yes! (Or even be as comfortable as she was just a moment ago enjoying some friendly banter with you!)

Keep the connections lively! Sometimes friendships that might have been wonderful begin to get stale because you keep having the same old discussions. No need to do that! You can introduce new topics or ideas, or do something besides meet at the same old watering hole time after time. The watering hole might be near a museum, or there might be a film that you really want to see, that your friend might enjoy seeing with you. If you begin to sense that things are growing a little stale, vary the menu!

Fix problems as they arise! Sometimes friends will disagree. One of the risks in early friendships is that there isn't much "positive capital" in the bank that will help the two of you survive a strong disagreement. Maybe it's the first time you've ever discussed religion or politics, or disagreed on something of importance to one of you. Maybe one of you failed to keep an appointment, or did something to hurt the other's feelings.

Since friendships are incredibly valuable, and really great ones take a long time to nurture, it's important to do whatever you can to keep one from drifting away. Sometimes letting a friend know that you feel badly about whatever it is that turned the milk sour is an important step. Just don't overdo it!

> **Caution!**
>
> Being "too cautious" can backfire in a friendship! If your friend really needs some honest feedback, but you withhold it for fear of hurting their feelings, they may feel that you betrayed their trust in you. Tact and care matter, but sometimes our best friends are the ones who tell us things we need to hear!

Set limits with friends. Sometimes friends are too "friendly"—if you know what I mean. A lonely person might become a bit too desperate, or press matters a little faster than you wish they would. This can be in the sexual realm, but it can also just involve being too open about personal things too early, or presuming that the person is more ready to open their life or home to you than they are.

> **Caution!** _____
>
> Sexual feelings can mess up a friendship! Sometimes it's better to deal with that sexual "tension" between you and someone else by finding a quiet (*but* public enough that you won't get halfway through the talk and jump on each other!) time to talk about it, than by acting on it impulsively. "Yes, we're attracted to each other, but it would wreck our friendship" is a sentence that has saved many long-term friendships.

If you just met someone and have had a couple of nice talks, and they suddenly want to know if they can spend the weekend in your place in the country, you might feel uncomfortable. (Or, of course, you might say "great!" and love it!) Setting some limits might be useful.

> **SI Tip** _____
>
> Friends from different cultures will almost always have different notions of what friendships involve, including how personal you can get, how much you can impose on each other, and so on. Even whether it's appropriate for you to be friends may be up for grabs! Be aware of cultural differences and, if you're in doubt, ask.

Limit-setting is mainly a matter of being aware that something doesn't feel right, and wanting to set some boundaries. The trick is in gently, tactfully expressing your concerns with that person. Generally, the more subtly you do this (at least at first), the better. Saying "Gee, I just don't know that I'll have time to spend with you that weekend" might be enough of a hint to the person, and is much better than expressing shock that they would have presumed to ask you to put them up.

Remember, the overall goal is to build friendships up. They grow by way of many good experiences. Painful or aversive experiences are difficult to overcome—it can take ten good memories to undo the damage of one bad!

It's What You Give

People sometimes fall into a psychological trap when discussing the benefits of friendships, because their natural inclination is to list benefits to *them*—instead of focusing on friendships as an opportunity to give something to someone else. While, yes, it's entirely "useful" to be in a giving role (helps the blood pressure, etc.), part of socially intelligent living is to value giving for its own sake.

Friendships are a primary place where you can enjoy this kind of giving attitude. Being a nurturing friend is an ideal that many people strive for.

Of course, being a caring and nurturing friend may mean coming through on the "big things"—you'll run into a burning building to save your friend and their kitten Fluffy; you'll donate a kidney to your high school pal, you'll mortgage your house to help your friend start their new widget business. But "heroics" aren't really required to be a nurturing friend most of the time. Rather, connecting, remembering them, and keeping in touch about the "little things" are a big part of the mix.

Some things that might enhance your "giving qualities" as a friend:

Remember personal facts about your friends. Keep track of their birthdays or anniversaries, their astrological signs, the names of their children or spouses, and so on. (Depending on what's important to them.) This is something that salespeople do routinely, for the sake of their business. It can be amazingly helpful in enhancing your friendships, and be a rich experience for you as well.

Keep a birthday card list or calendar. Many people make a monthly ritual of purchasing birthday or other monthly event cards, and sending them out to friends. If you're not that organized, simply keep a list in your address book of particular friends that you want to contact regularly. This can be a good way to remind yourself that this or that person needs an e-mail now and then.

Watch for news about friends' special interests and hobbies. Sometimes you will run across an article while reading the news online, and realize that a friend will appreciate hearing about this article, or will enjoy this joke. Some people have group lists of best friends that they send interesting things to.

> **SI Tip** _____
>
> One clever way to find out a friend's birthday is to ask, "What's your sign?" Whether or not you believe in astrology, you can joke about that for a minute and walk away with their birthday to put on your calendar as an annual reminder to let them know they're important to you.

Tell them you appreciate them. Letting a person know that you value them is a more personal, and even slightly intense, act. You may not need to do that very often, and there may be some friends with whom you only exchange those kinds of intimacies. However, both you and some of your closest friends may become even closer if you take the plunge and tell them how important they are to you from time to time.

There are no lifetime guarantees! Don't take your closest friends for granted. That includes spouses and children. You may be very good about remembering to tell your friend in Tucson that they are special to you, but have you told your nearest and dearest recently? In every relationship, it's important to express appreciation, and even love, in order to keep it thriving.

The Least You Need to Know

- There are many definitions of friendship, but the best may be that you decide to call someone your friend!

- Having friendships brings many benefits, but the best may be that your friendships help define who you are.

- Friendships don't just happen; you can consciously decide to create and deepen friendships.

- Friendship networks can be highly helpful and are often the basis for the most resilient friendships.

- Your friendships are strengthened by what you contribute to them.

Chapter 11

Love at First Sight—And the Other Kinds!

In This Chapter

- ◆ Romance and social intelligence
- ◆ Five ways to sink a romance
- ◆ Tips for new romantics
- ◆ How to deepen a bond

Ah! The romance of romance! Excitement! Mystery! Fun! And when you're really lucky (and do it right), a romance (yes, with real, romantic feelings!) can even last a lifetime!

Use a little SI and odds of a great romance are in your favor. In this chapter, we'll talk about how.

But first, let's check out your romance skills.

Check Yourself Out

This quiz is designed to help you assess your "romance SI." Read each item and circle the response that best describes you.

1. You're strongly drawn to two different guys/gals: one is stunningly attractive, but doesn't share your interests; the other is, well, okay looking—but he/she and you can talk for hours. Your best romantic bet for long-term success:

    A. I'd try to have sex with the stunner, and if the other one turns into a buddy, that'd be a plus.

    B. I'd spend my time with the person I "click" with emotionally and as a friend—sexual feelings will follow.

    C. I think I would drop them both and look for someone with the perfect combination of being hot and a great fit for me.

2. You are absolutely smitten with someone you met just moments ago—this person seems to be your perfect match! Odds of a happily-ever-after outcome?

    A. It'll never work out.

    B. My strong response tells me nothing either way—but it's fun!

    C. My strong response tells me we're meant for each other, whether the other person thinks so or not!

3. The best way to manage physical distance between you and that attractive stranger is:

    A. Move a bit closer and see what the stranger does in response.

    B. Move in closer than the stranger seems comfortable with—he/she secretly wants me to.

    C. Stay far back until I get a clear, verbal invitation.

4. In order to approach someone you're interested in, you should first:

    A. Hold back and let them come to me.

    B. Watch for nonverbal signals of interest—brief eye contact or a smile, then approach them.

    C. Practice my "opening line" so I can say it smoothly.

5. You're out with a new romantic interest for the first time and disagree about how to spend the evening. Best way to respond:

    A. Not agreeing isn't the end of the world—let's work out a compromise.

B. If it's happening already, we aren't compatible. Forget it!

C. I can be very persuasive—I use my social intelligence so well that people almost always go with what I want to do.

6. It's a good sign if early on in a romance your feelings about your new "potential partner" are:

   A. It's like talking to a good friend.

   B. I feel super-aware of how much I want to impress him or her.

   C. Almost 100 percent sexual attraction—amazing!

7. The best way to "deepen" your connection with a new romance is to:

   A. Give the person lots of "space" by not calling too often, etc., so he/she can "come to you."

   B. Start to give the person caring "advice" or information on how to be more successful.

   C. Get to know stuff about the person—it doesn't matter what, as long as it's stuff that person wants to share.

8. A great way to impress someone on that first night out is:

   A. Try to respond to that person's "signals" and tune in to them.

   B. Wear your most dazzling outfit or show that person your fancy car.

   C. Take the person to an amazing and expensive new restaurant.

9. The best "first move" when flirting and you want to get physical is:

   A. Give your partner a very specific, detailed description of how you want to touch him/her and ask his/her consent.

   B. Move close, signal with eye contact and body language that you're open, then wait for a response that says your partner is open to more.

   C. Seize them and start kissing—both women and men appreciate someone taking the initiative and feel it's more sexy.

10. After a great "first night" with someone you want to see again, you should:

   A. Wait for your date to get back to you so you don't "scare the person off."

   B. Buy your date a piece of jewelry or other gift signifying his/her commitment to you.

   C. Get in touch within a day or two and tell your date how much you enjoyed being with him/her.

Scoring: Circle your answers below, and tally how many you have in each column.

Item	MS	ME	SI
1. (Drawn)	C	A	B
2. (Smitten)	A	C	B
3. (Distance)	C	B	A
4. (Approach)	A	C	B
5. (Evening)	B	C	A
6. (Good sign)	C	B	A
7. (Deepen)	A	B	C
8. (Impress)	C	B	A
9. (First)	A	C	B
10. (Great night)	A	B	C
Totals			

Interpreting your results

MS 6–10: This stands for "missing signals," meaning the signals of potential romantic partners. If you have six or more answers in this column, you may be saying you don't tune in to a potential romantic partner's feelings very often. This can undermine your chances of a great relationship.

ME 6–10: This means "me," as in "me, me, me!" If most of your answers are in this column, you may be saying that the main person you want to fall in love with is yourself! Could you possibly be putting what you want in a relationship ahead of what a potential partner wants?

SI 6–10: The "socially intelligent" alternative. You are describing yourself as tuned in to the emotional dimensions of a great romance: rapport with a partner, the ability to "resonate" with each other, interest in him or her, and a healthy, comfortable attitude toward sexuality.

Even Romance Takes SI

Finding the right partner can be one of the most critical tasks in life. But success at romance isn't really all that mysterious. Many people are pretty good at it, and they aren't necessarily supermodels or living gods, either. But what they do have is the set of social skills and awarenesses that help them connect with potential partners.

What to do? Well, remember how we talked about needing the right tools or gear before setting out on your journey? Well, on the rocky journey to the land of love, make sure you pack your SI toolkit. Specifically:

Knowing yourself: One of the main reasons the "signs" on the road to love seemed so jumbled might have been because of all the confusion in your own heart. Are you confusing lust with love? Happens all the time. How about relying on all the bad maps that you received by watching confusing, or badly mangled, parental relationships?

Tuning in: You have to know how to decipher the signals that potential partners are sending. Do those downcast eyes mean, "I am being coy and flirting with you"? Or maybe, "Please leave me alone or I'll call the bouncer!"?

Connecting: Making, and holding on to, contact with another person takes more than good intentions (or mutual lust!) Knowing what to say, what not to say, and how to deepen the relationship are all necessary for the relationship to work. Then there are the advanced skills: working through conflicts, instead of just throwing in the towel when you and that special other are having a rough time.

Caring: Of course, the whole point of romantic relationships is to express caring for another person, and to be able to experience their care for you. Which sounds easy, right? Yeah.

> ### Social Science
>
> That strong, instant feeling that you get for a new person when you are madly in love with them is "limerance." The bad news is that it's a lousy predictor of a relationship's success, because it's mostly all about your own projections of all your own needs onto this semi-stranger!

Every one of these elements of socially intelligent relating is important. Let's look more closely at some of the science of romance.

Not only our bodies, but our minds react to potential partners on "automatic pilot." For example, we may be unconsciously matching potential partners to ourselves on various dimensions, from political beliefs to diet and movie preferences, to see if

def•i•ni•tion

Pheromones are chemicals our bodies produce and release into the environment that affect the behavior or bodies of others. For instance, early research suggests that male brains respond to estrogen-related chemicals secreted by females, and females respond to testosterone-type scents put out by males.

they will be a good fit with us. It seems likely that our biological heritage has also programmed us to look at potential mates (meaning, sometimes, every comely stranger we pass in the canned goods aisle) in terms of baby-making potential; for instance, we may respond to chemical scents or *pheromones* that can signal health and fertility. Or, we may be unconsciously observing how they behave in order to "assess" maternal qualities, or whether he will be likely to stick around and be a good provider.

And if dealing with the here and now weren't difficult enough, there is also the problem of hauling our childhoods around with us! Remember that we are programmed from infancy to expect and to long for certain kinds of attachment relationships.

Social Science

Many romantic feelings aren't under our conscious control. We think we're being "rational" when in fact our brains are transmitting signals back and forth from one neural center to another that say "Go for it!" and our bodies are surging with hormones that are preparing us for the fling of our lives.

If, for instance, you are a woman who had a great dad who was very affectionate toward you, you are much more likely to only accept affectionate guys as potential partners. If, on the other hand, your dad was something of a jerk to your mom and yourself, it may be very difficult for you to avoid getting hooked up with similar jerks, try as you might to avoid them.

Five Ways to Sink a Relationship

All that programming can result in some pretty effective self-sabotage. Responding by reflex to your own needs or habit patterns, without really tuning in to the other person and the signals they send, is generally the biggest mistake. But there are a zillion ways to play that mistake out. Here are five examples of common "new romance sabotage" patterns. Recognize anyone?

Too Much, Too Fast

Let's say you meet someone, and suddenly feel super attracted to her. What's the first thing you do?

Obviously! You glom on, and spend as much time as you possibly can with her! You invite her to meet your parents, or to take off with you on a romantic vacation, or to jump in the sack before the second drink. You start talking about your future together before it's even occurred to her that the two of you *have* a "future."

Whoa! Critical question: does she share your enthusiasm for this not-quite-started-yet relationship? Or are you signaling that you have some "issues" with *dependency*, which may cause the other person to back off?

def•i•ni•tion

Dependency means a tendency to cling or want to rely on other persons for attention, reassurance, guidance, support, or material things, to an unbalanced or unhealthy degree.

A socially intelligent person needs to be aware that in anything as complicated as a romantic relationship, each person will be responding back and forth with a great many signals. Focusing only on your desires, or on your fantasies about the relationship, will mean that you're not picking up the other person's signals.

Too Little, Too Late

If pouncing on someone is a big mistake, so is being oblivious. Someone may be signaling you that he's interested in a relationship, but you tune him out. Which isn't a problem, if you aren't interested in him. But what if you are?

You may feel that the other person couldn't really be signaling interest in you. Maybe your self-esteem is so low that it's hard to believe somebody wants you. Or you may just respond a bit too passively, or don't take any initiative to get to know the other person when you could have.

"Me. Me. Me!"

Being too focused on yourself and your needs is a high-potency relationship toxin. Being a total princess (or prince) will only attract masochists, and even they may not hang around long.

You may have learned that you should "expect" certain kinds of attention or affection in a relationship. Or you may secretly be pretty insecure about your desirability—and so try to reassure yourself by expecting that "royal treatment."

Baggage Not Checked at the Door

Every relationship is a new beginning … except when you spend your first hours together talking about your last relationship. Or better still, you make sure that this relationship will end the same way all your others have, by treating this person as though they *were* all your other partners.

This is what keeps therapists busy. Most of their caseloads are full of people who keep reliving old, painful relationships.

Old patterns die hard. At first you may not see that you're sabotaging relationships. Sometimes it takes a few mistakes before you can recognize the pattern. Sometimes it takes a best friend, a partner on his way out the door of your life, or your shrink to tell you. But if you're sharp and hone your SI skills (especially the "tune in" ones!), you may be able to prevent mishaps.

Trying to Fit When You Don't

You're telling yourself these little "signs" of problems between you, or your waning interest, are not so important.

Maybe they *are!* While a good relationship isn't all fireworks, there ought to be a few sparks at least. For instance, are you acting like you're great friends? Do you actually *like* talking to her—so much so that you can spend hours together? Researcher Dr. John Gottman points to that as a key question to ask yourself (based on his years of studying couples whose relationships succeed).

If you're not all that interested in each other, that's not a good sign. Neither is it so hot if your feelings of sexual attraction or passion are, well, not so hot. Come on, be honest: are there truly loving feelings there?

Are you really trying to hold on to the other *person*, or to your *fantasies* about the relationship? Maybe you should just let go.

The common toxic element in all of these "five ways" is really a violation of one or more SI principles. Most of the time, it's about failing to tune in to the other person because your own needs/feelings/issues are interfering. Being more needy than they want, ignoring their "come hither" or "be gone!" signals, and caring more about yourself than them—these are all relationship poison.

Okay—What *Should* I Do?

You're unique and so is every person you meet, which is why there isn't a one-size-fits-all answer to the question, "How do I start and succeed at a romance?" But there are some general SI principles that might smooth that rocky road for you.

Know who you're compatible with. Knowing "who you are looking for" is a good first step. Here's what the research says: for a short-term fun time, someone who is different from you may be a thrill. But for long-term relationship success, go with compatible every time. And this includes both interests and personality style.

If you're a scholarly sort, you'll mesh best with someone who also reads something besides the TV directory now and then. If you're really into sports, your best bet is another sports fan. Love animals? Look for another beast lover. Bank robber? Um ….

Shared interests are good predictors of a good fit, but similar personal styles and personality are even more important. We said before that there are happy long-term matches between introverts and extraverts. But generally, you'll have the best bet if you and your dream lover are a lot alike in personality.

In the end, knowing whom you're compatible with amounts to knowing enough about yourself that you can meet someone, get to know them a bit, and ask yourself, "Is this person a good fit with me?" If you know enough about yourself and your needs, style, and temperament, it's easier to predict how someone else will fit with you.

> **Caution!**
>
> Don't imagine that your dream lover will "fix" those depression or other problems! Won't happen—and you're likely to wreck a promising relationship. Romance can be a comfort but it's not therapy.

Get noticed. You walk into the party or restaurant and there he is! You noticed him right away. You're interested!

How come? What do you notice—what stands out—about strangers? How they present themselves physically? Hygiene, yeah, but maybe also hairstyle, clothing, how they move?

SI Tip

Few people look "perfect," so don't let your fears about your appearance inhibit you! Sometimes people "shut themselves down" physically because they fear they don't look "good enough." Pretend you look great, relax, and be spontaneous, and you'll be more successful than someone who is "perfect" looking but frozen stiff.

Now, look at you. Are you a slouch? What does that, "I'm with stupid" logo on your t-shirt say about you? And what about that tendency to shuffle off to the darkest corner of the room?

If you want to connect with someone, you have to do whatever it takes to get noticed. That doesn't mean setting off fireworks, or being so perfect that you intimidate people. (Supermodels sometimes have a hard time getting dates, you know! They scare guys off!)

Just a few simple things can mean a lot. The easiest, of course, is hygiene. Taking the best physical care of yourself that you can is also wise. Of course, using your best fashion sense to make yourself look good is always a good idea, but clothes are less critical than the fashion industry wants you to believe.

Put your best emotional foot forward. Rule of thumb: someone who looks neutral to pleasant will always be more appealing than someone who seems grouchy, sullen, or withdrawn.

Think about it in SI terms. We are wired to respond to potential danger by backing off or protecting ourselves, right? So if you're the guy at the lunch counter who always has that scowl on your face, who looks like he wants to intimidate anybody who crosses him, who are you going to attract?

Same goes for the morose woman who seems to have and want no friends. She may be constantly thinking "I'm so lonely!" but she may be doing everything humanly possible to push people away.

A pleasant, smiling person will tend to activate complimentary emotions in others. This is something that happens because of that brain-to-brain link people set up between themselves, without any conscious awareness. Generally you get what you give, emotionally speaking.

Make contact early and often. After a nice encounter with someone, connect with her again. Send a "great lunch!" e-mail, text her something funny, or call to see if she wants to connect again—or just to say hi and thanks. If you stay on her mind for a few days, the connection will grow.

Get closer. Proximity helps! The best way to develop a relationship with someone is just to be around them more. Look for opportunities to see them and talk to them—it doesn't matter so much what you talk about. Just do it!

Take a risk. Being overly cautious can mean you stay invisible. We are drawn to those who seem to have confidence, or even boldness. No need to be loud or foolish about it, though—just saying "Hi" is risk enough to impress most strangers!

Express interest. The trouble with "lines" is that they are one-size-fits-all conversation openers. People will usually sense it if you're not really interested in them, but are using a generic approach to meeting. (Not that they may mind that—sometimes *any* opener is all it takes! But the odds are more in your favor if you're sincere.)

> **Caution!**
>
> Don't crowd! Moving closer to someone is one place where you really have to use the SI skill of tuning in! Some people have a pretty low threshold for feeling threatened. If you're picking up hints of a "back off!" message, heed them.

You may notice some things about the person that pique your interest—often that's all it takes to start a conversation. But even just that old standby question, "How's it going?" is enough to express that you want to know more about the person.

Really *be* interested! This goes back to the "know thyself" principle of SI. Do you think you really would be interested in knowing this person? Is he doing, saying, or showing something that might suggest a good "fit" with you?

Do a mental experiment: if you could take sexual attraction out of the picture completely (pretend "he" is a "she" or vice versa, say), would you be interested in this person as a potential friend? Do you think you could talk with him for hours and enjoy that, if not for the sexual element?

> **SI Tip**
>
> "Test the waters" to see if someone wants to talk to you by asking a question that they can give either a short or longer answer to. "How are you?" works—someone can just say "fine, thanks" and move on, or they can stay and talk.

If you are really interested in them that way, it will show. Odds go way up they'll be interested back.

Show you care. Making contact means resonating with the other person's soul, her feelings, her concerns. Show concern. Remember her situation, the project she's struggling with at school or work.

Deepen Your Relationship

You're off to a great start! You've met this exciting person and the two of you are starting to spend time together. So far, it's great.

Now you want to deepen the relationship. What's the trick?

Every relationship is unique. What works for some couples won't work for others. But there are a few general guidelines.

Increase the intimacy. The core of the process of deepening a connection is to gradually increase your intimacy with each other. But what's "intimacy"?

People use the word to mean three main things: openness about personal things, a feeling of warmth and closeness, and sexual connection. Any and all are good.

Let's start with the openness. Getting to know how someone thinks, feels, what his interests are—these are half of it. The other half is letting him know the same things about you. Usually this is a gradual unfolding, an opening of heart to heart, over a period of time.

You may start by agreeing you love the same music or are both excited to be in chef school, but over time you will need to extend your knowledge of each other—and your openness with each other—to the whole of your lives.

Easy does it! But if every time you talk you reveal a bit more, it won't take long before you are enjoying that pleasant, peaceful state that comes with being connected and intimate with someone. (And yes, there is a long list of brain chemicals involved here!) In other words, much of the "warm cozy feeling" part can flow from the opening up.

Of course, sometimes that "cozy feeling" is also a result of the sexual connection you may have.

The sexy bits. People differ in how much they are okay with a sexual relationship early in a romance (or before commitment or even marriage). But whenever you both start falling into each other's arms and beds (or the back seat of the SUV), remember that sexual connections come with a whole menu of new feelings. (We go into sex in the next chapter. Keep reading!)

For now, the main point is that deepening a romantic relationship generally includes some kind of deepening sexual connection as well. And as that develops, it can trigger a stronger sense of closeness and a desire to open up more to each other.

Expect conflict. Conflict is just about having different ideas and finding a way to ensure that both partners get to express who they are. Sounds pretty easy, but it's not.

Being with someone means adapting to her, and not all adaptations are easy. You don't like Chinese food, she does. What do you do? How do you negotiate it?

> **SI Tip** _____
>
> One good way to handle conflicts in a new relationship is to talk about how you *want* to handle them! "What are you like in a disagreement?" might be a good opening question. "What do you need when we disagree?" is the other one.

Patience!

It takes time to make even the best new relationship work well. One trap to avoid is being overly negative and closed-minded when a partner frustrates you or doesn't respond as you want. "He'll never agree with moving to California so he's not for me!" may be true—or he may need some time to mentally explore the option (and what's your rush? You just met, for Pete's sake!) "He doesn't respect me!" may be true, or a "rush to judgment" that cuts off a relationship before he's even had time to absorb your concern and think about it!

Of course, if there are some truly fundamental incompatibilities between you, all the patience in the world may not mend them! If the issues are super important and nobody is going to budge after a few months of talking, you've got some decisions to make about the relationship.

It's a million small things. Great relationships aren't a matter of that surprise birthday trip to Mexico. Not if you neglect the small, day-to-day things—the phone call the morning after your great evening together. The thoughtful card or e-card. Remembering her favorite music or his favorite magazine. Relationships thrive on the small daily connections.

And this makes great SI sense: the more time you devote to the little things, the small exchanges of contact, the little intimacies, the whispered words of affection, the more you "build a shared neural network" that changes you from two separate individuals to two individuals *plus* one combined being that lives somewhere in that magical space between and inside both your brains.

The Least You Need to Know

♦ We're powerfully wired for romance—both our bodies and the unconscious parts of our minds seek out that ideal partner.

♦ Success at romance is largely a matter of skill, not just luck—people who are good at it are successful over and over.

◆ SI skills of self-awareness, connecting with others, and caring for them are the essential elements needed to be successful in romantic connecting.

◆ Keys to finding the best romantic partner include seeking compatible others, getting their attention, being pleasant and approachable, and making emotional contact.

◆ Deepening a relationship means opening up more to each other, being honest, and dealing with sexual feelings and conflicts that arise.

Chapter 12

Sex and SI

In This Chapter

- ◆ Sex is important
- ◆ Socially intelligent sex
- ◆ Your comfort zones—and theirs
- ◆ Enhance your sexual SI

Few things in life stir up as many feelings and as much downright insanity as sex. It can be both the best part of life and the worst.

And yes, once again it's your social intelligence skills that make the difference! So before we get to the naughty bits, as Monty Python called them, let's—*ahem!*—check you out!

Check Yourself Out

This quiz is designed to help you estimate your sexual social intelligence quotient. Read each item and circle the answer that seems best to you.

1. You're with a new, attractive person and make some overtures to get sexual. The best okay signal (that means he or she is willing/eager) is:

   A. He or she says "no," but of course he/she really doesn't mean it.

   B. You hear neither "no" nor "yes" but he or she seems "lost in themselves" as they let you grope them.

   C. Your partner actively responds—in fact, it's not clear who is initiating.

2. A guy is most likely being flirted with by a woman in a bar when she:

   A. Offers him her phone number using the "excuse" that she just dented his car.

   B. Is in the bar at all; just by being there she's saying she's available.

   C. Is physically expressive where he can see it, tousles her hair a bit, makes brief eye contact and smiles, then looks away.

3. You drive an attractive new friend home because he or she had "a bit too much" to drink; in the car he or she is pretty flirty and asks you to come up for a "nice time" and to "express his/her gratitude." It's best to:

   A. See the person safely inside, but under no circumstances mess around while that person is not sober—check on him/her tomorrow and see if the interest is still there.

   B. Sex is fine as long as you're a little bit "wasted," too.

   C. This is nothing but the booze talking—drop the person off and get on with your life.

4. With a partner you have difficulty performing sexually. Best way to handle it:

   A. It's probably a signal from your unconscious that you're really not attracted to your partner; back out of the relationship.

   B. If it bothers you, or you think your partner might have minded, find a quiet time to talk about what happened.

   C. Get your partner to be more stimulating or sexy.

5. Your boy- or girlfriend says they're opposed to sex before marriage for religious reasons, but you're not. You should:

    A. Tough call. Get to know the person better, try to be open to his/her preference but also consider your own beliefs and needs.

    B. The choice is clear. Either marry the person or find someone else.

    C. Suggest that the person's views are outmoded, and keep bringing up the value of healthy, open sexuality.

6. Which of the following "off limits" behaviors could be considered "socially intelligent" and empathic, under the right circumstances?

    A. Talking "dirty" to a consenting and involved sexual partner, or treating a sexual partner like an "object."

    B. Sexually harassing a co-worker.

    C. Getting up, dressing, and leaving without a word right after your orgasm.

7. What's the best way to proceed with a partner if you have kinky sexual interests, such as bondage or S&M?

    A. Don't do that stuff—it's not very intimate or caring.

    B. Talk about it first to make sure you both feel okay about it and know the ground rules and how to communicate if something feels uncomfortable.

    C. Talking about that stuff will spoil the spontaneity—just surprise your partner with handcuffs or a whip or slap, and talk later about how it went.

8. What impact might masturbating have on your ability to relate to a sexual partner?

    A. Could be positive if it helps me to build an image in my mind of a lively, mutual sexual connection.

    B. It might help me control myself later that evening, when I go out with them.

    C. There is no real connection.

9. You find sex hard to talk about with a partner. Best way to bring it up might be:

   A. Leave it alone—you're just not ready yet.

   B. Start by saying it's hard to talk about sex—and have a conversation about that!

   C. Just start asking your partner direct questions about their sexual feelings or thoughts.

10. You go to a friend's for dinner and want to get sexual. You are most likely to:

    A. Do nothing and go home without the topic coming up.

    B. Greet them with a hug that you turn into a kiss and fondling, before your friend knows what hit him/her.

    C. Move gently from cool to warmer, make eye contact and signal your interest, and see how your friend responds to these nonverbal hints.

Scoring: Circle your responses below, and tally how many you have in each column.

Item	Uncon	Push	SI
1. ("Okay" signal)	B	A	C
2. (Bar)	A	B	C
3. (Drive home)	C	B	A
4. (Perform)	A	C	B
5. (Religion)	B	C	A
6. ("Off limits")	C	B	A
7. (Kinky)	A	C	B
8. (Masturbate)	C	B	A
9. (Talking)	A	C	B
10. (Develop)	A	B	C
Totals			

Interpreting your results:

Uncon   6–10: This stands for "unconnected." If most of your answers are in this column, you are describing yourself as someone who has difficulty reaching out, responding to others' sexual messages, or is uncomfortable with sexual expression in relationships.

Push   6–10: This means "pushy." In SI terms, if most of your answers are in this column you may fail to "tune in" to others' messages (such as that they don't want to be sexual with you). This may mean you push things more than they are comfortable with. Caution!

SI   6–10: If your answers fall mostly in this column, you are describing yourself as able to tune in to others' sexual messages and to be responsive, balancing that with a considerate expression of your own.

Shh! Sex Is Important!

Not too many years ago, TV network censors had some rules about what couples on TV could do in the bedroom: they had to be married couples in single beds, and neither one of them could ever have fewer than one foot touching the floor. Needless to say, nudity and groping were completely off the table (and the bed, too)!

Yet, during the years when that "code" was enforced, advertisers sold thousands of products on TV by pairing up the image of their product with sexy models and actresses. Packs of cigarettes atop nude female legs danced across the stage, and scantily clad models leaned against big-finned cars from Detroit.

Clearly, we live in a culture that is pretty mixed up about sexuality. Indeed, *sexual repression* is viewed by many as a hallmark of our culture.

You could be excused for concluding that in much of the world, sex is semi-illegal! (And in some states and countries, much of what many people consider normal sexual expression *is*, in fact illegal!)

def•i•ni•tion

Sexual repression is the tendency of people to forbid or discourage any direct expression of sexual behavior or feelings—except when they're doing it!

On the other hand, we might argue that our culture is pretty sexually open. In the mid-twentieth century, researcher Alfred Kinsey began a large-scale survey of the sexual behavior, histories, and fantasies of ordinary Americans. He found that most Americans were far more sexually active than anyone had supposed.

Social Science

Alfred Kinsey's major best-sellers included *Sexual Behavior in the Human Male* (1948) and *Sexual Behavior in the Human Female* (1953). They are still considered landmark scientific works. Kinsey was portrayed by Liam Neeson in the 2004 film *Kinsey*.

The main thing we know is that sex isn't going away any time soon. It seems that we can't really suppress sexual feelings, thoughts, and behaviors.

Sexual attraction is a key part of psychological development. It helps us learn to relate in caring and intimate ways to potential partners. It also helps us to define ourselves, both as sexual beings and in terms of our core sexual attractions and orientations.

Social Science
Contrary to old legends, masturbating as a youth will neither cause hair to grow on your hands nor cause you to become "weak, spineless, and unhealthy." But it may help you learn to imagine and develop healthy relationships with partners, help your body and brain develop, and just feel good.

And sexual feelings nudge us to think about issues that we need to grapple with in order to become socially intelligent adults, such as how we balance our and others' desires, how to communicate about sensitive topics, and how to be intimate with others.

Sexuality and SI Skills

Some people see sexual activity as something to be enjoyed freely and without inhibition regardless of marital status or gender; others feel it is something sacred that needs to be protected by law, confined to married adults of opposite genders, or perhaps engaged in only in order to procreate.

Given these wide differences of opinion, it's even *more* important that you approach sexuality with the key social intelligence skills of self-knowledge, awareness of others' feelings and meanings, and compassion.

Comfort Zones: What It's All About

Consider a simple matter of a compliment. You run into an acquaintance who's wearing an appealing outfit, and without thinking, you blurt out "Sexy blouse!" There are a number of reactions that might flow from that simple action, ranging from "thanks!" to a hot romance, or on the other hand, to discomfort, screams, or hysteria. And what you meant by the compliment may have nothing to do with the response you get.

Caution! _____

It's wise to avoid even simple, innocent compliments in the workplace if they could even remotely be construed as sexual. Employers are not your friend, and the reactions of co-workers can be hard to predict. If you want to compliment co-workers, mention their hard work or something equally neutered.

And of course, when you move beyond basic compliments to actual sexual overtures and doing it with each other, reading each other's messages and being in sync are even more crucial. But by then, hopefully, the main reason for this close mutual reading will be that it feels so good, and helps you feel closer to each other.

Respect People's Boundaries—And Yours!

Most of us get a lot of schooling in the basics of boundary-reading by the time we're halfway through elementary school. "Don't touch other people's stuff without permission" applies to their crayons and the buttons on their blouse. "Be polite and ask before you grab something" applies to both your classmate's extra cookies and your boyfriend's belt buckle.

Of course, it can feel stilted and emotionally tone deaf to require consent before leaning forward for a kiss. Except in certain colleges where it's more or less the "law" to do that, the real-world key is being aware of context and body-language cues.

SI Tip _____

Talking about sex with someone, especially sharing your sexual feelings toward each other, is often perceived as foreplay. If you're talking about it at all, you've already _passed_ these boundary tests—or are in deeper waters than you know!

One of the complications about sexual expression is that it is seldom talked about directly. That means you have to be more skilled than usual at reading the nonverbals.

Of course, this is right up your alley as a skilled SI practitioner! Picking up cues of eye contact, subtle nods that yes, you can (or no you can't) take the next step in getting close, are crucial. This is also, in the right time and place and when you both feel okay with getting closer, part of the fun! For many people, this nonverbal mating dance is one of the most exciting activities in life!

Decide Where You're At

There's more at stake than the other person's sense of boundaries. You also have to consider your own.

"Know thyself," remember? Set your own boundaries—this actually is something you re-do every day of your life. As an adult, it's really your responsibility to communicate clearly, especially if someone isn't getting the message.

Improve Your Sexual SI

Researchers have compiled a ton of info on sexual skills and thrills—everything from "flirting" to intense tantric sex that can rock your soul and sear your brain. Let's sample their wares.

Flirting Secrets of the Masters

Male or female, you can become a master flirt with the application of some of your basic SI skills.

Flirting is actually considered by many to be an ancient art form! While it's undergone many changes (for instance, many modern young women favor more direct approaches—grabbing the boy's phone and punching her number into its memory instead of waiting for him to ask), the basics are the same. It's a matter of communicating and signaling interest, is all.

Let's review a top-ten list of great flirting techniques. You may develop a much longer list, but here's a start:

1. **Look appealing.** We respond to signs of physical health in potential mates. Shiny hair, nice skin, a well-toned bod, clothes that show you pay some attention—it's all gotta help!

2. **Send "Come hither!" signals.** Brief eye contact, showing off your bod by how you move, gesture, touch your hair, laugh with your friends (between darting glances across the room at that attractive stranger)—that kind of thing.

3. **Smile.** Not big stupid grins but the slight signals of warmth and interest. You know.

4. **Move closer.** If you're sensing interest or want to stir some up, get closer to your target. She may sense your move and signal back. She may not even realize you're doing it.

5. **Have a way to start.** Lines may be okay, but so is "hi." Be spontaneous. The less you obsess about it, the better.

6. **Manage your anxiety.** It'll be fine. Really. Besides, maybe all you need to do is to flirt with this person a minute or two, before fleeing into the night.

SI Tip

When flirting, it can help to view your target as "one of many" or "just practice." It can reduce your anxiety, and it gives *the target* just enough of a mixed message that your target may be motivated to try a bit harder.

7. **Have something to say.** Remember that stuff they always told you in home room about being an interesting person, reading the news, blah blah blah? This was why.

8. **Be interested in *them*.** Surely if he is worth all this work, there are at least two or three things about him you're interested in! Ask a question or two. Where's that accent from? Are you a student here? Need help getting that arrow out of your leg? You know—be alert and improvise.

9. **Use that eye contact.** Look into hers. (Tip: dart from the left to right once or twice—it suggests you're really looking deep into her soul.) Smile and nod in sync. It'll trip all sorts of circuits and hormones in her brain and bod.

10. **Learn his name—and use it!** There's something magical in hearing an attractive stranger call you by your name. (Unless your name is *waiter!*)

Moving Closer ... and Closer ...

Flirting is really the first step in *seduction*. Before we take the next one, it's important to be clear about something: seduction is ideally (and ethically) a two-way process. Okay?

When you flirt with someone and they notice it and respond, you've mobilized their internal sexual response systems. If they're flirting back, it means they've switched into a sexualized mind space and so are at least having some fleeting sexual ideas, feelings, or thoughts about you. You're both participating.

def•i•ni•tion

Seduction is enticing or persuading someone to do something that they may or may not have been inclined to do—usually with some sexual element present. It may not be seducing you to have sex—they might just want your vote!

Of course, that doesn't mean you throw caution to the winds and jump each other! (Especially not in Nordstrom's!) But it means you're both *considering*. How things move forward is generally a small step at a time.

Here are some milestones in the typical journey from hot eye contact to breakfast together tomorrow morning:

> **Caution!**
>
> Each of these steps contains chances for you to hit the *"abort!"* button if you decide that you want to stop the seduction process. But be aware that the other person might do the same thing. If the other person stops reciprocating, back off!

Moving closer. Flirting across the bar or boardroom leads to being closer to each other. You stand nearer and can see each other better.

Exchanging scents and whispers. As you talk, laugh, and smile at each other, or shrug a lot as you scramble through your English-Romanian dictionaries, you begin to signal that you're interested. You begin to share more intimate kinds of stuff. Someone may even mention feeling attracted. Your bods are getting more in the act and tension builds for, yes, that first actual touch.

Touching—stage 1. The first touches are generally "nonsexual." Remember that Nixon-era term, plausible deniability? Light, brief brushes of the arm, that first "nice to meet you" handshake that lingers and that's served with the longer than average eye contact. Generally it's best for some signals to go each way, lest there be any confusion.

Touching—stage 2. This stage comes several minutes (or sometimes, several years!) after the stage 1 stuff. You've either said you're interested or attracted, or else your hand brushes—then brushes and stays in contact with his. Hand-holding usually starts without talking about it, except among psychology majors.

Hugs and kisses. This needs no explanation, except to note we're not talking about the Hollywood air kiss next to your partner's ear. Air kissing is actually reverse flirting—a message that "sex isn't gonna happen, pal." Like air guitar, air kisses are going to totally shut down any sexual response.

But the other kind—lip to lip, then lip to lip with embraces and tongues and hands moving about, should generally be happening right about here. (If you've come this far, there's been a huge amount of "coast is clear, this is what I want" communication back and forth.)

Getting alone together. Everything up to this point may have been happening alone in your dorm room or apartment, or at a party with 50 friends present. The next stage is finding somewhere you'll have quiet and safety (remember Darwin and upping those survival odds during vulnerable moments, etc.)

Touching—stage 3. We have now moved to intimate touching—bodies, genitals, and so on. Clothing optional, but often frowned upon.

What clothing? This stage is the gateway to bliss. Dr. Alex Comfort, in his *Joy of Sex*, said that "skin to skin contact" was one of the most important aspects of sexual experience. Maybe you can't quite manage that in the backseat of your Subaru, but the move to shared states of undress is emotionally and sexually stimulating. It's also a vulnerable moment for most people—few of us feel great about our bodies, and we're exposing things that expensive wardrobes have been concealing till now. Show empathy for your partner—let your partner know that you're pleased by what you see (and feel, and taste …).

Passion—and passionate outbursts. Lovemaking may be a matter of intense concentration, fun and laughter together, and/or intensely passionate, emotional expression. You may be shocked to hear the words "I love you!" coming from your mouth—and to your greater surprise, you may decide you really mean them! If so, congratulations! But if not, or if it's only a passing fancy, don't worry—it's pretty normal. (Activated emotional circuits linked to the genitals, blah blah blah ….)

> **Caution!**
>
> Sorry to interrupt you again at such a critical time, but did you remember protection? From both sexually transmitted diseases and unwanted pregnancy (and the tap of Officer Friendly's flashlight on the side window)? Sexual arousal is an altered state, and in altered states we get careless. So prepare in advance.

But it's also a complex mix of feeling, awareness, and fantasy. You're feeling excited, stimulated, and yeah, stimulated *there!* So (hopefully! have you been following along with this SI stuff?) is your partner. You're having intense physical and emotional experiences of your own—but are also tuned in to the intense experience of your partner. And your partner's intensity will stimulate yours.

Lovemaking, in that sense, is the ultimate in SI fun—it's two complex intense states merging, pulling back, and merging again.

In addition, it's fantasy. Most men and women at least occasionally fantasize *someone else* when they're doing it with you. That doesn't mean anything bad about your relationship, your performance, or your potential future together. But it has led many sexuality writers to cleverly note that in the average act of lovemaking, there are no fewer than *four* people in the bed!

Afterward. A successful sex act with a partner tends to trigger a mellow, peaceful mental state (due to the various hormones and neurotransmitters that it releases, including oxytocin, which induces that state in post-coital lovers and nursing mothers, etc.). It's a good time to just rest together, or perhaps to share a quieter, more intimate kind of connection.

This can be a time of bonding (assuming that's what you want). It's when you can grow closer, when even silent touching, or listening to each other breathe, is *doing something* that builds the relationship.

Sharing Sexual Secrets and Desires

Before, during, or after sex, sharing sexual secrets, fantasies, and desires with a partner can enhance your relationship. The main rule is to be sensitive, use timing, and so ensure that divulging your thing for foot massages or tickling is a welcome exchange.

Sometimes you may want, or need, to bring up sexual experiences that you've found uncomfortable or even traumatic—perhaps related to events such as assault or molestation in the distant (or not so distant) past. Or perhaps it's just that the way your new partner does something squiks you. How to proceed?

As usual, with sensitivity, tact, and awareness of how they're responding. If it's about something they do that you don't like, choose a quiet time and mention that you need to talk about something. Share the good news (that you enjoyed your time together), but mention the things you're not comfortable with. Describe what you'd prefer, and stay gentle with each other if you can.

Follow up with a nice smile, a little kiss, a "thank you, pookie!" Or maybe, do all that, then go upstairs and practice the new, improved version together!

Tantric SI

The new science of SI is leading to some rethinking of some very ancient ideas about sexuality. In particular, the relationship between sex and changes in a person's self on a deep emotional and even spiritual level.

In ancient Indian traditions (especially Hinduism), *tantric* sexual rituals were an attempt to elevate sexual (and other, non-sexual) experiences to spiritual levels. For example, one description of this involves the use of "friction-less" sexual contact between lovers, such as embraces (or even "friction-less" intercourse) and long periods of eye contact, in a form of meditation in which the energies of both parties are joined and new, liberating spiritual states are attained.

def•i•ni•tion

Tantric, or tantra, refers to ancient beliefs rooted in various Indian religious traditions including Hinduism and Buddhism, that attempts to ritually experience and channel the energy of the Divine into human experience. It involves mantras, yoga, meditation, and rituals.

In contemporary Western thinking, the term "tantric" has often tended to refer mainly to tantric sex. (There is even a *Complete Idiot's Guide to Tantric Sex!*) But from an SI perspective, the main thing to think about is whether a sexual relationship can transform both your nonsexual relationship and maybe your deepest, most personal self.

Sex is, after all, more than friction on genitals. At its best it's about two (or more) people resonating together emotionally. When that happens, not just their bodies but their minds, their emotions, and maybe even their souls (whatever that may mean to you) are in sync. Paradoxically, it's a form of vulnerability that ultimately ends up making the partners *less* vulnerable, *more* resilient, and stronger than they once were!

The Least You Need to Know

♦ Our culture sends mixed signals about whether sex is acceptable—but from a SI perspective, it's normal, healthy, and a valuable part of life.

♦ You and everyone you know are entitled to set your own boundaries about what kinds of sexual expression is acceptable for you; the key is to respect others' boundaries as well!

♦ Flirting and getting sexually involved with someone requires the key SI skills of tuning in to your partner's "stop" or "yes … yes … *yes!*" signals, and being clear about your own.

♦ At its best, a sexual connection can go beyond merely feeling good to be a life-enhancing, or even spiritually transforming, experience for you and your partner.

Chapter 13

Marriage and Committed Relationships

In This Chapter

- ◆ Who needs commitment?
- ◆ How to deepen your bond
- ◆ Conflict management without (too many) tears

"Commitment." What does that word conjure for you? Cozy, lifelong partnership with the man or woman of your dreams?

Or psych wards, barred windows, and straitjackets?

Maybe both?

In this chapter, we'll explore how you can enjoy the first kind of commitment while avoiding the second. Your social intelligence skills can make all the difference.

But first, let's check your knowledge of what it takes to stay in a committed relationship and out of a straitjacket!

Check Yourself Out

This quiz is designed to help you assess your "marriage SI." Read each item and circle the response that best describes you.

1. Ideally, how many negative versus positive interactions do you think are best in a relationship?

   A. You should never have any negativity in your relationship—even if you disagree, you should keep things totally positive.

   B. You have to express your concerns for a healthy relationship: a 50-50 split sounds about right.

   C. You need to express some negatives but marinate them in lots of positives— about five positives for every negative is about right.

2. Your favorite way to pace managing a disagreement:

   A. Sometimes we take a break if we haven't resolved things yet—gives us time to ruminate.

   B. Ruminating makes a person sick—it's better to hang in there and see it through, if it takes fighting all night!

   C. It's actually better to avoid the fights in the first place, so if one of us can give in, that's best.

3. In principle, all conflicts between you:

   A. Can and should be resolved.

   B. We have no conflicts, so this isn't an issue.

   C. Most can be resolved, but we may never totally agree on some fundamental values or beliefs.

4. During an argument, you sometimes:

   A. Close your partner out while your partner goes on about a concern—you try to let it roll over you like water off a duck's back, without responding.

   B. Aggressively confront your partner's core, underlying personality problems instead of staying on the surface conflict.

   C. Neither—you prefer to stick to the "issue at hand" but stay engaged.

5. When things get heated and uncomfortable in an argument, you're likely to:

   A. That's never happened to us.

   B. Ignore it—we try to resolve things even if it takes yelling and screaming till we're exhausted.

   C. Take a 20-minute, cool-down break, or use some humor to break the tension.

6. The best you can realistically hope for in a marriage is:

   A. It will be a different relationship over time, but we'll still be able to be intimate, passionate, and committed to each other—maybe even in better ways.

   B. The love will fade, but if we aren't abusing each other and can still stand each other in 10 years, that's about right.

   C. Great times and great sex, hopefully, though we'll have stopped being polite and so will have our share of intense fights where we insult each other or are highly critical, too.

7. If you felt lonely, you would be most likely to manage that by:

   A. Connecting with my partner or spouse—maybe telling them I'm feeling lonely.

   B. Telling my partner that they're neglecting my needs again.

   C. We are pretty independent—I'd find someone else to talk with.

8. The last time you and your partner had to make a major, difficult decision together, one where you disagreed, you:

   A. It was a difficult argument—as usual, one of us ended up shutting down, getting overwhelmed, or forcing the other to give in.

   B. We avoided talking about it until it was nearly too late.

   C. We had some heated or difficult discussions that resulted in both of us modifying our opinions somewhat.

9. During the past day, which kind of interactions have you mostly had with your partner:

    A. Routine, with a few pleasant, warm connections.

    B. Some criticism and conflict—it's been kind of unpleasant really.

    C. We generally don't connect much in an average day.

10. During the time you've been taking this quiz, your feelings and thoughts about your partner have mostly been:

    A. Irritated, angry, or annoyed—I'm realizing how many problems we have.

    B. Haven't had any, really—I've been concentrating on the test.

    C. Pleasant or even reassured—our relationship is generally calming and a source of comfort to me.

Scoring: Circle your answers here, then add up the number of circles within each column.

Item	Discon	Confl	Balan
1. (Neg/pos)	A	B	C
2. (Pace)	C	B	A
3. (Conflict)	B	A	C
4. (Argument)	A	B	C
5. (Heated)	A	B	C
6. (Best)	B	C	A
7. (Lonely)	C	B	A
8. (Decision)	B	A	C
9. (Past day)	C	B	A
10. (Quiz)	B	A	C
Totals			

Interpreting your results:

Discon 6–10: Stands for disconnected. If you have six or more answers in this column, your relationship may be distant or emotionally uninvolved. At times it may feel like there are two loners living parallel lives, perhaps because that way you avoid painful conflicts.

Confl   6–10: Stands for openly conflictual. Your relationship may be marked by a high level of overt conflict. Most likely you grew up with this or think it's the only pattern you can follow, but you also know it's painful and even exhausting and overwhelming at times.

Balan   6–10: Shorthand for balanced. You're likely to have a fairly positive-feeling relationship. While not conflict free, you likely manage those disagreements in a fairly respectful, effective way, and your relationship probably feels fairly nurturing and satisfying.

The Urge to Merge—Who Needs It?

In most cultures the majority of adults pair up into relationships such as marriage or similar long-term arrangements. While there are other kinds of relationships (such as remaining "single" or *polyamory*) most people pair off. Usually, these pairs consist of one male and one female adult.

Why do we pair off this way? After all, this isn't something that happens throughout all of nature. In fact, only about 4 percent of primate species (humans and monkeys are primates) engage in lifelong pairings of one male to one female. (No, penguins don't do it—they take different mates every year.)

def•i•ni•tion

Polyamory means having more than one partner or spouse at the same time. Different varieties include polygamy, which means having more than one wife, and polyandry, which is having more than one husband.

But for us, it's a big deal! In fact, the pairing usually includes the idea of "romantic love" as well. Nearly 90 percent of all human societies studied (over 160 cultures) have a concept of "romantic love" that is part of this pairing up.

There are a number of reasons for playing this "match game," including cultural, religious, financial, child-support, and legal reasons—and the simple fact that "everyone else is doing it." But the main reasons seem to be psychological and, underlying that, biological.

As we've already discussed, we are strongly motivated for the experience of attachment to other people. This is something that starts during our infancy, and stays with us throughout life. We generally long for the feelings attachment brings. We expect to feel content, at peace, and fulfilled emotionally when we get our little "nest" together with the "right person."

And of course, we're just packed with juicy little hormones and genetically based urges that trigger feelings of longing, loving, and connection. It's an itch we just have to scratch sometimes!

def•i•ni•tion

Love maps are patterns of things we unconsciously look for in potential partners or mates. The term was coined by sexuality researcher John Money in his 1988 book *Lovemaps* (New York: Prometheus Books).

Social scientists use the term *love maps* to describe the pattern of things you unconsciously are drawn to, and repelled by, in a potential partner. Every person's map is different and unique to them—you may be drawn to women, someone else may be drawn to both women and men; you may like tall brunette introverts with tattoos, while someone else likes petite dark-skinned extroverts who cook.

When you spot that certain pattern, whoever has it may become that certain someone whom you long for.

What goes into that love-map pattern? How is it formed? It seems likely it's partly the result of your own childhood attachments. Ever hear the song, "I want a girl just like the girl that married dear old dad"? Both men and women seek traits in lovers that are similar to those in their own parents. (Even if you're sure you want nothing like dad in your husband, you'll resonate to qualities that resemble his. Sorry!)

But there's also our built-in "good parent selection system." Our evolutionary baggage includes a tendency to prefer partners who are good potential child-protectors and rearers.

When you meet a potential partner, you're probably noticing how considerate, caring, and empathic they are. These "good SI behaviors" are more than just signals that you'll enjoy that night at the ballgame or playing video games together. As psychologist Daniel Goleman (in his book *Social Intelligence*) notes, these key behaviors and feelings you have about the person are also good signs that they might be a good parent. (Again, just because you're saying, "Parent??? Me?? No way, José!!" doesn't mean your mind's autopilot systems aren't still checking!)

And so, Goleman explains, if all goes according to nature's plan, you and Dream Lover start doing more synchronizing together: you gaze into each other's eyes and so program your brains to sync together. You cuddle, and this triggers a lot of bliss hormones. You both start to regress, and call each other baby names like "snookums" and "pookie."

Where this leads, eventually, is the creation of a couple. Which is really something psychologically different than two individuals. By the time you think and act like a couple, you've begun to think alike, to anticipate each other's thoughts, to have a whole bunch of physical reactions and emotional links and bonds to each other. Even your brains are getting more and more wired to function as a kind of unit.

Do we need all this pairing up? The short answer is, yes. It does most of us a lot of good, both psychologically and physically—*if* the relationship is a healthy one! A recent study done by the Centers for Disease Control concluded that on most health dimensions, married people are healthier than divorced, widowed, never-married, or cohabiting people. Other studies tend to confirm that married people are more likely to benefit in many ways, from lower risks of experiencing violence (yes, including domestic violence) to better sex lives to longer life spans. Married people generally have lower stress for a variety of reasons, ranging from the fact that they have more support available on a day-to-day basis, to the fact that couples tend to be financially better off than singles. Both men and women who are married experience less depression and anxiety, and have generally higher levels of self-esteem than non-married individuals.

> **Social Science**
>
> When one member of a couple dies, the other person may suddenly have symptoms of memory loss. It's thought that partners divide up their shared key information, such as phone numbers and the location of important papers. So losing a partner means losing a chunk of your memories, too.

SI Skills for Deepening the Bond

In the last 10 years or so, we've learned a tremendous amount about what makes relationships work well—or not. Good SI skills such as knowing/managing your feelings, tuning in to the other person, connecting, and caring—are all core parts of the effective mix for good relationships.

It Doesn't Stop with "I Do!"

Fairy tales often end with marriage. Cinderella or Snow White or name your favorite—the stories are the same. Big journey or big villain to defeat or summer camp to survive, then at the end it's be fruitful and multiply and so there is the wedding. The Biggest Event In A Young Girl's Life. You cancel *Cosmo* and your bride magazines and live happily ever after in your McMansion in the cul-de-sac, because the rest is easy, right?

Um .... Not so fast.

Turns out, there's a whole lot to making marriages work. Most of it is all about the SI skills we've been talking about.

We have learned that relationships need deliberate, ongoing maintenance. Anthropologist Helen Fisher refers to this as a "continual courtship." Keeping a relationship alive and vital, making sure it is a nurturing home for both partners, requires tending it like a fire.

But that doesn't have to feel like a chore! In fact, if it *does* feel like a long slog up a hill with firewood on your back, you should wonder if you're doing it right.

Social Science

Psychologist Robert Sternberg has suggested that the most successful marriages include three core elements:

◆ Intimacy: feelings of closeness and warmth

◆ Passion: excitement about each other sexually

◆ Commitment: the conscious "decision" that you are in love, and later, the decision to stay with your partner

---

What Successful Couples *Keep* Doing

So what should you do?

Recent research, much of it done by Dr. John Gottman during a decades-long study of successful marriages, shows that there are some pretty clear do's and don'ts for making marriages a success.

Caution!

Don't try to avoid all conflict or disagreement in a relationship. But learn how to express disagreements in a way that doesn't cause lasting damage to the relationship. Manage your own emotional intensity, and don't launch instantly into an attack or criticism of your partner.

The most crucial fact may be that a relationship takes more than just not quarreling—it also means exchanging a fair amount of positive energy. If you've backed off from each other so far that nothing positive is happening either, you're going to start to look elsewhere for satisfaction.

One of the keys to success in any style has to do with maintaining a positive emotional bank balance in a relationship. After much research, Gottman has found that the key is a five-to-one ratio of positive to negative interactions. In other words, it takes an average of five positive contacts or inter-actions (including little things like a quick call to say hi from work, or a flirty little pat on the behind) to balance one negative or critical or disagreeing comment. If your ratio starts to get down to about one to one, Gottman has found, the odds are very high that you are heading for divorce.

> **SI Tip**
>
> Keep track of the number of positive and negative inter-actions you have with each other. Make a conscious effort to add positive moments each day. Ask your partner how they are, buy them a card, flirt a little. A constant trickle of little drops creates a mighty river!

Gottman's research has uncovered a number of things that successful couples do, or do more often than unsuccessful ones. (His book *The Seven Principles for Making Marriage Work* [with Nan Silvers, Crown Pub-lishers, 1999] is highly recommended.) For instance:

- ♦ "Enhance your love maps"—get familiar with your partner's world—what's important to your partner, what your partner's goals and fears and needs are, etc.

- ♦ "Nurture your fondness and admiration"

- ♦ "Solve your solvable problems"—not all problems can be resolved: you may dif-fer on core values or goals. But it's important to try solving those you can.

One of the most important tips may be to "let your partner influence you." Being defensive, warding off your partner's input or point of view, can be death to a rela-tionship. When each knows that the other values their input, it builds a firewall against the discouragement that can wreck relationships.

> **SI Tip**
>
> Make a list of five times when your partner has convinced you to change your mind, taught you something new, or been a model for something (a behavior, a belief) that you admire. Share the lists with each other.

Gottman summarizes much of his research by pointing out that happy couples tend to act a lot like good friends. There is the same kind of respect for each other; there is friendly affection and empathy for each other.

Not only that: as Gottman also points out, happy couples manage conflicts in posi-tive and gentle ways.

Managing Conflicts

Here's a paradox for you: the most fun, exciting, and interesting movie relationships would be the most horrible and life-shortening *real life* relationships, while the best *real life* relationships would *never* become movies. How come?

Movies are built around intense conflict. Screenwriters assume that movie viewers prefer life-and-death struggles on the screen. So they fill the movies with relationships full of "secrets and lies" (as Woody Allen said), or actual husband-wife gun battles (such as in *Mr. & Mrs. Smith*).

With all that movie data (and the memory of our own parents' fumbling attempts to resolve conflicts) rattling around in our heads, is it any wonder that most of us feel a bit, er, *under-prepared* for real conflicts in our relationships? That we approach marital conflicts with terror and dread, or avoid dealing with them until they're well past their healthy "fix by" date?

The result? Pain, misery, and a stratospheric divorce rate. At present, literally two-thirds of new marriages will end in divorce. Second marriages have even poorer success rates than first marriages. And as we've seen, the stress and the physical consequences of divorce are very high. So is the rate of extra-marital affairs.

Marital researcher John Gottman has found that it's possible to predict whether a couple will divorce with over 90 percent accuracy, with just five minutes' worth of observation of how they manage a conflict. Some of the things that predict divorce:

◆ Starting arguments "harshly." Instead of a gentle, empathic beginning ("Honey, would you mind if we talk about …?"), future divorcees leap right in and start to argue.

◆ Several kinds of highly toxic responses to each other, which Gottman has called the "Four Horsemen of the Apocalypse" for marriage: criticism, contempt, defensiveness, and stonewalling.

◆ Emotional flooding. Overwhelming each other with anger or anxiety, especially if it happens often, is a strong predictor of divorce.

◆ Failing to make enough "repair attempts" during arguments, or repair attempts that fail. "Repairs" include interrupting moments of tension with jokes or feeling-saving gestures, de-escalating the tension, and so on.

Gottman's findings make a huge amount of sense from a social intelligence standpoint. These behaviors are basically the opposite of good SI practice, which is based on emotional self-regulation (not "losing it" during a disagreement); tuning in to their feelings instead of steamrolling them with your own; and demonstrating care, empathy, and concern.

What are some keys to conflict?

First, one size doesn't fit all. Different styles work for different couples. Some couples avoid conflict and just "agree to disagree." Others prefer to wrestle each other into submission. Still others seem to be in competition for the Miss/Mister Congeniality trophy, affirming each other's point of view till the cows come home.

> **Caution!**
>
> Managing your emotional reactions is essential to resolving conflicts—and to survival! In a fight, couples may have increased heart rates, stress hormones such as adrenaline, and blood pressure. Take a 20-minute calm-down break if your bod is feeling the stress of a conflict.

And not all conflicts are solvable. For one thing, you can't get everything you want in life from one relationship, so if your conflict is really about why your partner can't be everything you want, it may be tough to fix. You may disagree on core issues, whether these are idea issues such as religions, or lifestyle preferences (slob vs. neatnick), or major decisions such as whether to move to the mountains or have kids.

But assuming you have a generally workable couple style, and the conflicts you're focusing on are fixable, try these SI tips:

Manage your feelings. While people manage to solve things while screaming at each other in movies, in real life it generally won't work. Neither does it work to hope the problem will vanish—more likely, your marriage will.

Researchers like Gottman talk about the dangers of stonewalling, tuning out or becoming *apparently* unresponsive to an arguing partner. Other researchers, studying brain processes during conflicts, have noted that the stereotyped shut-down partner (most often the male) who seems to be bored, inattentive, tuned out during a conflict, may in fact be very emotionally engaged, but not at a conscious level. Brain regions that register painful emotions such as shame and anxiety may in fact be at a red alert level, despite that placid, cow-like calm on his face. Work on being more responsive—get help from a counselor if need be.

Caution!

Odds are, you've unconsciously absorbed damaging habits of mouth as expressing contempt or criticism of your partner from your own parents: if your mom's voice dripped with contempt for dad when they fought, beware! When you're angry, guess whose voice you're gonna hear coming out of your mouth!

It's also important to manage your urge to blurt out critical, harsh feelings. They don't help. In particular, feelings designed to hit back or to hurt are tremendously damaging. As Gottman has shown, *criticism* (comments that attack the other person's character or personality or motives) and especially, *contempt* (which goes beyond criticism to include clear abuse, disgust, or insults) are destructive and toxic.

Don't get personal. Stick to whatever the conflict or disagreement is about. This may sometimes take some work, easy as it sounds! Consider this example:

"I don't want to go out again tonight. I'd rather stay home and order Chinese."

"You never want to go out! You're such a boring person!"

The thing here is that if you would never, ever call someone a boring person to their face, this may seem like an absurd example. But if you grew up hearing it, if you've said it before (and maybe gotten away with it a lot!), *you probably didn't even notice that you said it!* Or you told yourself it was "just a joke."

But you can be sure your partner noticed. And that it did damage.

SI Tip

Try this: Interrupt a disagreement with your partner and spend a few minutes each arguing the other one's case! Try to explain why their point of view makes sense or is right. Then check with each other and see if you got it.

If you do stick to the disagreement, things can go smoother. Especially if you follow a few other suggestions:

- **Stay tuned in to your partner's feelings and ideas.** Try to see if you really understand what they want, and why they want it. Take their point of view: can you see why their suggestion makes sense? Could you, if you needed to, act as their "lawyer" and argue for what they want to a third party, in their terms, even if it wasn't something you agreed with?

- **Look for areas where you can agree.** This can mean compromising—you can pick up a bit of Chinese takeout and also pick up a smaller pizza and everyone wins—or taking turns.

- **Keep the difference between the argument and the relationship clear in your mind.** Ideally, this should feel like friends having a conversation, perhaps weighing different options or ideas, fleshing things out so they can understand all the possibilities. If your style is more "I want to win you over!" than "Whatever you feel is best, honey," you can still make lots of room for hearing your partner out.

- **Watch the temperature gauge.** If things get too hot or too cold, do something to get it back in the "comfy zone." Some of this is what Gottman calls making "repair attempts." A smile, a diverting, off-topic comment, a joke or a kiss can all be ways to keep things temperate.

- **Reassure your partner that you care about his or her opinion.** There are a few ways to do this: listening and sending little "I'm listening" signals (a few well-placed "uh huhs" will do fine, as any therapist can tell you), or saying it outright. Or you can ask, "If we do it your way, how will we solve the problem of …?"

- **Take a break.** Not all arguments can be solved, not all conflicts resolved, according to the schedule of a 30-minute TV sitcom. Some take several passes, or are actually a "work in progress" for several years! Knowing when you've both said what you need to, that you'll come back to the matter, but that you can't solve it all right now, is okay. You may need time to think about the other person's point of view, to consider your partner's ideas, or to work up the gumption to say "You're right, I'm wrong."

The Least You Need to Know

- In almost all human societies, people tend to form long-term, committed romantic relationships—we seem to be wired to want such relationships!

- Well-functioning relationships are good for your physical health, while high-stress, poorly functioning relationships increase your vulnerability to stress-related diseases such as cardio problems, immune system dysfunctions, and so on.

- SI skills including emotional self-regulation, tuning in to your partner, and conveying warmth are associated with relationship survival and health.

♦ The best relationships are like close friendships: they include mutual warmth and caring, listening to each other, and good conflict management skills.

♦ Conflicts in relationships are okay—it's how you manage them that counts. Avoid destructive behaviors such as criticism, contempt, and stonewalling; tune in to your partner; keep the emotional "temperature" right; and look for compromises.

Chapter **14**

SI and Kids

In This Chapter

- ◆ Kids think differently than adults
- ◆ Skills for interacting with kids
- ◆ The emotional lives of children
- ◆ Tips for enhancing kids' SI

As a parent, a teacher, a relative, or a friend, relationships with children can be the most special of gifts, both for you and for them. Like other people, children respond best to the core principles of socially intelligent relating. And of course, you will want to nurture the SI of the kids in your life.

In this chapter, we'll talk about relating to children, and how to help those little socially intelligent critters grow into big socially intelligent critters.

But first, your quiz.

Check Yourself Out

This quiz is designed to help you assess your SI skills for relating with and helping children. Read each item and circle the response that best describes you.

1. You're with a three-year-old who suddenly starts to cry, and you don't know why. Your most likely response:

   A. Ignore her; it's probably nothing and she'll stop in a minute.

   B. Tell her to stop it—raise your voice if need be.

   C. Comfort her and ask her in simple terms what's wrong.

2. Your adolescent is pouting, angry, slamming doors, and doesn't want to talk to you. You're most likely to:

   A. Tap on their door, say "I'm concerned that something's wrong—if you want to talk, I'll listen."

   B. Insist that he get downstairs and tell you immediately what's wrong.

   C. Adolescents are like that; best to give the kid space—he wants you to back off, and will stop eventually.

3. Your child's elementary school calls you in for a conference and tells you that she's been bullying other children. The best response is:

   A. Grounding your child and telling her to stop it.

   B. Blame the teacher for singling out your child—after all, it takes two to tangle.

   C. Spend some time with your daughter, bring up the concern, and ask her to tell you what she can about what's going on from her perspective.

4. You just saw your child run in front of a car, which screeched to a stop and beeped at him. Your heart is pounding and you're angry and terrified. Your best response is:

   A. Make sure your child isn't left around cars any more.

   B. This is the "exception" to your "no spanking" policy—you need to put some fear into him!

   C. Pull him aside and talk about what just happened and tell him how scared *you* were—then help him understand the importance of being careful!

5. Your seven-year-old comes to you with a question about sex and babies, after she heard something confusing from a classmate. You respond by:

    A. Telling her that's something for when she's older.

    B. Answering the question she asked in terms she'll probably understand.

    C. Giving her a thorough talk about everything she needs to know about sex, pregnancy, virginity, and contraception

6. Your adolescent picks a college major that seems pretty much like a dead end, career-wise. You:

    A. Invite him to talk about his interest in this subject and how he sees it working out, and enjoy the conversation.

    B. Do nothing—it's his life.

    C. Tell him very strongly that he should major in something practical, like business.

7. Your philosophy of disciplining children who transgress is:

    A. It's always best to talk—to ask them what they were thinking, and to support them in doing the right thing.

    B. Of course, punishment—even strict punishment—is sometimes necessary; they'll appreciate it later in life.

    C. Nothing—let them find their own way.

8. Your little boy and the little girl next door, both age 6, are found under the covers in one of their bedrooms, stark naked. Your response:

    A. You're naturally alarmed; you express your anger at your child and tell them they're bad, and should never ever do that again!

    B. Let the kids play or do whatever they want—they're just exploring.

    C. Interrupt the play, quietly tell him and her to get dressed, and explain that they shouldn't play that game together.

9. Your son's high school teacher tells you that he bursts into fits of swearing and threatening others. When you tell your spouse about this, she remarks that that … um … sounds a little bit like you, honey. Your best response would be:

   A. Talk with her calmly about what she's seen in you, and do the hard work you need to change how you respond, as well as talking with your kid about how you both mess up.

   B. Ream out your kid for doing that and tell him not to.

   C. Laugh it off as "boys will be boys," and "he's a chip off the old block!"

10. You feel that the most appropriate way to relate to your child day to day is:

   A. As an authority figure—train them right!

   B. As an empathic friend—let them discover themselves.

   C. As an empathic guide and support—they need both understanding and guidance.

Scoring: Circle your answers below, and tally how many you have in each column.

Item	Miss	Flood	Balan
1. (Three)	A	B	C
2. (Adolescent)	C	B	A
3. (Bully)	B	A	C
4. (Car)	A	B	C
5. (Sex)	A	C	B
6. (Major)	B	C	A
7. (Discipline)	C	B	A
8. (Covers)	B	A	C
9. (You)	C	B	A
10. (Relate)	B	A	C
Totals			

Interpreting your results:

Miss   6–10: Stands for "missing the signals." Your relationship with children may tend to be distant or emotionally uninvolved. You may be trying to give them space, or may just not be very interested in kids' inner lives.

Flood   6–10: Stands for "flooding" a child—potentially overwhelming them emotionally by your reactions. Your strong reactions may sometimes overwhelm your kids. You may need to assess whether you're too intense at times.

Balan   6–10: Shorthand for "balanced." You're likely to relate to kids with a nice balance of empathy, curiosity, and sensitivity to what they're feeling, and some ability to be a guide, a teacher, and an active, secure protector.

Not Little Adults: How to Interact with Kids

Dealing with kids is both a delight and a challenge. So to talk about social intelligent relating to kids, and helping kids develop their own social intelligence, let's start out with a few "playground rules."

For one thing, we're about being realistic, not perfect. In parenting, it's not always easy to know what to do, or how to do it. Mistakes happen, and sometimes the only "tool" you may have is patience: the idea that eventually you'll either figure it out or your child will just outgrow whatever it is that's confusing you.

For another, support is important—both from friends and relatives and, yes, from your child or children (but more later on how children support your parenting.) It's okay to ask for help and advice from friends, relatives, pediatricians, teachers, and child and family therapists. In fact, it's often responsible parenting.

And be relieved to know that kids are usually pretty *resilient!* We used to imagine that all sorts of minor parental lapses and painful events would "traumatize" their delicate psyches for life. Not so! While no normal parent wants to injure their child, the fact is that if basic empathy, protection, and care are present, most kids cope pretty well with the ordinary stresses of childhood.

Finally, I'm not going to try to solve all your parenting dilemmas in ten pages. That would be silly. But what I can do is help "get your mental wheels turning" about how social intelligence skills might be useful for you in your role as a parent.

def•i•ni•tion

Resilience means the ability to tolerate and recover from painful or difficult events or conditions. Researchers have found that the average child is far more resilient than old-fashioned theories ever supposed. (Though of course, they're still pretty vulnerable. I mean, come on—they're just kids!)

Kids Just Think Different—At Every Age!

Kids' ways of seeing the world around them change constantly as they grow. A two-year-old and a four-year-old are light-years apart in their thinking styles! Even a 14-year-old, despite her ability to carry on adult-sounding conversations with you, has quite different thinking abilities than she will in two or three years.

> **Social Science**
>
> If you show most three-year-olds a jar full of jelly beans, then pour the beans into a taller, narrower bottle and ask if there are the same number of jelly beans, they may say there are more beans now! Their reason: the jar is taller!

From a social intelligence perspective, this poses a challenge for a parent, teacher, or other person interacting with kids. How do you tune in to kids, and how do you make connections and communicate with them?

So how do you connect with kids whose minds are constantly "changing?" For starters, let's review some of the "SI Basics" again:

◆ **Know thyself:** Not just your *ideas*, but your *feelings*. Kids inspire all sorts of feelings in adults, and the key is being able to manage your emotions for the sake of the kids. Because you connect with kids emotionally more, maybe, than logically, your calmness, confidence, and temper control (among other things) are the main things you're "saying" to a child most of the time.

◆ **Tune in to others:** That's what this is all about, right? Skilled parents may understand what their children "say," but kids mostly "talk to you" through their feelings.

◆ **Connecting:** Sometimes kids seem not to listen as well as adults. But even when they seem tuned out, they're more aware of your feelings, concerns, and messages than any adult. Look, talk, share!

> **SI Tip**
>
> One of the simplest and best pieces of advice for responding to children is the "24 carat golden rule" suggested by the authors of *Emotionally Intelligent Parenting*: "Do unto your children as you would have other people do unto your children."

◆ **Caring:** If you didn't, you wouldn't have read this far! Kids naturally seek out and get emotionally attached to adults. Adults naturally respond to those feelings and attachment-seeking behaviors. Caring for children is a fairly natural and even automatic response.

Most adults have a pretty good, basic level of empathy, especially for others' emotions. A good start in dealing with kids is to slow down and resonate as best you can to their *emotions*.

For instance, is that toddler smiling? Or does she look tired, cranky, in need of a nap?

How about that nine-year-old? Is he absorbed in whatever he's playing with, or is he looking confused, or feeling silly?

If you can tune in to their feelings a bit, you're well on your way to "getting" kids.

Tips for Connecting—Babies to Teens

Some of the skills for making contact and understanding children are the same for kids of any age—from birth to old age, actually. Other ways of interacting depend a lot on the age of your child.

Sound complicated? It is, sometimes. (Who was it that said parenting was easy?) But in finding your way through those tangled 18 years, you do have one major ally: your child.

The more you "get" social intelligence, the more clear it should be to you that your child is your natural aid to understanding her. Because, as I've said, SI is about understanding how much we're all natural communicators, and how wired we are for understanding each other.

We are primarily communicators and readers of *emotion*. If an infant or toddler needs something—almost anything—from you, he'll communicate it quite naturally through his emotions.

> **Social Science**
>
> Many scholars have speculated that the whole *point* of emotions is largely to make communication possible. Remember: we've probably only had spoken languages for a small fraction of the time we've existed as a species!

As your children's command of language grows, it will be *your* language. Not just "English" or "Dutch," but they'll be using terms, ideas, and meanings that they've already shared with you. So your understanding of much of what your children are trying to say will be much easier than anyone else's understanding of *your* children.

Finally, remember that without realizing you're doing it, you will be "adopting" the thinking patterns and understandings of your children as you grow alongside them. Moms sometimes talk about this in terms of being so immersed in the thinking of their toddlers that they have some difficulty adjusting when they suddenly have to converse with adults!

That's probably those old mirror neurons in action again, right? Your tendency will be to function automatically as a translator for your children, being the intermediary between them and the outside world. Without realizing it, you'll be fluent in both "toddler speak" and "adult speak" as you need to be!

Understanding infants: Baby books and grandparents have tons of advice for you, but if you had none of those resources and were stranded on a desert island with your infant, you'd probably do an okay job anyway. The key is to follow the basic SI rules: tune in the best you can. Don't panic when you don't know how to respond to everything right away—it's actually your calmness (as well as attending to basic physical stuff like changing wet diapers, feeding, comforting, and holding your baby) that does much of the "work."

SI Tip

Your baby will often focus on your face and will be pretty expressive emotionally. The best way to understand what he's feeling is simple: just match his facial expression, his frown or open-eyed delight, and that will trigger something like the corresponding feeling in your own brain! No language (or doctorate in baby counseling) required!

The other thing that you'll do fairly automatically is to process and digest your baby's feelings for her. How's that?

As you absorb a baby's feelings when he's upset, by noting them and feeling them a little bit yourself, you'll automatically use your own coping thoughts to change that icky mood in yourself to something calmer. So, say, the baby's fear turns into *your* fear. But then you calm *yourself* down.

The amazing part is that your baby, who has seen *you* pick up the fear, also notices in some way that you're growing calmer. Since you've been in sync, or emotionally locked in to each other's feelings, your gradual shift to a calmer mood tends to pull your baby along! They may orient to your calmer presence and gradually feel better.

You've heard this happen with other moms or dads. Baby is upset and crying and the first thing the mom does is say "What's wrong?" in an alarmed voice, right? "Oh, my, what's wrong?" But then she'll shift to a soothing tone, like "there, there, there …", and what happens? That, and a bit of cuddling and patting, and baby calms down, too!

Like that.

Toddlers and preschool: Imagine you had amnesia for everything you've ever known about yourself and the world. And that you were plopped into a new culture where you had to learn a complicated language, to walk and *talk* all over again, and to learn every part of the culture you were in—all while going through rehab so you could relearn to control your bodily functions, wash yourself, drink out of a cup, walk, and relearn skills like fastening buttons and opening jars. Now suppose you managed to learn all that stuff in just three or four years! You'd be darned proud of yourself, right? You'd probably make the cover of *Time* and *Newsweek* as a newly discovered prodigy!

Meet your toddler!

In the short space of a few years, a toddler must master all those things, and more. All the while growing cuter every day!

Fortunately, communicating with this little genius is quite possible. Again, much of it is about those emotional exchanges you're having every day—sometimes every minute. Toddlers still communicate much or most of what they need and feel through emotions, even though they are also learning language. In fact, one of the main things you'll be teaching him is how to put into some kind of words what it is he's feeling.

The more secure a toddler feels, the more sure she is that you're tuned in and present, the more she feels free to explore her world. This tendency to be connected (or even to cling) to you, and then, as you seem reliably "there," to gradually creep a few inches away to look at the bug on the rug or the cartoon character on the TV, then back to you to see how you're responding, will be a core part of your connecting.

Elementary schoolers: By now you're probably a parenting pro, right? Your child can talk (and talk and talk! sometimes) and is starting to really explore what's out there in the world. Such as—other kids!

During these years your child is facing many new challenges. He has to leave home for longer periods than ever before. This may delight him, or he may feel quite frightened of leaving the security of home and your constant presence. But each step toward more independence will also be a step into adventure and interesting new things, and most kids are pretty resilient about managing these shifts.

One of the big new events that may start in preschool if your child goes there, or else in elementary school, is learning to understand other kids. Of course, if there are already brothers or sisters or neighborhood play friends around, this has already been happening. But this is a great time to help your child develop more ability to have empathy for others.

> **SI Tip**
>
> Ask your child about his friends—their names, what they're like, their interests, and even some of his friends' concerns. It'll help you expand your awareness of your child's thinking, concerns, and social world, but also give him practice at being socially aware, attentive, and perceptive.

Social Science

Years ago, "authorities" believed that adolescence was always a "stormy" period of conflict with parents. In fact, research shows that the average adolescent is, most of the time, fairly un-"stormy" and functions pretty well, as long as things are basically healthy at home. (Your mileage may vary! Of course, even the best-adjusted kids can have their intense periods.)

Early adolescence: By now your child has become an old pro at basic functioning out of the home. She knows the way to school, how to function for whole days away from home, and how to form friendships and play and work with others.

The main challenges of this period include coping with more difficult and complex school and other social environments, with harder academic work and other challenges, and with the new and suddenly pretty "major" issues around her growing awareness of sexuality. Also on tap: your child will begin to need to "separate" a bit more from you and to develop a more unique, personal sense of identity.

There's a psychic shift in loyalties to some extent, in which she may come to view peers as the most important people in life, with you relegated to more of a supporting role (or sometimes, you being the enemy). Probably, you know all about this—you've been through it yourself. (Remember that "Mom's voice is coming out of my mouth!" problem? This is your prime time to go through that, since the "Mom's voice" you disliked most was probably the one you heard during adolescence.)

A key goal during these years is to keep the lines of communication open. Your child will be feeling more ambivalence about your relationship, but it's a myth that they will automatically start to have a constant conflict with you about every little thing. (Well, there may be days like that ....)

Later adolescence: At this point (roughly, age 15 and beyond), things may calm down more, but the stakes have never been higher! Your child is becoming a little adult in many ways. She can drive, travel alone, and is making plans for adult life. She's also able to get in trouble more creatively than ever before! Your years of sleepless nights, as you wait to hear her key in the door, have begun!

On the other hand, this can also be a time of great pleasure in your relationship. Your kids are at an age where they're more mature, more able to reflect on stuff like "who they are" and "what life's really about," and you and they can have some nice conversations about that kind of thing. It may happen only occasionally at first, but if you're open to it and have built some basic "let's talk" habits into your relationship, it's likely to happen.

One of the main challenges for parents at this age is facing the fact that increasingly, their role is more that of advisor than controller. Knowing how to "back off" helps when your children really need your advice and support, but not direction. To some extent, they do need a bit of time to learn from their own mistakes.

Tears and Moods: Feelings in Children

As I've said, children start off having a range of emotions, and their main way of "communicating" with you will often be more through emotions than through words. (This is especially true when they don't know any words yet!)

A lot of your time as a parent will involve helping children learn to manage the intensity of their feelings. This isn't something you do by lecturing them, of course—you do most of it by conveying empathy when they're upset, and by being calm yourself. The very fact of tuning in to their upset feelings is probably the most powerful intervention you can do to help them.

One of the main things you'll want to protect your child from is emotional *flooding*. It's possible for a person (adult or child) to be overwhelmed with emotion—for his emotion to be so powerful that he literally can't tolerate it. Believe it or not, this can be damaging to a child both physically, in terms of the amount of stress it triggers in his body, and by creating a traumatic reaction that might lead to avoidance of the overwhelming situation or object, phobias, or other strong responses.

def•i•ni•tion

Flooding is a strong emotional response that overwhelms someone. When we're emotionally flooded, our brains are literally on overload and so our ability to regulate our emotions or to think clearly are compromised, or totally absent. It's extremely painful.

For a child, something might be seen as threatening that you might not perceive as frightening at all! You may see a harmless little dog, and your child bursts into tears as she's afraid it might bite her.

They Get It from You: Teaching SI Skills to Kids

Yes, they do get it from you! And of course, as most parents realize (and forget daily!), 90 percent of the social skills you "teach" your kids are taught by example. Or perhaps more accurately, by trial and error. (This is where social skills are different from practical skills such as skydiving and handgun safety, where teaching by trial and error is a really bad idea.)

But how about the other 10 percent? Here are some tips for teaching your kids social intelligence skills. Since there is actually no limit to the teaching possibilities for this kind of thing, just consider these some "starter ideas" that may inspire you.

Have regular "talking together" times. This can be at bedtime, at dinner, or a weekly thing—it's a time to talk about just about anything: school, favorite TV shows, weekend plans. The key is making sure there are minimal distractions (TV off) so you can tune in and actually talk together.

> **Caution!** _____
>
> If you have problems controlling your angry or depressed moods, it will have a big impact on kids' sense of security and safety. That's why doing everything you can to be well, healthy, and fairly calm yourself is important.

Ask about—and express—a wide range of feelings. Don't just focus on news, events, and ideas. Asking a child how she *feels*, using words she'll understand (e.g., "are you sad that Tommy can't go with the rest of your class to the carnival?"), helps children develop the skills of understanding the emotional parts of their experience. And expressing your own feelings—not just the intense and angry ones but quieter, gentler feelings as well, is important.

Do little emotional check-ins. Asking "What's up, sweetie?" and really waiting for an answer is a great habit to develop. Ask follow-up questions or do other things to draw your children out a bit more. The key here is you're helping them get used to talking with you about how they're feeling and what they're thinking, and they're learning that this is generally an emotionally positive interaction. (Their spouse will thank you some day!)

Get down to your child's level. This means physically as well as intellectually. When having a heart-to-heart moment, kneel or sit so you're not forcing them to look up to talk to you.

Talk about some of their fears or concerns indirectly. Sometimes children prefer to hear how imaginary animals or other creatures might manage a difficult problem. (That's why kiddy shrinks have rooms full of dolls and toys!)

Create special times together away from the usual, everyday environment. Taking your daughter or son out for a day trip to a favorite museum or movie, then a stop for a snack or lunch, can give you a nice time to talk together.

Focus on positive emotions, not just problems. Helping your children develop an awareness of their emotional life includes their positive feelings and experiences. Peaceful or relieved or excited feelings are good to know how to identify and share.

Ask for their input. No need to always be the one with the plan, or the answers. "I don't know what to have for dinner tonight. What do you think?" might be a simple example. But even more complex issues, such as "I'm not sure how to help you with this disagreement with your teacher—what do you think would help?" can lead to productive discussions. Of course, they want to be reassured that you're competent and not relying on them to solve family problems—but that's different from letting them know that you value their input.

Convey openness and availability, even around sensitive topics. Your children will have many times when they're not sure they can or should talk to you about concerns. It's rarely crucial to force the issue but always important to convey respect for their choice about whether or not to share with you. If you let them know you're available if and when they want to talk, that's usually enough.

Get a feelings chart and use it. You've maybe seen these—charts that have little smiley-type faces, but showing 20 or 30 different facial expressions with the right "emotion word" underneath. Small children in particular might enjoy using these with you as they learn to identify their feelings. (But older kids, and sometimes spouses!, can also sometimes benefit!)

Model positive interactions. This includes how you deal with your kids, but also your spouse and others. Show them how you and your partner might discuss a decision that involves some problem solving or even a disagreement (of course, doing it with all your excellent SI skills!) They'll learn a lot from seeing you in action together.

See this as a long-term process. Sharing feelings, helping your children become centered, self-aware individuals is a lifelong journey. You'll appreciate it when they come to the nursing home for their weekly visit and start the conversation with "What's up, Mom?" and you recognize that "mom voice" coming out of *their* mouths!

The Least You Need to Know

◆ Children have totally different thinking processes than adults—your best guide to what they think is often what they feel.

◆ Especially with infants, mirroring their feelings when they're upset can allow you to help them shift to more calm and less "flooded" emotions.

- Part of tuning in to your child is asking them how they're feeling and what their concerns are. Build the habit of having these conversations early and often!

- Communicating with your child will help develop their social intelligence awareness and skills.

Part 4

Social Intelligence in the Workplace

Remember the old Roman galley slaves? You know—the guys who sat on long benches pulling oars while the boss cracked the whip and beat the drum to signal either "slow" or "the captain is water-skiing!!!"

In those seafaring jobs, social intelligence skills weren't super important. But things are (slightly) different today. Most workers now operate in a social environment, and much of our work consists of dealing skillfully with others. Whether it's getting along with co-workers, managing our own ~~galley slaves~~ (*ahem!*) associates, dealing with clients, or wrasslin' with office politics, high-powered social intelligence skills can make all the difference between sitting on the bench and tugging the oars, or being the one on the stool with the megaphone.

In Part 4, we explore social intelligence and the wonderful world of work. Take the quizzes, read the chapters (faster! faster!!), and learn all you can before Monday morning. Let's row!

I FEEL LIKE I'M IN SOME SORT OF *OUT-OF-CONTROL* METAPHOR.

Get to Work!

In This Chapter

- ◆ Social intelligence and career success
- ◆ Assessing workplace SI challenges
- ◆ Tips for improving your workplace SI
- ◆ Getting personal at work

Your social intelligence is often the real secret to your career success and satisfaction. In this chapter, we'll explore some of the keys to growing and using your SI skills at work.

But first, let's see how your SI skills really operate down in them salt mines!

Check Yourself Out

This quiz is designed to give you some idea of how well your SI skills operate in your work environment. Circle the item that comes closest to describing your *typical* response.

1. On Sunday night you find yourself thinking about the challenges at work for the coming week. Usually that means you are thinking mostly about:

    A. The anger or tension I feel about some of the jerks at work—I dread Mondays!

    B. The zillions of tasks I have to accomplish.

    C. My mind goes back and forth from tasks and projects to the people involved, and how to make things work well with them.

2. Before your next performance review, you'd want your boss to know that you:

    A. Are a thorough and hard worker—you get projects done!

    B. Just don't want him to be too critical of you, is all.

    C. Get your work done, but also that you see your job as helping her do *her* job well.

3. Much of your workday is spent:

    A. Either doing my main tasks or connecting with others, to get their help or to help them with their tasks.

    B. Biting my tongue as I try to get work done despite some of the hassles people at work cause me.

    C. Closing my door, ignoring my phone and e-mails, trying to work without interruptions.

4. How would you describe the kinds of personal relationships you have with people at work?

    A. I don't "poop where I eat." I avoid personal relationships at work.

    B. I have some friendships at work, but try to maintain a balance so they don't complicate my work life or main roles.

    C. Work is a big part of my social life, though I admit that sometimes this causes some problems at work.

5. How much can you be yourself at work?

   A. I am pretty much able to relax and show many sides of myself, though I know there are also lots of things that it's best to leave private.

   B. I'm reluctant to share very much about myself or my life, or to express feelings about anything—you never know when it might backfire!

   C. I blurt it out and don't care who knows, whether it's a feeling or a personal fact.

6. There's tension in your office or shop between a couple of key people—voices have just been raised! Your most likely personal response will be:

   A. Their tension will affect me all morning.

   B. Burrow down harder into my work so as not to notice, if I can.

   C. I'll sense the tension and do something so it doesn't get to me, like take a quick break for coffee or step outside for some fresh air—or maybe check in with one of them to see if he's okay.

7. You hit "send" on a work-related e-mail to a co-worker but now realize it might look a bit more harsh than you meant it to sound. You are likely to:

   A. Actually, I probably wouldn't notice until they tell me that it bothered them—that's my most likely mistake.

   B. I may re-read it, and send a follow-up apologizing if my last one sounded more impatient than I meant it to.

   C. Well, I was and am impatient—I stick to my guns.

8. You're part of a team or committee trying to get a big project done. At your next meeting, you realize you feel like you've been doing your job but some folks on the team aren't doing theirs. Your most likely approach at the meeting:

   A. Ask them how it's going and see if there's something they need or are concerned about, and try to problem solve it together.

   B. Mention your concern that they're not getting their parts of the project done, and encourage them to try harder.

   C. Stay focused on your piece of the project—update the group, and let them sort out their own difficulties.

9. Your work involves managing or keeping track of a huge amount of information and handling help requests from many people. How do you cope with the workload?

   A. I dig into the work and keep at it till I am ready to drop.

   B. I try to organize the best system I can, prioritize what I try to get done, and make sure I'm fairly fresh in order to be able to respond well to the calls or requests of the clients or people who call me all day.

   C. I spend a lot of time telling my clients/students/customers or co-workers to be patient, that I'm doing the best I can; I admit sometimes I sound impatient.

10. Your boss ignores your improved way of doing a task or assignment and lectures you about how you didn't do it the way you were instructed. Your response:

   A. Just give up and do it the way she says—who cares?

   B. Argue with her, or comply but be angry in your own quiet way.

   C. Manage your frustration and do it as she asked, trying to understand the pressures she's under, even if you know you're still right.

Scoring: Circle your responses below, and tally how many you have in each column.

Item	Task	Confl	SI
1. (Sunday)	B	A	C
2. (Perform)	A	B	C
3. (Workday)	C	B	A
4. (Personal)	A	C	B
5. (Yourself)	B	C	A
6. (Tensions)	B	A	C
7. (E-mail)	A	C	B
8. (Team)	C	B	A
9. (Info)	A	C	B
10. (Boss)	A	B	C
Totals			

Interpreting your results:

Task 6–10: This stands for "task focused." You may be more focused on tasks than on people. You'll have to decide whether your work is helped or hindered by ignoring some of the key people dynamics (and your own emotions!) at work.

Confl 6–10: This stands for "conflicts." You're probably tuned in to others—but you get into conflicts with them. Remember that SI means having good control over your own emotions, and that the people around you have feelings, too!

SI 6–10: "Socially intelligent," of course! You're probably tuned in to both your own emotions and the emotions and concerns of others at work—without sacrificing time and energy needed to maintain some task focus. And it's the balance that counts, right?

SI and Career Success

In *On Writing* (New York: Scribner, 2000), a book of advice for writers, Stephen King says, "People love to read about work. God knows why, but they do."

Actually, it's no dark, spooky mystery. For most people, work is not just what we do, but who we are. Our jobs or professions are the first things many of us mention when a stranger asks us to "tell me about yourself." In fact, we're apt to mention our careers even before we share our marital status or whether we have kids!

We often spend more than half our waking lives at work. And most often it *is* fascinating, Stephen! Whether you're a brain surgeon, a carpenter, a sanitation engineer, or a waiter, there are usually hundreds of details, skills, techniques, problems, schedules, challenges, and dilemmas to master in order to do your job.

A big part of most people's jobs involves the most interesting and challenging puzzle of all: *other people!* Even if you're an independent worker, stuck in a cubicle, painting a fence along the highway, or (ahem!) a "solitary" writer, your success at work (and many of its pleasures) will depend on your interactions with others.

We often forget how central dealing with people is to our jobs. We're apt to focus more on the number of widgets we've built,

> **SI Tip**
>
> Carry around a notepad or index card, and make a count of *every* person you interact with at or about work, from the time you get up in the morning until you hit the rack that night. Odds are you'll be amazed at how many people you connect with!

the memos we've written, or the other, more tangible tasks. I've even known university professors who've said that their jobs would be great if it weren't for the students! But of course, without those students, their jobs wouldn't even exist!

The problem occurs when people get so wrapped up in the non-people parts of their jobs that they do resent, irritate, or just fail to work and play well with others. Because in most jobs, once you start to treat people as obstacles and irritations to your work, instead of your essential partners or the people you're there to serve, you're sunk!

Let's consider an example of how ignoring the social part of work can hurt you.

Suppose you're a genius—no, I mean it! You're not only super, super smart, but you're one of the world's great experts in something. Let's say you're an expert in triblet building and shipping—you know more than anybody about how triblets are manufactured, what they do, and how to get them out to the triblet stores.

So one day you get a call from the CEO of Triblet International, who wants you to solve their "triblet building" mess. Things are in chaos in triblet-land, and everyone everywhere agrees: you're the one to fix it! You get an amazing offer in the many-figures, and so you start work at TI, Inc. the next Monday.

You swing into action. You check out the triblet fabricators at the plants, read the stats, do whatever other fact-finding you need, and you ID the problem. You start making calls, sending e-mails, giving orders, and making waves.

Within a few months, two things happen. First, triblet production at TI has skyrocketed. Your plans and repairs have worked!

Second, the CEO calls you in and tells you that … you're fired!

"What?" you ask, amazed. "Why?"

"It just hasn't been working out," she says. "Sorry. You're smart, but nobody can work with you. We appreciate your help, and good luck!"

Dismayed, you go out and invest part of your severance bonus in hiring a consulting psychologist or coach, who agrees to help you diagnose the problem. He meets with you and surveys your former co-workers. He finds out that:

- People thought you came off as arrogant—you never let them forget that you are that "big triblet genius."

- Your subordinates felt that you constantly pressured them to work faster—nothing they did was good enough.

◆ Managers in the triblet factories thought your e-mails were too critical—they started to call you the "grand triblet poobah" behind your back, and they didn't mean it in the nice way!

◆ The vice president you reported to felt that you were constantly hinting that you were after his job.

◆ Nobody wanted to work with you anymore—even your secretary thought you were "kind of weird!" (And you thought *she* was kind of weird!)

So even though you tripled triblet production, your social functioning was considered too costly for the company.

Grow Your Workplace SI

In the preceding example, the "genius" might have saved his job with just a bit more social intelligence. One of the most obvious (in retrospect) SI facts would have been that good working relationship skills are often more important than triblet skills. In fact, you can almost never thrive in a job if your SI skills are really poor!

Caution! _____

You may pay for blowing off social expectations. Not that you should give up your creativity and great ideas, but don't ignore the need to communicate your genius in a way that other people can appreciate (or at least tolerate!) it—and you!

As a *consulting psychologist*, one of my jobs has been to help employees and professionals function better in their work environments. Like the example above, it's not unusual to get a call from a manager or supervisor or someone in HR who has a concern about an employee. Generally, the concern has nothing to do with their technical skills. Rather, their interpersonal gaffes have become serious problems for them, to the point of jeopardizing their jobs.

def•i•ni•tion _____

Consulting psychologists are psychologists (experts in behavior) who help individuals, organizations, or groups function more effectively. Often their clients are the organizations or companies that hire them, instead of individual patients like in psychotherapy.

As with the imaginary example, the first step is to get the lay of the proverbial land. Getting an assessment of a person's work style, particularly his social intelligence and how he's been using (or not using) it, can help identify the key growth areas or areas needing change.

Let's walk through the basic steps you can take in your own work life to "ramp up" (business-speak for "improve") your SI skills!

Assess Workplace Challenges

If you (or your boss) were to hire me to help you improve your workplace SI, we'd first sit down together and do an assessment. (Actually, if it were your *boss* who brought me in, I'd sit down with her first, and find out what her concerns were about you. But you'd be the next stop.)

The first thing we'd talk about would be your perception of how well you function with other people at work. We'd do a complete assessment of your strengths and places where your SI could be tweaked a bit. Then we'd pick out a few major goals for you to work on, and set up a plan for making improvements in how you deal with others in your workplace.

> **Social Science**
>
> Workplace coaching and consulting with employees is a growing and highly regarded business practice. Many companies have found that the return on investment is huge from helping employees improve their social intelligence skills.

This chapter will help you do a miniconsultation on improving your workplace SI. First I'll give you some self-assessment questions (in addition to the quiz you did previously); then we'll talk about goal setting and follow-through. The corner cubicle may be only a few SI tweaks away!

(Of course, doing a self-assessment from a book isn't exactly the same as hiring a real consultant. But it may get you thinking, and you can probably ID most of your key issues or red flags. Working solo gives you all the time you need, and it's more private. We'll also talk below about how to find your own consultant or coach if you need one.)

Probing Questions: Grab a notebook or open up a new computer file or project (pick whatever software you're most creative in.)

Here is a 10-Question Self-Assessment to help you sort through your social intelligence "issues" in the workplace:

1. Write a description of your job—what do you do, day to day? List your main tasks, and then circle or highlight those that involve working with people. Be sure to describe your *real* job—it may be different than the one in your official job description.

2. Write a brief overview of your whole work history. How did you get to this job, and to this point in your career? What strengths, talents, and skills have you developed?

Caution! _____

This assessment project is private! Don't leave it on the office computer if there is *any* chance your company might ever audit or read your files! Same at home—it'll work best if you know you've got a totally private work space, so you can be honest with yourself.

3. Now make a list of the people (e.g., clients, patients, engineers down in the triblet department) you work with. Include everyone from superiors to people who report to, or work for, you, including the guy who brings the coffee cart by every morning (everyone counts!)

4. List some of the interpersonal issues, concerns, and challenges that you've run into. List things like:

   ◆ Formal feedback you've received about your interactions

   ◆ The kinds of relationships you have with people at work—are you friendly, businesslike; are there tensions?

   ◆ List *every* conflict or personal/work disagreement you've ever had with anyone in school or work (or if the list is huge, just list the top or most recent five or so). Any patterns in there? Flag 'em.

   ◆ What do you like about your co-workers? Your boss? Your subordinates?

   ◆ What do you dislike?

   ◆ What do you think are your strengths and weaknesses, in terms of how you relate to people at work?

5. Is there a way to get any feedback from co-workers, bosses, or subordinates on how you work with them? Such as by, say, asking?

6. What are your goals? Write down your current goals for your career, for the short term, the intermediate term (the "five-year" goals for your work life), and your ultimate, big-picture goals. Take some time on this one.

7. Now the really big question: how are your "people smarts" connected to your success—or lack of it—at work? Look for anything in all these notes that might have a bearing on that central question. For instance, look for things like:

   ◆ Feedback about your interpersonal style. (Feedback can be formal, but it nearly never is—until it's too late! Usually it's what you've noticed, picked up, or sensed from people over time: do they like you? Do you get included in the invitations or the jokes? Are you someone people trust with secrets?)

   ◆ Opportunities you've gotten, or missed, because of your interpersonal behavior. (It's usually easier to spot the wins: they flow from your good relationships as people invite you in, or send you word of a good job, etc. The ones you miss are harder to know about—people don't call to say they *haven't* referred a client to you because they think you're an abrasive jerk.)

   ◆ Concerns you have: do you feel left out of the loop? Are you comfortable with your co-workers? Do you often regret those nasty-sounding e-mails after you hit "send"?

   ◆ Places you'd like to expand yourself: What would be your dream "self" interpersonally? When you watch that mental movie of yourself functioning at work, what do you look like? How would that "best version of me" relate to others? What would you have to change to be like that person?

   ◆ Some people like this common question, used forever in self-help tomes (such as in Stephen Covey's *Seven Habits of Highly Effective People*): if you were to die and then "lurk around" at your own memorial service, what do you think people from work would say about you? Okay—how about afterward, in the bar, when they said what they *really* felt about you? (The self-help books don't mention that second "little chat" but it might be the most revealing!)

Social Science

Consultants use a "360-degree feedback" instrument to assess employees' interpersonal performance. Bosses, peers, and subordinates complete questionnaires about the employee's behavior, style, strengths and weaknesses, etc.—then the consultant presents all that anonymous feedback to the employee! It's super helpful to discover what others notice about you!

8. What's the worst thing that might happen if you don't change? For instance, if you don't stop letting that little edge of sarcasm trickle out in your e-mails?

9. What might you *gain* if you could make your SI glitches vanish? Suppose you *could* behave in meetings like your "best-case-scenario self"? Suppose you *were* great with clients, popular with peers, the person the Grand Poobahs called when they wanted input from their best "little people"? How might that enhance your career?

 SI Tip _____

Brainstorm the worst-case scenarios for your most pressing interpersonal gaffes. Might your shyness lose you customers? Might your "edge" at meetings, or your habitual halitosis, lead to mass layoffs of all those sloppy, cranky programmers? Remember, it's the people who *don't* anticipate the worst that get hit with it!

10. Now do the math: the difference between your "worst-case scenario" outcome and the "best-case scenario" outcome (in salary or success) is the likely cost to you of not making the changes in your SI! Corner office vs. unemployed? Clerk in cubicle 34A in Scranton vs. running the Honolulu Field Office as a VP? The choice is yours.

Set Goals and Make Changes

Now that you've conducted this cut-rate assessment (Actual consultants might charge you or your company thousands of dollars to walk you through the same list of questions! Heck, I would!), the next step is turning your results into an action plan.

What are the main changes you might want to make? Think of it in terms of our four key SI areas. Are you, for instance, inclined to:

◆ Not "know" yourself—especially your emotional hot buttons or reactions? What emotions do you infect the people around you with? Is self-control or self-expression more of what you're hung up on?

◆ Do you tune in to others, or are you so wrapped up in your work tasks that you forget to notice their feelings, concerns, or how hard *they* are working?

◆ Do you make contact? Make a connection? How? Where can you do it better?

◆ What's your caring level? Might you remind yourself to be a bit more engaged, involved, interested in your co-workers? Do you bother to ask how things are going, and really to feel it? Do you think about, visualize good things for, express concern for, or pray (if it's your thing) for your co-workers?

If you did this assessment with a consultant, they'd give you a nice binder with your results. The most important page would be where your particular change targets or goals were listed. So now, ask yourself whether you need a formal set of goals, or just to remind yourself and be aware of how you want to make changes. For instance, you might want to:

♦ Develop more relationships or connections with people at work. Get to know people a bit better.

♦ Make a habit of asking your co-worker/assistant/whoever, how her weekend went, how they're doing, etc.

♦ Take steps (such as relaxation training) to reduce your social anxiety or shyness with people, if that's an issue. (Or to increase your assertiveness, or any of the other issues noted in our early chapters.)

♦ Get a handle on your moods, if they are intruding at work.

♦ Smile when talking to clients on the phone—it will come across in your voice!

♦ Insert some of your ideas here: _____

_____

Get a Coach!

You may decide that you're not sure what changes you need, or you may have an opportunity to work with a *coach* or consultant on your SI changes. As I mentioned previously, many companies have discovered that coaching can not just help workers who are "in trouble" but that most key employees can benefit—and that these benefits can actually improve the company's bottom line!

People who can help you enhance your workplace SI include consulting psychologists, coaches, counselors, and similar folks. Your HR department may offer services or referrals. There are internal coaches in many organizations; in addition, people may use the word "coaching" to include anything your boss or supervisor helps you to do to improve your performance. (Frankly, I think the word is a bit overused

def•i•ni•tion

A **coach** is a trained professional who helps enhance the interpersonal or other work performance of employees. Coaching is the process of helping people assess, develop, and improve their performance. There are both business and life coaches who do this work with people.

and trendy, but that doesn't mean a good coach can't be amazingly helpful. Pick your coach with care, is the usual advice.)

See Appendix B for web resources where you can find a coach.

Personal Relationships in the Workplace

A big part of social intelligence is being intelligent about the nature of your relationships—and being able to predict what kinds are helpful or harmful. (Your grandma used to think of this in terms of whether people had "judgment" in their choice of friends.)

This is important not because you're a bad person, but because in modern times, *your employer is not your friend.* Generally, they're indifferent to employees' friendships and emotional lives, unless and until there is even the tiniest little threat to them (such as the possibility, say, of their being named in a harassment lawsuit.) At which point, any loyalty you've thought existed between you and them will generally prove to have been just an illusion.

While most workplaces allow for a reasonable amount of fraternization, it's critical to be clear about both the official boundary rules and the actual, unwritten rules in your organization's culture. (The *actual* and more relaxed rules may be operative, for instance, unless or until somebody gets mad at you.)

So it's good sense to be careful how you relate to people. Here are five tips and one Golden Rule for managing your social relationships in the workplace. (As usual, these are just suggestions—your workplace may vary.)

1. Know the rules of the place—including both the workplace culture and whatever HR says are the rules.

2. Don't ever assume you'll be able to explain, give your side, or back out of the consequences if something gets messy between you and a co-worker. Especially in a corporate workplace, the accuser usually wins.

3. Watch e-mail comments: your e-mail may be monitored, things always get forwarded to the wrong person, and it's a permanent record of your indiscretions, if you make 'em.

4. Affairs at work are almost never a good idea (though if you are peers or in different departments and the rules say it's okay and neither of you reports to the other of you and so on ... you know).

5. Beware of TMI—too much information. Some sharing may not be welcome or wise. Some people use the term "business personal" to refer to what's okay. The fact that you spent the weekend gardening or had a cold is okay to share with anyone; the fact that you spent it fighting with your spouse, or strapped to a rack in Lady Domina's House of Pain, is not.

And finally, the Golden Rule: *Always assume that everything you do and say at work will end up in your personnel file and that this will be seen by all potential future employers as well as your significant other, and that a complete copy of the file will be given to your daughter or son some day.*

The Least You Need to Know

◆ Your interactions with people are as crucial to success on the job as your performance on work tasks and projects.

◆ Improving your SI at work involves assessing your social strengths and blind spots, tuning in to co-workers and others, and setting goals for change.

◆ A coach can help you improve your workplace SI—and may be a huge asset to your career; just be sure you pick a competent and well-trained one!

◆ You can be friends with co-workers—but be sure not to violate your organization's formal or unwritten (culture) rules or to do anything that might damage your or their career.

Chapter 16

Network Everything

In This Chapter

- ◆ Networking and survival in the arena of life
- ◆ Networks and your career
- ◆ Mapping the terrain
- ◆ How to expand your "net" worth!

Your career success—and the pleasure you get from doing it—may depend as much on the network of relationships you build, and how you maintain those relationships, as on your other skills.

In this chapter, we'll explore the connection between social intelligence and networking, and help you organize and expand the effectiveness of your "me-net."

Let's start with a quick self-assessment.

Check Yourself Out

This quiz is about your networking skills. Read each item and circle the answer that best describes your *typical* response.

1. You attend a conference where there are many people who work in your field. Your typical style of interacting is:

   A. I like meeting people so much that even when I'm talking to someone I'm looking over their shoulder at who else is around to meet.

   B. I keep to myself, hunker down, and take notes.

   C. I usually connect with several people and learn about their work, interests, who they are, and then make plans to stay in touch.

2. There's a "company bag lunch" on Fridays, where the director of your branch office invites everyone to spend the hour just talking about whatever. You will:

   A. Just keep working—nobody notices when you show up at those, and who has time?

   B. Always show up, mainly to score points for being there.

   C. Go to those sometimes, to get better acquainted with the director and other people from the office.

3. How do you generally use e-mail at work?

   A. I use it to connect with individuals—try to stay in touch, but I do it individually.

   B. I spend a lot of time e-mailing a lot of people to stay in touch by sending cartoons, announcements, and so on.

   C. I read what comes in, but rarely write to anyone—at work I'm too busy.

4. Whom would you call if you lost your job and needed to find a new one today?

   A. I wouldn't call anyone—I'd look in the want ads first.

   B. I have a select few people I could call who would probably be able to help me, or who'd know what opportunities are around.

   C. I would have to call a hundred people or more—luckily, I have all their numbers!

5. You meet a new person in your workplace. As a rule, you will:

    A. Learn who she is and what she does, and whatever I can personally about her.

    B. Say hello, then get on with my job.

    C. Make sure she knows who I am and what I do at the company.

6. If you want to make a new acquaintance part of your "network," the best way is to:

    A. Look for an opportunity to get in touch with something useful to him.

    B. Send him frequent e-mails or blurbs about myself and my work.

    C. Only contact him if I really need something from him.

7. You move to a small town and don't know anyone. In the first month or so, you're most likely to:

    A. I'll only meet the people at my job, if I have one.

    B. I'll seek out some of the main "hub" people—folks who know lots of people, such as clergy, hairdressers or barbers, or small business owners, and get acquainted.

    C. I'll blanket the town with blurbs about me.

8. Do you think it's better to be rich, famous, or well connected?

    A. If I'm "well connected," I can probably get rich or famous if I want to.

    B. Fame, fame, fame! If you're admired, you're in luck!

    C. Rich—I can buy the rest.

9. If you could pick just one, which "scientific invention" would you give to a "pre-scientific" society, to give it the best chance of thriving?

    A. The microscope—they'll be able to see what things are really made of.

    B. The scientific journal—people will be able to exchange information about discoveries.

    C. The science of "advertising"—the important people can have a lot of influence that way.

10. If you wanted to get rich building better mousetraps, you'd focus your energy on:

A. Designing that great mousetrap—the world will beat a path to my door.

B. Advertising my mousetrap everywhere.

C. Creating a network of people who can help me launch my mousetrap: experts in engineering, exterminators, someone to lend me mousetrap money, a mousetrap marketer, maybe a cat or two, and so on.

Scoring: Circle your responses below, and tally how many you have in each column.

Item	Isola	Indis	SI
1. (Conference)	B	A	C
2. (Bag lunch)	A	B	C
3. (E-mail)	C	B	A
4. (Job)	A	C	B
5. (New)	B	C	A
6. ("Network")	C	B	A
7. (Town)	A	C	B
8. (RFC)	C	B	A
9. (Invention)	A	C	B
10. (Business)	A	B	C
Totals			

Interpreting your results:

Isola   **6-10:** This stands for "isolating." You may tend to isolate yourself instead of developing or participating in social networks. The good news may be that you've excellent concentration, focus, and expertise; the downside can be that you don't have the social resources that could help you succeed.

Indis   **6-10:** This stands for "indiscriminate" social networking. While you may work hard to make a social splash, your efforts might be undermined by either being too "shotgun" and indiscriminate, or by a tendency to not make very sincere-seeming, thoughtful connections. Sometimes "knowing everybody" is less effective than really connecting well with a well-chosen, well-liked but smaller group.

SI   **6-10:** "Socially intelligent" networking of course! More than five responses here suggests that you're aware of the value of a good network of co-workers, colleagues, or community; you're interested in real relationships and connections, not just quantity.

Networks and Career Success

"Whatever comes out of these gates, we've got a better chance of survival if we work together. Do you understand? … If we stay together, we survive."

That's the advice given by Maximus, a Roman general forced to fight as a gladiator, in the hit film *Gladiator*. What follows is one of the most exciting battle scenes in movie history, as a small group of outnumbered gladiators manage to defeat a larger and more heavily armed group of opponents.

Maximus's advice is a great example of ancient wisdom. It's likely that the most important survival skill of our ancestors was their ability to work together as a group. This would have enabled them to defend themselves against larger and more dangerous predators (animal or human), to divide up complicated food-finding or growing tasks, to locate resources such as water and shelter, and eventually to organize into larger tribes, then nations. (Some even claim that the modern corporation is the culmination of this ability to work as a coordinated group.)

This *networking* skill of humans is probably the main reason why our brains are about seven times larger than they would need to be in mammals of our size! Why do we need all that extra braininess?

In general, the size of animals' brains are strongly related to how much networking they do. The "top" or most advanced parts of our brains—the so-called "neocortex" and in particular, our frontal lobes, are super large, relatively speaking. And this is where the networking stuff happens. Both primates (such as great apes, or little apes like us) and other animals (such as some species of hyenas that have complex social networks) tend to have larger brains than comparable animals (like other kinds of hyenas) that operate as soloists.

def•i•ni•tion

Networking means communicating or interacting with others to exchange information, resources, skills, etc. A network is either an informal or formal arrangement of relationships between people, which allows them to exchange information, help, news, and other resources.

You need all those brain cells because keeping track of complicated social networks is very complicated. How complicated?

Consider just a few of your nearest and dearest—say your five closest friends or relatives. Grab some paper and start jotting down *everything* that you know about each of them. Start with physical stuff: height, weight, hair color (and in some cases, *real* hair color—and all the other colors it has been!). Go on to birthplace, main facts of his or her growing up, key relationships, job, love life, favorite foods ....

Give up? I bet you didn't even finish the exercise. Why? Because the amount of information you have about *just those five people* is probably mind-boggling! Imagine the amount of brainpower you are currently using to store all these "sets" of data about social networks:

Social Science

Most people's "inner circles" of friends or connections tend to consist of five people. The average person can keep track of a social network of about 150 people—that's the main list of friends, relatives, and co-workers you're likely to list as "everybody I know and interact with."

- The relationships between your top five people—who knows whom, their relationship history, the feuds and love affairs, and who borrows whose library books

- Who was who, and who hung around together in your high school—all the love affairs, feuds, big events, that time Carrie burned down the gym ...

- All the "family dynamics" in—yep—your family

- The networks that exist in your workplace, corporation, job, or profession

- All the networks or cliques in your church, mosque, temple, MENSA chapter, or favorite AA group

And of course, you've filed away the whole social *worlds* in perhaps dozens or even hundreds of TV shows, movies, novels. Plus the places you've worked, studied, interacted ... Your mind contains universes!

So what?

Good question. Why is all that data stored on your mental hard drive? Cuz you need it. Because most of your survival, even in a modern society, depends on it. It's that complicated society, the vast networks of people you know or can get access to, that provides you with all your food, shelter, safety, financial, emotional, social, sexual, and other resources. And that society is really nothing but a complicated network of people.

When it comes to work and career issues, you're not likely to be very successful if you neglect "the net." Meaning your network of professional relationships and connections.

Your network is probably worth a literal fortune to you. Author Daniel Goleman, in his book on *Working with Emotional Intelligence*, calls our networks our personal *capital*. It's both our wealth and our main tool for increasing that wealth.

What are some examples of uses for your network at work or in your career? Here's a top-10 list:

def•i•ni•tion

Capital is money or anything else that you either have or can use to invest in building or supporting a business, project, or career.

1. **Getting advice and mentoring.** Teachers, old friends of the family, and friends of yours are all part of your network that can help you find the right book, think through a career interest, etc.

2. **Finding crucial information.** Want to know whom to call to get help, an application, an answer to a puzzle? Tap your network.

3. **Getting a job.** More people find jobs through networking than through want ads. I've never gotten a professional gig, either as a psychologist or a writer, that didn't come from my network of colleagues and friends. (And heck, I'm super introverted!)

4. **Political insights.** Who's who, what's happening at work, who's in and who's out? Your *only* real intel will come via your connections.

5. **Client leads.** Have to sell anything—widgets or services? Most of your clients may come through the net (meaning *your* network—not the Internet!)

6. **Resources for work.** You need to know where the funds or the paper clips are? Who you gonna call?

7. **Expertise.** You have to find out what? By when? Research shows it's about five times faster to get key info via a good network than via solitary hunting in the stacks.

8. **Safety net.** If you lost your job, or someone got really mad at your memo on the boss's pet catastrophe plan, your political support may be what saves your bacon.

9. **Emotional support.** In rough times, and just to keep that smile on your face, the give and take of connections can't be beat! Social support is literally more powerful than antidepressants in keeping you afloat.

10. **Creativity.** Your ideas blended with other people's ideas can be much more powerful, creative, and effective than just yours alone.

Remember Ben Franklin's "Junto"—his little group of friends and business associates? They met weekly to improve themselves, share news, and brainstorm how to make improvements in their businesses and community. This was an example of deliberate network building.

Time and again research has confirmed the effectiveness of what Franklin and other business people have done. A great network is something successful business people actively cultivate. They consider it part of their jobs to spend time staying connected to associates—just making calls, sending e-mails, sharing clippings from the news, even! And needless to say, this is where _all_ your social intelligence abilities come together!

Map Your Network

You've probably seen network maps in movies or TV shows without knowing what they are. Think back to a scene where the cops are in their offices talking about that organized crime syndicate. Remember the bulletin board where they hang pictures of the mobsters, with lines connecting one thug to another? Maybe they even put the "top banana" at the top of the map, and then draw lines under that to his subordinates—the "little fish" (and the guys who are "sleeping with the fishes")?

That's one kind of network mapping. But you don't need the big white board or fancy FBI computer network to track your own network. A big sheet of paper, your address book on Outlook (if you're a PC type), Entourage (for Macs), or even better, some professional-grade contact-management software (like Goldmine for PCs, or Daylite for Macs) can help.

One of the things that separates the pros from the amateurs is how well they keep track of their networks. Whether you're in business, academia, college, run a lemonade stand or paper route, or just have a big, extended family to stay in touch with, being deliberate about keeping track of your connections is important. At the very least, you'll want to know that if you need to talk to Uncle Ernie about babysitting over the weekend, that his phone number (taped to the fridge, remember?) is current!

So do you actually *need* an FBI-style "network map," or does that Christmas card list in your desk drawer do it for you? How do you decide how much work to put into your "map"?

The best rule is probably the one most people follow anyway: don't make a more complicated system than you need—*and that you'll keep up.* If you live in a small, stable community, have the same job, and hang with the same friends and family from one year to the next, just keeping up the phone numbers and adding the occasional new name to your book will be fine. Your real networking work, then, is being a good citizen, neighbor, friend, and relative: stay in touch! (And maybe, if you haven't, make up that long overdue birthday list.)

But if you're moving to a new community, running a business, working in a large organization, researching a complicated project, or have to do a lot of outreach to the community—in short, if your work (or new lifestyle) depends on building up a large network of contacts, you'll need to spend some serious time developing, tracking, and enhancing a web of relationships. In that case, you might actually want to make a visual map of your connections, to brainstorm a list of possible contacts who can help with a project, or to invest in some heavy-duty customer relationship management or contact-management software.

Let's look at some further skills and ideas for developing and nurturing your network.

> **Social Science**
>
> Skilled networkers learn to make links (on their CRM software, for instance) between people and projects, so that when they open a project file they see everyone who is part of the plan. This saves time and ensures they won't accidentally cut someone out of the loop.

Skills to Grow Your Network

By now it's probably clear that the time you spend consciously developing your "net(work) worth" is a good investment. In fact, you'll often get more benefit—*and do more good!*—from an hour spent networking than you will from almost any other career support activity (such as, say, shopping for your work wardrobe). But for most people, networking is more than a support activity for their careers—it's the very heart and soul of their careers.

> **Caution!**
>
> Don't ever put connecting with others low on your priority list! Even if your job is mostly working by yourself writing or filling in forms, maintaining your relationships with co-workers, clients, colleagues, peers, and others is a daily must!

Here are some ideas for building up, and enjoying, your network:

- Get addicted to business cards! Collect 'em from associates and add them regularly to your address book, list, or software. Add notes on who the person is, where you met, how you might help them, etc.

- Make links between people. Some researchers have found that the most effective networkers spend most of that networking time helping people connect with other people in their networks. If I know a good web designer, and a landscaper in my network wants to get a website running, calling her with the designer's name is a great way to help both of them out, and to keep connected myself.

- Learn and remember what your associates' projects, concerns, and problems are. That way, you can help—and of course that helps you, too.

- Don't be a "smarmy salesperson" type—really *care* about the people in your network. There's way too much insincerity in the world, and it's not SI!

> **Caution!**
>
> When networking, take pains to avoid negative gossip, or any other kinds of negativity. Remember that your bad vibes will spread through *that person's* network like a struggling fly's panic spreads through an entire spider web. You'll only get yourself bit eventually!

- ID the "hub people" in your network. I know three or four friends and colleagues who, between them, seem to know just about everyone else I might need to connect with in my work universe. They are excellent networkers—well-liked, highly credible people whom I also happen to like a lot. They're also the people I call first whenever I have a question, need a lead, or just want to share some news of my own. Who, among your zillions of connections, are these "hub people"?

- Review your lists as part of your weekly work routine. Decide whom you need to contact, whom you haven't seen or talked to in a while—and put their names on a weekly "to contact" list. Jot down something to say when you call—maybe just "hello" or maybe you want to follow up on their work problem, or whether that web designer worked out.

- Which reminds me: whenever you do make a referral, give advice, share a phone number, or hear of someone's stressful work situation, it gives you an automatic reason (and sometimes even an obligation!) to call them and follow up. Great!

◆ Avoid the "cc" key. If you send *me* a cute cartoon or a quick hello, I feel special. But if I'm one of a zillion folks on your mailing list, all I feel is spammed! (Exception: family members—it's nice to feel like we're all enjoying the photo of "Sparks the handsome genius dog" together. It's not so cute when a business associate does it.)

◆ Never overlook the value of old-fashioned paper and pen. Some politicians (like the first President Bush) are renowned for their habits of sending personal, handwritten notes to vast numbers of friends, colleagues, and supporters. In this day of quick, easy e-mail, a handwritten note can really stand out.

The Least You Need to Know

◆ Almost nobody succeeds without the help of a network of friends, co-workers, colleagues, and clients.

◆ Networking isn't manipulating people (unless that's how you think about it!)— it's just being human.

◆ A big part of network success is helping the people in your network connect with each other—and really caring about the people!

◆ Maintain your network deliberately—use technology tools but mainly your SI skills to create and maintain pleasant and effective connections.

Chapter 17

Managing Others

In This Chapter

- ◆ SI managers don't just "boss"!
- ◆ What socially intelligent leaders do
- ◆ Tips for building your management skills
- ◆ How to coach others

Once upon a time, being the big cheese was easy. You could just snap your fingers and snarl, and all your little Bob Cratchits would scribble even faster (and be grateful if you gave them Christmas off!)

But we aren't in a Dickens novel, and as you know, your cheese has moved. Besides, it's likely that the most socially intelligent managers have always gotten the best results—even in Dickens's day. In this chapter, we'll explore what the science of social intelligence is teaching managers and leaders about the best ways to help others do their jobs well.

First, time to reflect some on the main person you have to manage well: yourself. Pop quiz:

Check Yourself Out

This quiz is designed to help you assess your "management SI." Read each item and circle the response that best describes you.

1. You're about to hire a new assistant. As a general rule, you pick the person who:

   A. Has the best technical skills.

   B. Will be loyal and follow my lead in most things.

   C. Balances technical skills with the ability to give me honest feedback when I need it.

2. One of your employees has been making some mistakes. So you:

   A. Sit down with him and focus mainly on what he's doing well, with an aside about needing some corrections.

   B. Come down pretty hard on him about the mistakes, because employees generally need that kind of direct, clear feedback.

   C. E-mail him a list of corrections.

3. Quality in the department you manage has been slipping. Your preferred intervention would be to:

   A. Fire the lowest-performing 5 percent of employees, so the others will "get the message."

   B. Ride it out for another quarter—there are always going to be cycles of poor and good performance.

   C. Express your concerns with the staff as well as your confidence in them, and invite them to help find ways to improve quality.

4. Your own boss has just come down hard on some of your staff. You want to calm things down but are concerned about contradicting your boss. So you:

   A. Say nothing to your workers; they'll "get it."

   B. Force yourself to side clearly with your boss, even if you may disagree.

   C. Focus on finding a way to "connect" supportively with your workers, and helping them improve what they need to in their work.

5. You're the president of a company with a number of offices around the nation. You have reliable info that one of your office heads has been "blowing up" and being inappropriately threatening to staff. You:

    A. Let her continue—maybe they needed it.

    B. Hope it was a one-time incident—you don't want to second-guess your best staff.

    C. Order a more full evaluation of the situation, but if this proves true, you'll have to intervene.

6. You're a very introverted person whose technical skills just got you an offer of a promotion to manage a department full of outgoing, bright, and contentious people. You:

    A. Turn down the promotion—it wouldn't be a good fit for you.

    B. Take the job, because once you're the boss, they'll have to pretty much do what you say and so you can use your expertise to get things done right.

    C. Take the job if you feel you'll be able to connect with your employees and get their support, despite your different styles.

7. You "lost it" in a meeting with your staff today, reaming them out over something that in retrospect wasn't entirely their fault. So you:

    A. Pull together another brief meeting and apologize, and give them a chance to express what they felt about the meeting, then invite them to work the problem with you.

    B. Don't apologize—it will convey weakness—just be careful in the future.

    C. Say nothing about the blowup but do let them know that you have found new information that shows it wasn't all their error.

8. When starting a new and challenging project with your employees, the most important thing you have to convey is:

    A. Lines of authority and organization—so they'll know who decides and who can authorize actions or expenses.

    B. Technical information—the key details of the project, steps, info they need, etc.

    C. The value of the project—why their contribution is important.

9. If you're totally honest with yourself, you like "being in charge" because:

   A. You like connecting with employees to get things done.

   B. You enjoy being able to control people's actions.

   C. You enjoy the intellectual challenge of being on top of things.

10. You would prefer to follow:

    A. A firm, no-nonsense, and clear boss.

    B. Nobody—I just like knowing what my job is and doing it.

    C. Someone who inspires me and others to do our best.

Scoring: Circle which answer you chose here, then add up the number of circles within each column.

Item	T/A	Bossy	SI
1. (Assist)	A	B	C
2. (Mistakes)	C	B	A
3. (Quality)	B	A	C
4. (Boss)	A	B	C
5. (Blowup)	B	A	C
6. (Introvert)	A	B	C
7. (Lost it)	C	B	A
8. (Project)	B	A	C
9. (Honest)	C	B	A
10. (Follow)	B	A	C
Totals			

Interpreting your results:

"T/A"   6–10: Stands for "task-focused/avoidant." Your management style may be highly task focused, or you may tend to avoid connecting with employees much at all. You may be super devoted and effective, but not so interested in the SI dimensions of tuning in to workers or connecting with the people you manage or lead.

"Bossy"   6–10: Stands for … you guessed it. Your management style may be more traditional—you may prefer to give orders and assume employees obey.

"SI"   6–10: You're describing yourself as wanting to understand your employees' motivations and to apply what some people call a "resonant" style of leadership in which you and your workers "resonate" emotionally to each other. Leaders like this tend to inspire loyalty, confidence, and trust.

More Than Barking Orders

In modern times it's come to be understood that managing people is more than just giving orders. Modern managers may sometimes feel that they have to be part expert in the jobs of everyone they manage, part marketing genius, and part psychologist. And there's some truth in that.

In fact, one of the most important skill sets of a leader or manager is social intelligence skills. Leading (and I'm using the terms "manager" and "leader" inter-changeably here—the differences aren't so critical to our discussion) is largely about mobilizing the energies and skills of others. And mobilizing energy is as much an emotional as an intellectual task.

Old-Style Management

Ebenezer Scrooge's management theory probably made a great deal of sense to the other bosses of his era. In Dickens's day, most employers treated employees as little more than slaves. (The main difference between slaves and employees, of course, being that employees could quit their jobs.) Bosses assumed that workers needed constant oversight, prodding, and even scolding to get them to work.

Even in the early twentieth century, leaders such as Henry Ford believed that workers would do the least work possible, so that constant supervision and designing jobs that would accommodate "lazy" behavior were the keys to success.

Nowadays, notions of management and leadership are quite different. In fact, bosses from Dickens's era wouldn't understand why today's effective leaders behave as they do. Modern leaders motivate workers by focusing on the positive aspects of their work and using more emotionally "resonant" styles of leadership.

Why the shift? Mainly because the old style never worked all that well. Henry Ford was *partly* right: if your style is bossy and authoritarian, workers *won't* be very inclined to be good little serfs. They won't want to be near you, they won't do more than the minimum, and they may even undermine or sabotage you or your organization. They surely won't put in the extra time, effort, or creativity that a modern competitive business needs in order to be successful.

Social Science

Research confirms the importance of social intelligence for leaders. A study of CEOs who were fired in several countries showed that the main reason they were let go was due to poor social intelligence—they were not able to get along with boards of directors, direct reports, or others.

SI Tip

Make a list of the bosses you had on your first jobs. Jot down notes about their leadership styles. What did you like or dislike? What motivated you to do your best for them, or made you angry and resentful? Reflect on what they taught you about being in charge.

But even knowing all this, it's true that a modern leader may sometimes fall back on old, Scroogey ways. It can be hard to maintain an effective, SI style of work. Some reasons:

- **Early training:** If you were raised in a family where "dad was boss" and you had to obey— or else!—it may be hard to see why you should treat your workers any differently!

- **Habit:** It may just be the way you've always done things, or the way your first boss treated you.

- **Organizational climate:** You may work in an organization where bossy bossing happens from the top down. It can be hard to buck the culture, even if you want to.

- **Anxiety:** You may worry that things will fall apart if you change, or that people don't respect wimpy bosses.

- **Stress:** When the going gets tough, the tough sometimes get ... tougher. You may feel that being patient and connecting with your employees is a luxury you can't afford when the ship is sinking and everyone has to bail.

Leadership involves making lots of judgment calls, and you can't always please everyone. But as a rule, the more you develop your social intelligence, the better leader you'll be—and the more responsive your employees will be to you.

Socially Intelligent Bossing

So what's the difference between socially intelligent and generic management? Like many things in life, it's all relative. Even non-SI-focused managers are probably more socially intelligent than they may realize, since we're so deeply wired to be attuned to and to connect with others. Besides, it's hard to get into a leadership position without having at least *some* SI skills.

Management researchers are now saying that it's emotional sensitivity and other SI skills that separate successful from unsuccessful leaders. Technical skills just get you in the door. It's like running: strong legs and good cardio fitness may help you qualify to run a marathon—but it takes a complex combination of conditioning, training, and in the end, attitude factors to finish the race. In leadership, the key attitude factors are often your social and emotional intelligence.

SI Tip

Use a leadership mantra. Not to meditate off in a corner, but to remind yourself, like a token on your keychain, of an essential attitude or habit of mind. Your recommended mantra, from Daniel Goleman's book on leadership and emotional intelligence: "Emotions are contagious." That means your emotions, boss!

Drilling down more deeply into management skills, we'd again expect the most socially intelligent managers to have some mix of the big four elements of SI:

Know thyself. This is what many business writers, probably starting with Daniel Goleman, call "emotional intelligence." Specifically, a good manager has to have some awareness and ability to manage his or her emotions.

So, for example, it's essential to manage your own anxiety or anger when dealing with problem employees. And being able to feel and convey emotions such as enthusiasm when you need to hit a big sales quota, or toughness and perseverance when the water's rising to deck five, are all essential to helping your staff cope with stress.

Not only is it crucial for you to be emotionally self-aware, but it's only by knowing how to tune in to your own emotions that you can reliably tune in to the emotions of your employees. (That's why the best shrinks—the only ones I'd trust with my family members, anyway—have been through their own therapy. It's so they can learn what feelings feel like!)

Tune in to others. Of course, you want to have a pretty good sense of what your employees are feeling, right? When you come in to work and feel something distant and icy from an assistant, alarm bells had *better* be going off in your emotional brain!

Caution!

Learn to read signs of trouble among employees! While most workplace frowns and grumbles are over personal matters (which are probably not your concern), a recurring or widespread ripple of discontent definitely is important to a manager or leader. Get to the bottom of it, if you can.

We'll talk in a bit about some ways to enhance your tuning-in skills, but let's talk for just a bit about an important topic: why employees might *not* want to share everything with the boss.

This may seem like an obvious point, but it probably gets less obvious the longer you're in the boss's seat. A simple fact of life in the workplace is that you're a threat to your employees. You have power over them that they don't have over you. And so no employee with any social intelligence of their own is ever going to forget that you can make or break their job.

Sure, you know you're a nice guy or gal. Sure, you care about their welfare. "Provided that they …," right?

That's just it: there's always a "provided that." Because you're not their dad or mom. Their sole purpose, in some senses, is to get a job done. So if they let it all hang out emotionally, that might not be so good for their careers. And they know that.

But take heart. That doesn't mean you and your workers can never connect. As long as you and they are pretty much in agreement, which most people generally can manage, that *of course* there's a "power difference" but that doesn't mean anything bad, then you can work together.

Listening to employees and tuning in to their emotions are only part of the picture, too. It's also crucial to tune in to their core assumptions about their jobs, their roles, and what they assume you owe them in return. This is what some experts call the *psychological contract.*

def•i•ni•tion

The **psychological contract** is the unspoken, implied agreement that employers and employees assume they have with each other. It's broader than formal contracts or job descriptions, and includes things like how much respect employees expect, what constitutes fair treatment or the right workplace attitude, and what each feels they owe the other party in return.

Employees generally bring a wide range of unspoken expectations to a job. The more you can understand about these contract matters, the better able you'll be to anticipate and address staff concerns.

Make contact. Everything you do communicates something to employees. And it's not just your speeches or what you say when you stand across the desk or the punch press from someone, or the e-mails you send. The way you dress (are you a tie- or silk blouse–wearing boss, or a work shirt and jeans type?), the way you get your coffee (or have someone get it for you), the speed with which you get back to someone ... all of these are ways of communicating.

The main contact-making skill is finding ways to create emotional resonance between yourself and your staff, and communicating back and forth about your and their work goals. Your job is often to keep things well defined and on course, the way a ship's captain has to continually monitor the vessel's location and adjust its course. Or you may have to solve problems, such as when workers tell you things are getting behind schedule because they can't get parts.

But whatever else you're doing, you're managing the emotional temperature of the workplace. Are people doing okay?

And this leads to an important philosophical point: emotional climate management is not a one-directional process. For one thing, while you're managing your employees, they're also "managing" you in a thousand, often highly sophisticated ways. If they *don't* trust you or your motives, they're managing the information you get, managing the impressions of them and their work that you get, and doing things to steer you either away from them, or toward conclusions they want you to draw. (And they may *not* be doing this consciously, any more than your kid is when they "forget" to show you their poor report card.)

But all things being equal, your employees generally want to work with you, not at cross purposes. They may share your goals, or even feel that they have as much or more commitment to building good widgets as you do.

Meaning that they will look to you continuously to find out things like: are we all okay? Is everything okay here at the factory? Is the boss worried about anything— and if so, is it going to affect us? Is he or she mad? Are we doing well?

Some of these worries may seem childish to you—after all, you have a newspaper to put out (or a Pentagon to run!). But never underestimate the power of the unconscious, of the "inner child" of your employees. Or really, of the "reptile brain" of your workers—that part of all of us that's wired to continually, always, always be sensing any signs of danger, of threat. Because in a modern world, even a hint of disapproval or anxiety from an authority figure is a form of threat. It's like they say of presidents: when they sniffle, the stock market gets a cold.

Caring. These remarks should help make sense of what might otherwise seem very un-Scroogelike in a business discussion: why caring—really caring—about your employees is important.

In a word: they're wired to need it. Just like you are. And when they have a sense that there is some real concern for their welfare in your bossy heart, things will generally go better.

Psychologically, we all function better when we have what developmental researcher John Bowlby used to call a "secure base." When, as children, we feel secure and safe in the knowledge that our mom or dad are there, watching out for us, we relax a bit. Our brains go down to "condition green," and so all that energy that was being used to "watch out for danger!" is freed up. So as toddlers, we could relax and explore our surroundings, see what's going on a few feet away, notice the cat playing with some string. (When a toddler is anxious, the cat is just another threatening object.)

As adults, when we feel reasonably secure in our jobs and that things are okay with our employers and co-workers, it frees up our energy. We handle more stresses as an adult, and our defenses or coping skills may mask more of this from our conscious awareness. But basically, it's the same game: if we feel that our boss is in our corner, and that he or she really *means* it, we'll generally be much more productive.

Hone Those Management Skills

There are tough ways and easy ways to learn anything. Ebenezer Scrooge had to learn about emotional sensitivity, empathy, and opening up to the lives of his workers the tough way—it took three ghosts, a long night of reviewing his life, and a death threat.

Fortunately, it's much easier for most managers to improve their skills. For one thing, you're not starting as far back in the race as Scrooge! You've already got a heart and a ton of emotional sensitivity, or you wouldn't be in a position to manage a cub scout troop, much less the … well, whatever it is you *do* manage (or hope to manage in the future. Maybe even all of Widgetcorps.)

And for another, you're probably already familiar with many contemporary theories of management—all of which have hefty doses of understanding people and ethics in them.

So you're off to a running start. Let's talk about some ways you might enhance your skills as a socially intelligent manager or leader.

What the Best Managers Do

Most people in managerial roles are actually talented, high-achieving people. (If you're a manager, you can blush and bow now.)

In addition to being present, what are some other things the best, most socially intelligent managers and leaders do? Herewith some suggestions:

Avoid negativity. I had a professor once who was fond of saying the only feedback students remember is negative. It's not true, and mostly what we remembered was how disliked he was. People *do* remember positive feedback, and it generally has more impact on their behavior.

Focus on motivation. That doesn't mean patting people on the heads or giving out candy. It does mean remembering that your main job as a leader is often to help manage the *energy* of your staff, not just the technical details. An energized person will work to figure out the details; a demoralized one won't do so well even if they know the technical stuff.

Listen well. Good listening means focused listening. It means *communicating* that you're listening, not just listening. You can do more good managing just by asking a follow-up question or two than you sometimes can by explaining the answer to someone.

Ask what works and what doesn't. If you design a new form or procedure, or just want folks to do something differently, check in with them about it. Find out what they think will work and what won't about the change. Not only might that give you some valuable input, it will show that you're interested in their input.

Maintain—and convey—your own positive vision for a project. As a leader or manager, you're like the director whose task it is to convey what the movie is about to the actors and crew. So a big part of your job is to have that clear picture in your mind—and to find ways to impart that to your employees. Whether it's truly a movie or just making sure that Bob's Hot & Tasty Donuts are truly hot and tasty, you're the main definer of reality and goals for the staff.

SI Tip

A little regular reading up on SI can go a long way—it will help you stay tuned in to the latest developments, but best of all, it will keep you tuned in to your own behavior and to ways you can hone your SI skills. (See the appendixes for good places to start.)

Know things about your employees—like their names. This is probably obvious, but worth noting. From a SI perspective, something important lights up inside our brains when we hear our names, or when an important figure recognizes us.

Avoid the appearance of "politics." I do a lot of work in the area of employee satisfaction surveys, and have to tell ya: the biggest complaint in many, many workplaces is often about politics. Meaning people feel that the real decisions are being made in some kind of illicit or illegitimate way, behind everyone's back. Make sure people feel they can trust you and that the reason for decisions is as clear as possible.

> **Caution!**
>
> Employees are sensitive to the perception of bias, and will monitor your behavior to make sure there is no unfairness going on. It's 10 times more important to avoid even the appearance of favoritism as a boss than it is for anyone else in the workplace.

Apologize. You're going to blow it occasionally. Practice the words "I apologize for ..." and say them whenever the occasion arises. It's really not all that hard, once you get the hang of it.

Coach Others in SI Skills

It stands to reason (and the trend in the research bears this out) that an organization full of high-functioning, socially intelligent employees will function better than the alternative. Which means that as a leader or manager, part of your job is developing the social intelligence of your employees.

> **Social Science**
>
> When staff is experiencing high rates of burnout, their feelings of dissatisfaction, frustration, and loss of concern for clients or customers will adversely affect their work and reduce customer or client satisfaction. Like other emotional factors, burnout's negative effects are contagious.

This can have several tangible benefits. It can help facilitate the working connections between employees. It's likely to prevent burnout, and to help employees feel more energized and motivated. Finally, it'll generally ease *your* stress and workload—who do you think it's easier to be around and supervise: a group of emotionally sensitive, self-regulating, good-communicating, and caring individuals, or the other kind?

So what can you do to encourage and foster higher levels of social intelligence, emotional awareness, and connection among your staff?

Foster a climate congenial to SI. Don't penalize honest self-expression. (This is one of those "one strike, you're out" rules. First time someone is penalized for, say, telling you they're angry at you, no one will *ever* take that risk again!)

Be patient. You can't train people to be more socially tuned in overnight.

Make SI behavior part of performance expectations. Use a style of gradual encouragement to help people "get" that being emotionally self-aware, tuned in to others, and able to work well together is part of their job.

Ask how you can help. Let employees know that their success is important to you, as two human beings, not just as "boss" and "lackey."

Model SI. Goes without saying.

The Least You Need to Know

- Successful leaders are generally gifted in social intelligence.

- Employees generally avoid, and seldom work hard to please or support, bossy and authoritarian managers.

- Some keys to effective leadership include managing your own feelings, setting the emotional tone for employees, tuning in to their concerns, and conveying your caring for them.

- SI leaders are better able to maintain workers' focus on the organization's goals and how their efforts contribute to meeting them.

Chapter 18

Your Clients *Are* Your Career!

In This Chapter

- ◆ Who are your clients?
- ◆ Tune in to your clients and their needs
- ◆ How to strengthen your client bonds

Whatever you do, wherever you work, you have clients. Anyone you sell to, help, or provide a product to is a client. And while there's no substitute for "giving 'em what they paid for" in terms of great goods and spectacular service, it's also important to remember that there's no substitute for connecting, understanding, and caring for your clients.

Social intelligence is super critical to good client relations. In this chapter, we'll talk about the best ways to tune in, connect with, and satisfy your clients, whoever they are.

But first, some self-assessment.

Check Yourself Out

This quiz is designed to help you get some idea of your social intelligence when dealing with clients. Read each item and circle the answer that best describes your typical response.

1. On arriving at your second visit to a client's office, you are thinking about:

   A. How to get her to buy more of what I sell.

   B. Her assistant's first name and the top three problems the client needs help with today.

   C. I've got a laser-like focus on the details of the client's problem, but not much else.

2. If you were (are) a teacher, you'd want to spend your time:

   A. Focusing on the contents of the lessons my students should learn.

   B. Making friends and connecting with the students.

   C. Balancing the lessons with having a mentoring relationship.

3. If a client says "no, thanks" to an offer, you:

   A. Treat her response as feedback that teaches me something about her needs.

   B. Persist in trying to convince her.

   C. Move on to the next client.

4. Your new clerk is telling you about her first day on the job. You tune in to see if she mentions:

   A. How many units she sold.

   B. How well she's relating to me and what she noticed about the customers.

   C. Persuading any reluctant customers to buy.

5. As a clergy person, the best way to convince someone to join your church would be:

   A. Connect with them as a human being.

   B. Point out the theological correctness of my church's views.

   C. Cajole them into making some visits to the church.

6. The real key to succeeding with your current boss is:

   A. Good work combined with a human connection with him.

   B. Regularly doing things to impress him with how loyal I am.

   C. Work my buns off!

7. If you were a physician, you'd want to make sure every patient of yours:

    A. Got technically excellent medical care.

    B. Had time to talk with me about whatever was important to them.

    C. Was "sold" on the superiority of my practice and facilities.

8. Meeting with an executive in her office about your new products, she starts to talk about a concern that her daughter is ill. Your most likely response:

    A. Table everything else and listen to her concerns—even if it means leaving without discussing the agenda.

    B. Bring the conversation back around to what I'm selling when the chance arises.

    C. Cut the meeting short and reschedule—obviously she's too out of sorts to be bothered today.

9. As the head of a small-town library, you have to hire a person to do check-outs and reference work. Best bet:

    A. Hire the person who knows book cataloging and books backward and forward, but who isn't very sociable.

    B. Hire that quiet, helpful "readerly" high school grad who lights up when I talk about reading to him, who knows his way around the stacks.

    C. Hire that skilled "sales" type who loves to engage, but who has minimal "books" aptitude or interest.

10. The guy or gal you should hire after interviewing customer service job applicants is the one who:

    A. Knew the most about the products we sell and our company—I feel lots of confidence they know their stuff.

    B. Was the most outgoing and charming—I really enjoyed her company.

    C. Spent most of the meeting interviewing *me* about my product and concerns, then gave me some honest and thoughtful pros and cons about hiring him or her.

Scoring: Circle your responses below, and tally how many you have in each column.

Item	G/S	Push	SI
1. (Second)	C	A	B
2. (Teacher)	A	C	B
3. (No)	C	B	A
4. (Clerk)	A	C	B
5. (Church)	B	C	A
6. (Boss)	C	B	A
7. (Physician)	A	C	B
8. (Daughter)	C	B	A
9. (Library)	A	C	B
10. (Hire)	A	B	C
Totals			

Interpreting your results

G/S 6–10: This stands for "goods or services only," meaning a tendency to focus primarily on the good, service, or task you are doing and to ignore the human connections needed in a client relationship. You are describing yourself as someone who may be excellent at "getting the job done" but who may strike clients as uninterested, uninvolved, or even cold.

Push 6–10: This means "pushy." You may be inclined to try to force some kind of connection, relationship, or sale on your clients. They may sometimes feel that you're the stereotyped obnoxious salesman, and pull back from dealing with you.

SI 6–10: You are describing yourself as balancing the need to give good service or do your job for clients, with a socially aware, empathic, and tuned-in style. Whether you're selling cars or dropping by with the bottled water, your clients probably look forward to seeing you.

Who Are They and What Do They Want?

When books on emotional intelligence first hit the scene about ten years ago, they were instant hits in the business world. Soon there were scads of websites and books on using emotional intelligence to sell anything to anybody.

While it's understandable that salespeople in particular would swarm to anything promising better profits, the emphasis on using EI to increase profits might at times tend to get a bit *mercenary*. So before we start our discussion, let's hit the "reset" button and discuss who clients really are, and what they want and need from us.

def•i•ni•tion

Mercenary means being super-focused on making money, often at the expense of ethics or concerns for clients.

This is important in part because a core part of social intelligence is having a real concern for the people we work with and for. Our brains are wired to have empathy for others, and our clients' brains are equally well designed to sense when we have—or lack—that genuine concern. I don't know about you, but I just don't want a card shark or dishonest saleswoman using her EI or SI skills on me! And neither does anyone else!

But who are we defining as clients? To start, I'm using the term broadly here, to mean *anybody for whom you provide any kind of goods or services.* In short, almost anybody! A short list of people we might consider clients:

- A barber's or hairdresser's customers
- A priest's parishoners
- A comic strip's readers
- A purchasing dept. secretary at the Pentagon
- Medical patients at a clinic
- Callers to a tech support line
- Voters, for a politician
- People buying lemonade at a kid's stand
- Your co-workers when you're helping them find something
- Your boss (even if you see yourself as a "freelancer" at heart!)

In short, anybody whose needs you might attend to.

Okay, then! The next question becomes, "What do these folks need and want from me?"

And of course, *half* of the answer to that question will be all over the map—it will depend on what specific good or service you provide. If you repair shoes, it's a new sole. If you're a minister, it might be a saved soul. If you sell missile guidance components to the Pentagon, it's whatever's in those little black boxes.

> ### Social Science
>
> The emotional processing areas of the brain (yours, mine, and your dog's) are not the same as the verbal processing areas (which are pretty small for your dog. Yours are bigger.) We sense emotion signals such as warmth, empathy, or anger, even when our conscious minds are focused elsewhere.

But as long as they are human beings (or, arguably, mammals that share some of the characteristics we do, such as the ability to tune in to emotions), part of what they want is an emotional connection! And that's true whether or not they consciously realize it!

As a socially intelligent person, you recognize that everyone you work with or for, every client, is first and foremost a human being. So while you may not focus all your time on your relationship, you need to remember the first key to working with any client, of any sort, at any time:

The relationship is the container for the work!

Meaning your connection with them is kind of like a container—everything else you do, everything you sell to them or repair for them or consult with them about happens inside that container. Keep that rule in mind, and the rest will be easy!

Connect and Assess Client Needs

As we've discussed before, the first thing you do when you get around other human beings (if you're pretty socially intelligent) is to tune in to them. That's basic to all relationships, but it's the heart and soul of interacting with clients, customers, patients, or anyone you might want to work with or for.

Any good salesperson will tell you that learning about client or customer needs is the key to being effective. So this may seem like pretty obvious advice—not worth the price of this page of the book, right?

Except, think about it: How often do vendors, experts, salespeople, and others tune in to *your* needs? What's the overall track record there?

If you're like me, it's probably a mixed bag. In an average day, we're likely to have these experiences:

◆ **"Your call is important to us…"** Whenever you hear that, you're being lied to. Somebody designed a system to make sure a human being would not be available to interact with me—so really, how important is my call to them?

- ◆ **Spam e-mail.** I get 'em, and so do you—hundreds of e-mails a day that clog our systems, and more junk mail in our snailboxes, all supposedly there to "help" us. All it does is hurt.

- ◆ **Oblivious sales clerks.** A bunch of places I go have developed the rule of "no human contact unless absolutely necessary" to an art form.

Of course, there are also great experiences. My favorite bookstore in Vermont, where I'm known by the owner and treated like a real human being. My favorite restaurant, where I go not for the great eats, but because the staff is friendly and asks me how I'm doing, and knows me well enough that I believe they mean it. A barber who's pleasant and friendly and gives good conversation. The garage where my car is serviced, where the owner calls me the next day to check that everything went well—and always takes care of things if there's an error or that "clunk" is still there.

The point is, I may get the technically needed service from the "your call is important …" vendors, but I only use them because I'm a captive audience. First time somebody seems actually interested in me and has the same service, they'll get my business instead.

So lesson one about tuning in: real human presence counts.

Lesson two: use those mirror neurons. Again, salespeople all get taught this, but many other providers of goods and services do not. (And not all salespeople actively use the advice!)

What we're talking about is tuning in. Having active curiosity about clients. So active that you make eye contact, try to gauge their moods, and ask questions about their concerns. That you actually put yourself in their moccasins and see what mildewy, wet moccasins feel like, before you start trying to sell them spike-heeled shoes. (You might decide that what they'd really prefer is a pair of dry, comfortable hiking shoes.)

> **SI Tip**
>
> Face to face wins every time. Whenever you can, connect with clients in person. It's the best way to pick up important info about them and their response to you, and will help you provide better service.

> **Caution!**
>
> In the interest of efficiency or uniformity, you may try to script or manualize your service to clients. The danger is that this will tend to override real interest and empathy for clients—you'll scan their first few words to spot the generic solution from the manual, and stop tuning in!

Of course, the main threat to tuning in is our own concerns and anxieties. If we're in a selling situation, those can include concerns that we're not going to make the sale, but they can also include concerns about how we're being perceived by the client. (It's embarrassing to admit that the first time I consulted with a corporate vice-president, I spent the whole meeting worrying if my suit and briefcase looked okay!)

SI Tip

Remember the main truth of human emotions: they are contagious! Walk in to a client meeting with discouraged feelings swirling around you, and they'll be feeling it too within moments.

Sales pros are particularly aware of this, and the best of them are expert at managing their own moods when they're interacting with clients. This does fall under the heading of "emotional intelligence" but also under the SI heading of "knowing yourself." For instance, how do you cope with that anxiety about meeting a new client?

Here's a suggested mental sequence of steps for preparing to meet with a client:

1. Check your mood at the door. What are you feeling? What do you *need* to be feeling, in order to meet with and help this person?

2. Are there any special feelings, moods, etc., you need to be resonating with this client? (If they've just lost their mom, being super cheerful might be off-putting, right? On the other hand, I used to have a clinical supervisor who told me he would do push-ups before seeing a particularly low-energy, depressed client, so he'd be fairly energized when he met them in the hopes that he could impart some of that feeling to them.)

3. Review what you need to know about the client and their situation (and maybe company, industry, medical condition, whatever). Be reasonably primed when you meet them with helpful ideas and knowledge ... but not so much so that you don't bother to listen to them.

4. Start with an appropriate, generic greeting, and ask them something that fits the reason for your meeting. That can range from "Did you get the e-mail on those parts?" to "How's that lumbago feeling?" to a simple "How are you?" Then, tune in to their reply—but also to the emotional cues they send you!

5. Ask follow-up questions as need be.

Of course, what you actually do will depend on your particular job. And many clients don't want to talk when they expect some kind of action from you—whether that's advice, the part they ordered, or the information they called for. But as a general rule, whatever else you're doing, it's always good to at least find some half-second to ask, even if by a look or a glance, how they're doing and what they need from you.

Again, the biggest mistake you can make is to ignore the human part of your relationship. And most of the time, people do that mainly because they assume they know the answer already.

This tendency, to *assume you already know* what your client is thinking, needing, or feeling, may have some kind of evolutionary roots, as well. For instance, it may just be a better survival move to assume that if you see a lion on the savannah in front of you, that it may attack you. Of course, you may have run into one of the friendly (or more likely, not too hungry, or lazy) lions out there that won't bother you. But if you want to survive to breed, you're better off assuming that all lions—including this one—are dangerous!

> **Social Science**
>
> The tendency to fill in the blanks or the gaps in our knowledge is natural and human. It was something studied by gestalt psychologists, who noted that we tend to mentally connect the dots and see figures (such as constellations in the night sky) where there actually aren't any.

A few years ago I met with a doctor who recommended some medication to me for a minor condition. When I said I wasn't interested in it, he turned to the medical student who was shadowing him and started to explain that patients (meaning me) won't use this medication because it's not paid for by health insurance—clearly assuming he knew my reasons for refusing. What he didn't know (because he didn't ask) was that I'd already had a long discussion about that medication with my regular nurse-clinician, and we agreed that the side-effect risks (like destroying my liver) weren't worth the minor benefits. The doctor *assumed* he knew all about me, and so gave the student a patronizing lecture about "patients' motives." Since this seemed to be his general style of working with patients, I fired him.

Once more: you don't know anything about your client until they tell you. Got it?

Strengthen Client Connections

Time can be your ally in strengthening your connections with clients. This is related to your own development, to the way relationships deepen over time, and to the secondary benefits of having longer-term client relationships.

To begin with, let's consider you.

Most people tend to increase their relationship-enhancing skills over time. When working with clients, we're talking about learning to sense and to manage our feelings, in order to enhance our contact with others.

When I was in grad school, someone asked one of our better teachers how to manage the anxiety they were feeling as they were beginning to meet for the first time with new clinical clients. To our surprise, the teacher (a well-known expert in helping depressed patients) confessed that he, too, still got anxious whenever he was about to see a new client. In fact, in the shrink literature there's even some theorizing that says that therapists unconsciously want their new clients not to show up at all! Because that anxiety is *always* going to be present—and we don't want to be around whatever makes us anxious.

Clients can trigger all sorts of unhelpful feelings in most of us, from rejection to tension. They may cause delays, stubbornly refuse to be helped or satisfied, or give us the runaround.

So you're constantly going to be learning and practicing the skills of patience and resiliency. Learning to manage rejection, discouragement, and self-doubt takes time, but if you persist (and get support from colleagues if need be), things should get better between you and clients.

The second way time helps you is in deepening your connections. Again, what that means, exactly, may depend on the kind of clients you've got. Where the human relationship is generally understood to be pretty important (such as, say, if you're a teacher, a counselor, or a member of the clergy), it's probably pretty obvious that getting better connected emotionally with clients over time is the way to go. But suppose you're selling widgets? Or running one-time-only workshops for sales employees?

Caution!

Avoid burning bridges. While it may be satisfying to storm out of a job or to tell an annoying client where to stick it, odds are high that you'll run into them again! And even the least likable client has several hundred friends, including some of your future clients!

Fact is, even those relationships tend to have longer life spans than you may assume. People take your workshop or buy your widgets, then later decide to try a second workshop with you. Or they run out of widgets. Besides, you just never can tell when a former client may turn up again, in a different capacity. It's a smaller world than you think!

And finally, yes, there is the "net." Most of your clients in many fields will tend to come from client referrals. So as you further develop relationships with people, they'll start to pass the word along to others. The longer you're part of people's lives, the broader your network will grow through their efforts.

More Tips on Strengthening Client Connections

Let's say you've got a new client—whether it's a customer at your bookstore or dough-nut shop or a guy who just bought a used car from you. What would the social intelligence literature suggest to help you strengthen the relationship you have with him or her? Here are some ideas to get your own thinking going. Adapt these to your situation.

(Of course, we have to assume that your books are good, your doughnuts are fresh and tasty, and you didn't sell the guy a lemon, right? Nothing in SI will make up for lousy product.)

Interact like a human being, not a robot. This isn't always as easy as it seems. We tend, when in professional roles, to wear our professional demeanor. And it comes across in our body language, in the subtle tensions in our voices, in our ways of making eye contact. People generally expect and accept that at first, but if it continues beyond a certain point, they'll pull back, because they don't feel that they really know you.

Another way to think about this is again in terms of emotional contagion. If you're reserved and distant, and don't open up, then that's what you'll get back from clients. But since you're trying to learn all you can about a client so you can see how to help them (or how to help them decide to buy something you have for them), you're cutting off the flow of information by being distant and too professional yourself.

Convey your interest. That means let them know that you want to know what they need, and what will satisfy those needs. Do they like your selection? Were they hoping for something different? But more broadly, convey your interest in them as persons.

Learn about their needs. Not just for this sale, but for the future. And it's not just about the doughnuts. Have you noticed that your customers' needs are a bit different than you assumed? Such as: if they buy coffee at your shop for five people in the morning, maybe you ought to sell those larger containers of coffee, like Starbucks does. If your patients have problems dealing with insurance, you might need to hire someone to help them.

Be human. Meaning be yourself. Share a bit of who you are with clients. Gratify a bit of curiosity, and help them see that you're human, too.

Follow up. Find some way to ask them later if they liked the service. Even if something didn't work out, they'll appreciate it. (As I was writing this, I got a call from a company that had sent a guy over two months ago to discuss some home remodeling. We concluded they had nothing for me then, but it was still nice to get the call from the woman who had been interested in my problem back then. I may not have hired them, but you can bet I'll recommend them.)

Hook clients up with other clients if you can. This goes back to the networking chapters, but some researchers have said that it's one of the main ways certain professionals expand their business.

Stay in touch. Clients can be one-shot or for life. When possible, find ways to stay in touch. But the trick is not becoming just more spam. What makes the difference? If I have a feeling that you and I are really connected, I enjoy hearing from you— even if it's via mass e-mails. For instance, one woman I know has been a huge help to me as a computer consultant in the past. When I get one of her mass e-mails about some new service, it's a treat, not an annoyance.

Really see clients as people, not just as customers. Your best clients will appreciate feeling like you enjoy them and are interested in them for who they are. But more important, you will actually enjoy your relationships with them, person to person.

The Least You Need to Know

- A client is anybody for whom you provide any kind of goods or services.

- Social intelligence isn't something you can just use on somebody to get them to buy from you—it involves genuine caring for them as persons, even if that means you don't get their business.

- *The relationship is the container for the work.* Everything you do with and for clients happens within the context or container of a human relationship.

- You can strengthen connections with clients by such means as interacting in a more informal, human way, learning and remembering things about them and their needs, and staying in touch.

Chapter 19

Office Politics

In This Chapter

- ◆ Politics happens!
- ◆ How to decode political signals
- ◆ Be a socially intelligent politico!

"Wherever two or more are gathered together …" things will get political. People working together have to develop all sorts of relationships, networks, and connections in order to get things done. When these networks are formal, they're called an organizational chart. But the *real* organizational chart is the invisible web of political lines that crisscross the organization in every possible direction.

In this chapter, we'll talk about politics in the workplace—the good, the bad, and the downright nasty. And we'll discuss how a socially smart person such as yourself can learn to understand and master Politics 101 in any work (or school, or even family) environment.

But first, let's do our quiz.

Check Yourself Out

This quiz is designed to help you assess your political SI. Read each item and circle the response that best describes you.

1. You're flooded with work in your job and afraid you may be about to burn out from the overload. So you:

    A. Take a bit of time to assess how you can change your job to make it manageable, then work out a plan to line up support to make the changes.

    B. Go to your boss and show her how much you've done and firmly demand that you get a break.

    C. Dig in harder—who has time to do anything else? Besides, it's your own fault for not being efficient!

2. The best habit to build if you want to increase your influence in your job is:

    A. Spend as much time as you can impressing the "top dogs."

    B. Be sensitive to the politics but build good relationships with lots of people.

    C. Avoid doing anything that looks political by staying on task and waiting to be noticed.

3. After an out-of-town meeting, you end up sharing a long ride in the van to the airport with the CEO of your company. So you:

    A. Introduce yourself and find a way to let her know about your great work.

    B. Avoid talking to her.

    C. Say hi, introduce yourself, and then follow her lead about talking further.

4. In a meeting, someone seems to shoot down your suggestion. So you:

    A. Clam up and try not to feel bad—the worst thing you can do is to look injured or deflated.

    B. That stirs up your fighting instinct and so you show you can defend your ideas, even if it means getting a bit rough.

    C. You try to be receptive to the feedback, and to have a productive back-and-forth if there is something you still think is good about your idea.

5. An associate is having some trouble figuring out how to do something at her computer, so you:

   A. Help her, then share the incident with your boss and suggest to him that you might need to supervise her work.

   B. You don't risk making her uncomfortable, so you let her figure it out.

   C. You volunteer to help her, if she likes, in hopes that you're strengthening your relationship as well as really helping her out.

6. For maximum political effectiveness, your work network should include:

   A. People all over your organization, and in related fields in other organizations.

   B. Just the people in your closest work area—otherwise you might look too "aggressive" or "political" and that's not very socially intelligent or strategic.

   C. You should focus on knowing and impressing superiors, bosses, and any other people who have the power to help you.

7. When you hear negative gossip about someone at work, the best response in terms of "politics" is:

   A. Don't join in the fun and risk being tagged a gossip, but if there's a chance to tactfully support the victim of the stories, take it.

   B. Reciprocate with gossip of your own, but use some strategy about whose reputation you're trashing.

   C. Forget you heard it.

8. The best reputation to cultivate in order to win promotions is:

   A. You'd want to be seen as the most competent and well connected—maybe even as a good "political operator."

   B. You think looking nonpolitical, even a bit naïve, actually helps as long as you're also known as a diligent worker.

   C. You can't answer that unless you know something more about the organization.

9. The fastest way to succeed in a new job or school is generally:

   A. Learn and do your job, but also be sure to spend time getting to know people and developing a sense for the place.

   B. Spend a lot of time learning the players and the politics, even at the expense of getting some of your work done.

   C. You think you should focus on doing your job first—the networking stuff can come later!

10. After you're passed over for a job you wanted, the best strategy might be:

    A. Quit and find someplace where your talents will be appreciated.

    B. You'd feel hurt, so you'd know to go off and lick your wounds for a long time and focus on your work.

    C. When you're feeling okay, go ask your boss or a mentor what you might do to have a better chance at a future promotion or change.

Scoring: Circle which answer you chose here, then add up the number of circles within each column.

Item	Ob	Ag	SI
1. (Burnout)	C	B	A
2. (Habit)	C	A	B
3. (Van)	B	A	C
4. (Shot)	A	B	C
5. (Associate)	B	A	C
6. (Network)	B	C	A
7. (Gossip)	C	B	A
8. (Rep)	B	A	C
9. (Speed)	C	B	A
10. (Passed)	B	A	C
Totals			

Interpreting your results:

"Av" 6–10: Stands for "avoidant." Your political style or skills probably tilt toward avoiding the whole matter of politics. Perhaps you feel that being political is wrong, or maybe you just feel intimidated. But politics happens everywhere, so you might be ignoring some threats, or missing chances to have a bit more control over your work life.

"Ag"   6–10: Stands for "aggressive." You may tend to be a rather aggressive political player. In some (e.g., already highly politicized) settings, this may work well, but in many settings you may be at risk for being seen as a bit too manipulative, self-seeking, or threatening.

"SI"   6–10: Your political style is probably fairly balanced: you recognize that politics are important and often unavoidable, but also that most of the time this is mainly a matter of people working well together to accomplish more than they might as individuals. You also may use your SI skills of sensitivity, self-management of emotion, and connecting with others to help them, your organization, and yourself.

"Politics" Are Everywhere

People often think that the best working environments would be totally "politics-free." When employees are surveyed about their workplace satisfaction, it's often the case that where workers say there is a "lot of politics" in the company, they're pretty unhappy in their jobs. "Why can't we just all do our jobs and get along?" might be the typical plea.

And yes, it would be a great world if only there weren't the poisonous, energy-draining politics that often crop up. But the real question is whether it's even possible to be totally politics-free, and if so, whether it would really be all that perfect.

We are political animals. We're wired to be political. Our brains, as we've already discussed, are designed to keep track of complicated social networks, to recognize patterns in how others are interacting, connecting, affiliating with each other. Even children can be master politicians!

Whether it's kids on the playground, seven stranded castaways maneuvering for resources or the best way to find food, or a church choir, people have agendas. They also communicate with each other about these agendas in subtle and complex ways—fleeting moments of eye contact between two people across a boardroom table can make or break alliances, library budgets, careers, or billion-dollar deals.

> **Social Science**
>
> Social psychologists have found that any group of three people will tend to split into an unspoken pattern of a dyad plus one. Two of the three will team up around some topic, issue, or even just based on good rapport. It's a usually unconscious pull that is one of the simplest forms of politics.

def•i•ni•tion

Machiavellian means manipulative or cunning, particularly in a political and unscrupulous way. The term derives from Niccolo Machiavelli, whose book *The Prince* (1532) teaches that one should use devious and unethical methods to get and hold on to power.

So don't panic if the world seems to be too political or *Machiavellian*. It can be, at times. But that doesn't mean you have to give up, give in, or become a victim of schemes. It's possible to develop your political skills and savvy—they are, after all, a part of your social intelligence tool kit!

Our first stop is a discussion of the different ways politics may function in a workplace (or other group or community). Some settings truly are toxic and dangerous, but in others, "politics" is just another word for "we work pretty well together around here."

Toxic Political Environments

A woman works long hours and weekends to provide good services to an agency's clients. Meanwhile, a colleague who is supposed to be sharing the load sees hardly any clients and spends a lot of his time schmoozing with a superior. Yet when finances are tight, she's the one let go.

A man hired to be director of a university program is promised a substantial raise the next academic year by his dean, only to be later told that he'd first have to tell the dean what other department's budget the raise should come from.

A new boss feels threatened by a staff member's superior knowledge of the department and client needs—so she's demoted to a lesser job in a basement office.

These are good (and real-life) examples of working in toxic political environments. When you work in such environments, you can feel like you're in a lifeboat full of starving people who are discussing cannibalism. You're not sure whether you can lower your guard, be yourself, or express your opinions.

Social Science

A recent British survey found that politics has become the biggest cause of stress among managers, surpassing high workloads and poor management styles. Estimates are that politics cost billions in wasted time and corporate resources every year.

When employees complain about "too much politics," this is what they have in mind: environments where good, hardworking people are ignored or even punished because they didn't play the game, while the "players"—less talented and less interested in the good of the organization or its customers—get the promotions, the praise, and the big salaries.

What causes toxic political environments? There are individual, leadership, and organizational causes. For instance, people who get rewarded for obviously competitive, sucking-up behavior can create a toxic waste pool in their company as others take notice and resentment grows. Bosses may reward overtly competitive or nasty behavior, perhaps not realizing that the nice young man who keeps showing up with great ideas has been lifting them from colleagues. Such successes tend to create unspoken rules in the company that the way to succeed is to be like that snake, Charlie.

Organizations under stress can become more political, as scant resources are suddenly up for grabs. But toxic politics can just be part of an organization's tradition. Many people in business are trained to see business, and life, as being all about competition. They were raised on that toxic "Darwin made me do it" belief that ultimate survival for human beings requires a claw and tooth mentality. (As we've discussed, newer science tends to see that as a half-truth—humans are generally more effective when they cooperate with each other than when they view every other human as someone either to defeat or to control.) But organizations tend to have cultures that may persist, that may over time solidify so that it's hard to imagine them *not* being jungles loaded with predators.

They may not be the kinds of places you want to live out your (short, unhappy) work life! Fortunately, it's not all like that!

Even Good Places Are Political

Suppose you're a cyclist who relies on your bike to get to work every day. Your route down Main Street is sometimes pretty hazardous, with speeding cars that seem oblivious to bikes.

You may have two choices: either you keep risking your life—the passive approach. Or you decide that your town needs a bike lane on Main Street. But to get the lane, you'll need help. You may go to your city council rep. He or she says they're supportive if you can show that other folks in the community also want the lane.

So you go out, talk to some friends. Biking friends are especially enthused. You form a committee—the "Main Street Bikers Alliance." You get signatures and lobby other council members. Soon you have a small grass roots movement. You hold a few community meetings at the school and set up a website.

Next thing you know, you've gotten a nice, safe bike lane. Traffic still flows smoothly, but now you have the satisfaction not just of getting to work, but seeing families riding their bikes safely down Main Street. (Plus, you've made a ton of new friends with connections.)

Congratulations—you've just become political!

The moral of the story: politics isn't intrinsically evil or sleazy. Almost everything in life depends on the many small steps taken by groups of people working together. People have to form alliances, people have to work in ad hoc groups to get things done. It's one of the things humans do best.

Characteristics of a healthy political environment are many, including:

♦ **Cooperation:** People are comfortable taking the time to help each other on projects or when they're stuck. So there's a lot of flow from one person to another.

♦ **Productive networking:** People build networks to accomplish goals. Networks may form and dissolve without formal notice, once a project is accomplished or abandoned.

♦ **Openness:** If you're not in favor of something a group is doing, you're free to argue the other side without having to fear for your career. It's also fairly easy to find out who's pulling for one or another option—all you have to do is ask.

♦ **Transparent criteria for advancement or rewards:** You can predict what you have to do in order to get a promotion or a raise. You almost never hear anyone suspiciously or resentfully ask, "How did *she* get that promotion?"

♦ **Healthy stress:** People may be stressed by the fact that they work hard, but not because they toss and turn worrying about "What's *really* going on here?" (Psychologists call this healthy stress *eustress*.)

♦ **Just rewards:** In a healthy political environment, kind, hardworking people are rewarded for their work, not because of whom they're sucking up to.

♦ **Leadership:** Healthy political environments are generally led by people who set the tone for effective political processes. They don't tolerate destructive politics, but support and encourage employees who work and play well with others.

> **SI Tip**
>
> A great way to hone your political skills is to get involved in some community project or movement. Volunteering at the library or helping with a recycling drive can teach you more political skills than a Bachelor's in political science!

> **def•i•ni•tion**
>
> **Eustress** is a psychological term meaning "healthy stress levels." Stress researchers agree that no stress is actually pretty stressful and unhealthy—it doesn't develop resiliency or coping skills. You need a moderate level of stress to function best.

This is the kind of place you probably want to work in (unless you're really comfortable with, and adept at functioning in, more toxic environments). If it's where you already work, great! Hold on to that job!

But if it's not so rosy and perfect for you, maybe you can enhance your political skills.

Figure Out the Secret Codes

The first thing you have to do is to develop your political awareness. If you've never noticed all the politics going on around you, be prepared to feel like the blind man who suddenly got sight! You may be surprised at how much "stuff" is going on!

There are all sorts of complicated politics in some companies—even the masters of the game can spend a lot of time trying to decipher the clues. But generally, just a bit of extra social intelligence will pay big dividends in insight and knowledge.

So time, once again, to dust off that famous bit of advice from the Great Sage of the Ages, Yogi Berra, who said, *"You can observe a lot just by watching."* That's indeed the key!

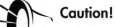

Caution!

Keep your new interest in your company's politics to yourself! At least, be discreet when discussing it with others. The term "politics" sounds vaguely sleazy to many people, and so you could give them a bunch of wrong ideas about your motives.

The best way to learn about your environment is to start with a few specific questions. For instance:

- What's your general "take" on the politics in your workplace? Do you suspect there's a lot of it? Why?

SI Tip

Keep a *private* notebook—*not at work!! and not on your workplace computer!!*—where you can jot down your observations and speculations about the politics of your workplace. Understanding political processes is a slow, detective's job of tracking your observations across time. The best tool is a good set of notes.

- How "toxic" or "healthy" do the politics seem? What do your co-workers do or say that may give you hints about whether the place is "too political"?

- How do people accomplish things at work? How do projects and ideas get approved or shot down?

◆ Who are the key "players" or people with the most influence? How do they operate?

◆ What are the other main questions or key issues in your workplace that you should be collecting observations on?

Trust your hunches. Our brains do a lot of processing of information subliminally or unconsciously. You may find that your gut feelings about your workplace or about a specific co-worker or situation are dead-on accurate. If so, it's because you're picking up cues from them or others. Check in regularly with your gut!

Understand your organization. Do you know the main issues, concerns, and challenges your company or agency is facing? Budget problems? Personnel upheavals? Drop in the stock price? These issues are the main context or threat environment in which politics are happening. It's normal to see changes in how political things get when external realities shift. (Which they always do! That "cheese" is always moving!)

As people get more anxious about the company's problems, it mobilizes more of their reptilian brain processes. Suddenly, the majority of a company's employees may be coping with activated anxiety centers such as the brain's limbic system; and so sloshing around with higher levels of stress hormones like adrenaline and cortisol. Everyone is "sensing" it, even if few say it. (Which also means everyone is going home and acting stressed, so that fragile marriages are getting strained, fights are happening, kids are acting up, and so people are coming back to work more frazzled.) In situations of such danger, people's most paranoid fantasies start to get activated.

In short, if your company is stressed, look for people to be more stressed and defensive, and for politics to get a bit more icky. (At such times, talking about it as a group may actually help. This is something you might share with superiors, and it's a classic time when well-run companies may bring in HR or outside consultants to help people manage the stress.)

Understand your co-workers. In your notebook, make a list of the people you know at work. Think about what each of them is probably most concerned about, what they hope, what they need. What are their projects? What stresses them? (You don't need extensive notes, but you're building the *habit* of being aware of individuals and their situations. That is the core of being skilled at tracking politics.)

SI and Political Skills

If you've come this far, and begun to develop some awareness of the political processes in your workplace, you're well on your way! Now it's time to put these hot skills to some use!

"Use? For what?"

Why, to get you to your goals, of course!

The reason anyone is political is to help them achieve goals. As mentioned before, sometimes these goals are just self-defense: in a toxic political setting, your job may depend on knowing where the mines are buried and which snakes not to pet.

But assuming an average-to-good political setting, there are still important reasons for honing your poly-sci techniques.

List your top five work goals. It's fine to mix "selfish" and "altruistic" goals here: helping the Tectonics Division make their numbers can rest easy next to "get my income above six figures within two years." (After all, your company's goals probably include both "do good" and "make a bundle." Why shouldn't yours?)

Got the list? Swell. Next is formulating some strategy, which is nothing more than a flexible game plan for getting from where you are now, to where you want to be. The trick is to both plan some specific steps to get there, and to be *alert to opportunities that arise.*

> **Caution!**
>
> It's not wise to make someone else's destruction one of your goals! This is both bad karma and bad politics. Your animosity will be apparent to others (you're not the only one with intuition!), and people will not trust you. Your evil plans *will* leak out, so don't make any!

Some goals are things you get to by a quick action, but many require months, or even years, of baby steps. One promptly returned phone call, an unexpected thank-you or sympathy card to a co-worker, or taking coffee breaks regularly with folks in your "network" will, over time, keep you "in circulation," make sure that the right people know you, and show others that you are a team player, a help to others, someone whom co-workers trust and like. That can be critical when a promotion opportunity arises and suddenly the fact that co-workers know and trust you may count for more than the impressive resumé of an unknown applicant with an Ivy League MBA.

Example: Say you want to help your boss achieve his goal of increasing sales in your department. (Helping your boss achieve his or her goal is generally a pretty safe and well-rewarded political goal, by the way!) What can you do?

Look around. Find opportunities to be useful. What seem to be the three main obstacles to achieving this success? Ask your boss, even—go chat about what you can do to help. Then make some plans, get busy, and start helping it happen.

Often, this is where being political starts to mean connecting with other people a bit more. For instance, you may notice that some of your co-workers are less effective because of not knowing how to manage something in their work-flows. Is there a way to be helpful with that? If someone's project "crashes" at five on Friday, can you volunteer to stay till midnight to help them get it fixed?

How about any extra work you can do that will get noticed, as long as it doesn't also annoy or threaten co-workers too much? (If you look like a classic brown-noser, your efforts may be undone.)

It's also important to know the difference between being the helpful one whom people recognize as a trusted, reliable colleague, and being the office doormat. You can help people, but for heaven's sake, have some boundaries! Always mumbling "okay" and slinking out in the rainstorm when "Scott the up-and-coming star" asks you to "go get us some coffee before the meeting, will you, hon?" is a bad move. There are times when the best response may be a loud, publicly embarrassing (to Scott) "Ex-CUSE me? Isn't it your turn to go out for the coffee?" This may even be a career-saving move.

Do you have ideas? Sell them—using all your SI skills! Do you have alliances? If not, build them! This is essential—politics is not a solo sport! And it's fine to make sure you get well-deserved credit when it's your idea that made the difference. (And if someone manages to steal the credit, use it as a learning experience, and don't let it happen again!)

A thick skin can help—people won't always flock to your swell idea. (This is where the emotional intelligence skill of regulating your emotional responses comes in handy!) You may even be wrong, or missing a big piece of the puzzle (maybe a piece that's actually a secret). So don't take it personally if someone shoots your idea down.

Helping others is generally the most powerful "tool" in any politician's arsenal! (Why else do you think your senators have constituency services offices? It's so they can do the same kinds of things any local politician—or mafioso!—does in a big city ward: favors bring connections and influence!)

SI Tip _____

Great advice from Kathleen Reardon, in her super book on organizational politics titled _The Secret Handshake_ (New York: Currency/Doubleday, 2000): _"You do have power, even if it doesn't seem that way at times. One of the last things you want to make a permanent state in your life is the feeling of powerlessness."_

A key SI skill is learning to identify the areas where you can have some influence. Just remember that working with others is the real key to success in any group of two or more humans, and you're on your way!

The Least You Need to Know

♦ "Politics" just means "people working together to accomplish goals"—and they happen all the time.

♦ Toxic political environments exist where they're tolerated by leaders, when organizations are stressed, when management decisions are made without enough transparency, or when an organization's culture has a long history of requiring unsavory politics for survival.

♦ The first step in enhancing your political skills is to learn about how things really get done in your organization.

♦ Most effective politics involves building alliances, helping people out, and being clear about how you will move toward your goals, with the help of others.

Chapter 20

Conflict Control

In This Chapter

- ◆ You can't escape conflict!
- ◆ The social intelligence of conflict
- ◆ How to beat swords into plowshares
- ◆ Mending fences the SI way

Many people think that in a perfect world there'd be no conflict. Actually, a conflict-free world would soon become a dull, lifeless place. Sure, when they're bad they're awful, but good conflicts are the basis for creativity, stronger relationships, and personal resiliency. If you know how to handle it with social intelligence, a certain degree of conflict and disagreement in life can actually be a plus.

In this chapter, we'll talk about conflicts that don't work and those that do. We'll also talk about some tips for mastering conflict situations in the workplace (though they work anywhere.)

First, let's explore your conflict IQ with a thought-provoking quiz.

Check Yourself Out

This quiz is designed to help you get some idea of your social intelligence when dealing with conflicts. Read each item and circle the answer that best describes your typical response.

1. At the first meeting of a new association, you suggest that everyone say something about their reasons for wanting the new group. Your associate Hal jumps on that, says it's a waste of time and let's get planning. So you:

   A. Acknowledge that it may take time but patiently point out that it may help us all "be sure we're on the same page," then ask what others think.

   B. Come down hard on the guy, point out he's already trying to take control of the group.

   C. Mumble "okay" and hope someone else agreed with your suggestion.

2. You're assigned to share responsibility for leading an important committee with Isabel, whom you see as too timid and overwhelmed to handle the job. So you:

   A. Say nothing since she gets anxious so easily; you hope for the best.

   B. Find an early time to ask her if she's comfortable with the group, and ask if there's anything you can do to help her.

   C. Confront her chronic and frankly tedious insecurities and suggest she either get them under control or not lead the committee.

3. A student in your class seems sexist and you think he may intimidate and stifle the female students. You:

   A. Try to expel him from the class to protect the young women.

   B. Allow the young women to manage things if they're bothered, while making sure to both support and challenge him if he needs it.

   C. Don't think it's your job to get into that stuff.

4. You put a new roof on and now your gutters are dripping and leaking; when you call your roofer, he says it's nothing he did. So you:

   A. Call a gutter repair company and eat the cost for repairs—what's the point in arguing?

   B. Ask the roofer to come by and help identify the problem, and stick to your position that you want him to fix or repair damage he clearly did.

   C. Go ballistic and threaten to sue him and report him to the Better Business Bureau.

5. You're most likely to express anger at a co-worker by saying:

   A. "I'm angry."

   B. You wouldn't say anything—not to her face, anyway!

   C. "You're making me angry."

6. The project meeting left you feeling really mad! Afterward you would typically:

   A. Take a few minutes and figure out what got you so peeved.

   B. Fume about that (expletive deleted) co-worker.

   C. Jump into work to take your mind off things.

7. As a manager, you'd feel things were "on the right track" among your creative and hard-working staff when:

   A. You went a year with no disagreements or conflicts.

   B. You had disagreements or conflicts, and usually managed to air them out and use them to grow new ideas.

   C. People have learned that you expect them to stifle disagreements and get the job done.

8. Tempers are high! One group wants to bring the wagon train through the desert, which is dangerous; the other wants to take the long way around, which may mean getting stuck in the winter snows in the mountains. As wagon train leader, you:

   A. Tell people to go whichever way they want, and good luck!

   B. Pick the best chance and get everyone in line to follow you—now!

   C. Gather everyone together and calm things down, then say you want to get the best consensus you can about which way to go and let everyone air their concerns.

9. You've paired up two staffers, each with great talent and creativity, for a project, but their style is like oil and water. Soon each of them is complaining to you about the other, and both are complaining to *your* boss. So you:

   A. Ask each if they can compromise, and try to find the positive areas of agreement.

   B. Say "Enough's enough!" and just tell them to get along and make it work.

   C. Schedule a meeting where you'd have each of them say what they dislike or disagree with in the other's position or style, and stick to it until things are resolved.

10. You're concerned that a co-worker's behavior with clients is unethical. So you:

    A. Keep your concerns to yourself.

    B. Talk about it with other co-workers and maybe report him to HR or someplace.

    C. Seek him out, close the door, and privately share your concerns—and try to understand what his perception of the situation might be.

Scoring: Circle your responses below, and tally how many you have in each column.

Item	Squeak	Roar	SI
1. (Hal)	C	B	A
2. (Isabel)	A	C	B
3. (Sexist)	C	A	B
4. (Gutters)	A	C	B

Item	Squeak	Roar	SI
5. (Angry)	B	C	A
6. (Meeting)	C	B	A
7. (Manager)	A	C	B
8. (Wagons)	A	B	C
9. (Oil/H_2O)	A	C	B
10. (Hire)	A	B	C
Totals			

Interpreting your results:

Squeak 6–10: As in "mice." Your conflict coping style is probably to anxiously avoid any. You may be overly inclined to back down and give in, even if it costs you; or you may block out any awareness that there are disagreements brewing in order to feel safe.

Roar 6–10: This is the column for beasts who roar. You probably try to manage conflicts aggressively. The main danger is that aggressive styles can backfire, particularly in a workplace. Be careful!

SI 6–10: You are likely to have a more socially intelligent conflict style: you recognize that conflicts are part of life and so face them head-on, and you've got good skills at managing the interpersonal challenges of resolving conflicts in win-win ways.

There's No Demilitarized Zone

Don'tcha sometimes wish there was a conflict-free zone or two in your life? Does it seem like all that disagreeing and hassle isn't worth it? Well, you're not alone.

Most people tend to wish there were no conflicts in life. After all, disagreements can be painful. They can threaten friendships and the peace in neighborhoods.

In workplaces, conflicts cause a whole lot of problems: increased workplace stress and anxiety levels, strained or unproductive working relationships, employee turnover, decreased productivity, client dissatisfaction, disability, absenteeism, worker sabotage, and sick leave.

So with "conflicts" being so costly and icky, why don't we just stop them?

> **Social Science**
>
> It's estimated that the average cost for replacing an unhappy employee can run from 75 percent to 150 percent of their annual salary!

If only it were that easy!

The truth is, it's nearly impossible to avoid conflicts, in almost any realm of life. That's partly because conflicts have so many causes. For instance:

♦ **Internal causes:** Most of us are walking barrels of conflicting desires and urges—each side vying for control. I want to go out, I want to stay home; I want to rest, I want to work out. Much of our life is a love-hate relationship with just about everything.

♦ **Frustration and being thwarted:** If you slip into the lane ahead of me and I have to hit the brakes, this triggers a natural response in my brain that, putting it as politely as I can, makes me want to kill you. (I used to have a little plastic death ray button on my car's dashboard for just such occasions!) Our "reptile brain" responses of anger and the desire to strike out are activated whenever anyone, for any reason, frustrates us. So imagine five of us in a room, working out disagreements for a work project!

♦ **Competing interests:** Even if we didn't have those "reptile brains" and inner conflicts, we'd have competing interests and goals. As director of a college counseling center, if my budget went up, someone else's had to go down or get a bit frozen. Of course, I deeply believed in the importance of my department's mission. So did the other department heads—they believed in my mission, but they probably believed even more in their own! Oops.

In addition to these reasons, there are scads more, both rational and irrational. How do you classify different cultural norms or expectations? These can be the usual and customary ones we talk about, such as the differences people grew up with, religious or ethnic beliefs, and such. But how about the differences in ethics and values, say, between people who see themselves as primarily business persons (whose primary goal is making money for stockholders) and their professional employees whose codes of ethics stress primary loyalty to their patients, clients, or customers (such as teachers, physicians, nurses, psychologists, or journalists who work for those business types)?

> **Social Science**
>
> One recent study found that over 40 percent of managers' time is devoted to resolving conflicts.

See? There are so many reasons for conflicts, it's impossible to keep up! And many leaders do, in fact, spend a lot of their time on conflict management.

But is all conflict bad? What about its positive benefits?

For instance, conflict can energize you. It can bring out clear thinking, both in an individual (who wants to make her clearest case to her teammates or for the jury), or it can cause people to step back and get clearer on the decisions they're making. Old, moldy assumptions are questioned and discarded. Fresh thinking and new, creative resolutions may suddenly occur. People can get more innovative, or develop better "human" qualities of learning to listen, to have empathy for another person's point of view, or to sometimes yield gracefully on something that isn't so important after all.

In short, creativity, maturity, and better social intelligence skills may all blossom from the stinky piles of conflict in your life.

SI Keys to Conflict Control

The real question is not "How can we eliminate conflicts?" but "How can we improve the odds that our conflicts will be more helpful than harmful?"

That's where your social intelligence skills come in! If you can manage your emotional response to a conflict, tune in to the other person's feelings with genuine empathy, and make contact in a way that facilitates a respectful give and take of opinions, many conflicts can become *win-win* situations.

Let's look at a simple example of a conflict. You and a colleague have to plan a training meeting for junior staff members. You want to break the meeting into small groups so they can practice their new skills and ask questions. Your colleague, however, just wants to do a full day of PowerPoint presentations.

def•i•ni•tion _____

Win-win solutions are those in which each side benefits.

This triggers a fight! You insist that the staff needs to really practice and discuss this stuff—it's too new and complicated. Besides, you personally dislike watching or giving PowerPoint talks—you think they put everyone to sleep! Your co-worker is irritated, though he doesn't say anything direct. You don't resolve the issue but wander off onto other topics, but when he writes up a memo to your mutual boss on the status of the workshop plans, he writes "We'll do a PowerPoint presentation, and may have some time for discussion afterward." You feel sabotaged, and enraged!

(Feel free to imagine things escalating from here—up to and including your car's front end dented in, and white chalk outlines of your co-worker on the pavement of the corporate parking lot!)

Or ...

... you could play it differently. Let's replay the scenario, only this time you wear your Social Intelligence Traveling Cap (the red one with the little propellers on top!)

So ... going back in time ... your colleague and you disagree about the format. At this point, you realize you're having a feeling! Ick! It's an angry feeling. Frustration. Vague sick feelings as you imagine sitting through—yes, that's it!—another one of his long, boring PowerPoint thingies, all bullet points and no real point.

Good: so far you're doing some internal processing of your emotions. (You haven't shared any of this with him, right?) You take a moment to calm down, then pull Biff aside.

"Ahem," you start. "Biff, it feels to me we're starting to have some tension about this decision, and I'd appreciate if we can take a few minutes to talk it out."

SI Tip

It can be more effective to start by saying, "I have some feelings about this," than to just launch in. It's also important to state your own feelings, instead of labeling the other person, or saying they've "made" you angry. "I'm uncomfortable" is more helpful than "You're making me uncomfortable."

Great job! Now, you're off to an open, honest start. Because you've stated something he was probably already sensing: that you're getting angry. Most of the time, if you've presented this in a caring, controlled way, and opened it up for a mutual discussion, he ought to respond fairly well.

From here, the discussion might go in a few directions. But the next thing you are careful to do (you SI genius, you!) is to *tune in to Biff's feelings.* Sure, you know he's sometimes a bit full of himself, and so he wants to get up and make speeches all day. But let him give you his version of that. It may surprise you.

For instance, you may say, "I get the sense you really enjoy giving presentations."

Then you nod, listen as he talks about how when he was a small boy growing up on the farm back in Iowa, he used to go out to the pond at night and talk to the frogs, and they'd all grow quiet and listen.

Whereupon you'd say something empathic—but also gently assertive—about hoping you can find some creative way to blend his skills (you *don't* add, "at frog-whispering"!) with adding some variety for the students. "How can we manage that?" you then ask. "Because," you then say, "I guess I'd want to have some time with you leading my small group, too, so I could check out my understanding of your ideas and get your input."

Or something like that. Generally, it's a blend of eliciting feelings, sharing your own, and looking at the pros and cons of the different choices. But the main thing is that you are *working to keep Biff engaged*, instead of triggering defensiveness.

Of course, your mileage may vary. But assuming Biff is not a walking powder keg in addition to a frog-whisperer, you may find that he'll respond well to your emotionally self-regulated, empathic, assertive statements, as long as you've also given him the chance to express himself and to problem solve with you.

Remember, emotions in you trigger emotions in him. If you can create the right emotional tone of respectful listening and give-and-take, and maybe even make this an enjoyable heart-to-heart talk, your odds of a successful solution are greatly increased.

Tips for Conflict Management

The first step in dealing with any conflict is recognizing that there's one going on! That may seem obvious, but in real life, it's not always so easy! Sometimes you only figure out much later that someone was waging a war with you! Or that people or a group were working hard behind the scenes to sink the great plan that you were all enthused about putting into operation.

If you had some kind of workplace command and control center with a huge world conflict map on it, you might map all of the main areas of your work setting on it. These might include an organization chart, a list of the major processes or projects people are working on, and so on.

Then you might start to put little red flag pins on the map where each of these things is happening: overt complaints by one worker about another; sarcasm; indirect criticisms of various people or departments; downshifts in productivity in some areas; sabotage, undermining, or passive-aggressive behavior; tension between people; people avoiding working with each other; stressed workers or departments; deadlines being missed; poor or deteriorating communications; actual backstabbing or formal complaints (which may have nothing to do with the actual reason for the conflicts.)

What would your company's map look like? How about your personal conflict map?

SI Tip

Jot down three of the top areas of conflict in your current workplace. As you read on, fill in any signs or symptoms of conflict that are mentioned in the text that you realize are part of these real-life situations of yours. Then brainstorm any other warning signs that may be present.

Once you have developed your conflict map (keep it up! there will always be new outbreaks!), use some of the following suggestions to improve your management of the messes.

Manage Your Urge to Go Rambo!

Conflicts create frustration, and frustration gives you that automatic, reptile-brain "smash the candy machine if it won't give me my goodie!" response. As you review your list of conflicts, or realize you're in one, you may start to feel your blood boiling.

This is when it's important to handle those angry emotions like the virtual flasks of nitroglycerine that they are! Unmanaged anger (or other intense feelings, such as anxiety) can lead to rash words and actions, which will damage your credibility and ability to work together with others.

> **Caution!**
>
> Be extra careful when e-mailing anyone about workplace conflicts! It's easy to leak negative feelings, even if what you write seems technically neutral or fair. Don't leave a permanent record of your peeved feelings that may come back to haunt you!

It's not that you shouldn't ever be angry at work! You can't be a robot, and if you're never peeved at someone or something, you're probably asleep at the emotional wheel.

But strong feelings can be damaging if not handled well. If nothing else, they may just undermine your credibility with co-workers. ("He's the one with the temper!") Eventually, this can interfere with your career. And as they say in the CIA, you can usually expect blowback for angry slashes against your co-workers.

Take a long walk, vent in your journal (not the one on your work computer!) or to your local bartender. If you can't manage the intensity of your feelings on your own, you may need to consult with a pro, such as a workplace coach, a consulting business psychologist, or someone outside the workplace.

Also remember that avoidance of feelings is a problem, too! Because while you're telling yourself "it doesn't bother me," your voice and body are probably telling other people that yes, it sure does bother you!

Assertiveness and Empathy Skills

The key is to find the balance between asserting your own opinions and having empathy and concern for others in the workplace. When it comes to managing conflicts, this blend is truly the magic elixir.

When you're working with people and run into a conflict, it's the blend of assertiveness and empathy that can help you to bring up, acknowledge, and talk about the fact that there is a disagreement or conflict going on. Then it's often useful, especially if things don't pretty quickly sort themselves out, to acknowledge your understanding that the other person or group may have some pretty strong feelings about the situation.

> **Caution!** _____
>
> Try to be honest when you're saying that you "understand how they feel." People get tired of form e-mails and customer service scripts that involve being told how sorry "we at the corporation are" that their computer just crashed. Nobody believes business dishonesty.

Approaching others with assertive empathy opens the door to the real work of conflict resolution: finding those win-win solutions.

Finding the Best Win-Win Wins!

Most things become clichés with good reason, and the phrase "win-win solutions" is one of them. A good reason for a cliché is that it's usually, actually, a really good idea, but then everyone repeats and overuses the term.

So let's take a moment and appreciate the real potential beauty of a win-win solution.

A win-win is a solution in which you've really gone to the mat, if need be, to fully express your best ideas about a problem—and also heard the other side(s). This requires not just a discussion of the issues, but a team approach that includes opening up as much as need be about what the real meanings, concerns, and feelings about the issue are.

A group might brainstorm a problem, for instance, and spend enough time so that all the opposing viewpoints and concerns are pretty well aired. If the process happens among a group of mostly socially intelligent people, we'll see these things happening in that process:

1. Everyone will be tuned in to both their own and the other folks' feelings, as well as really working hard to "get" their suggestions and opinions and ideas.

2. This will mean that everyone will have dramatically expanded their understanding and grasp of the problem—it's complexities, different angles for viewing it, and so on. Essentially, this will be the equivalent of everyone in the room sharing or linking their brains, to create a collaboration that is "bigger than any

of us." (Note, again, the importance of everyone feeling free to be honest for this process to work. Since emotions are truly contagious, one person's anxiety will be a distorting field on the process.)

3. As people continue to explore, generally some new, better ideas may be expected to come out of this stew of input. Often, these new ideas, at first even wild-seeming ideas, can turn into the truest and most creative solutions.

When this process is really understood, it becomes clear why it's actually much better than a simple compromise, though compromising may, indeed, be one of the outcomes. At best, it's a creative and new solution—and not just a cliché!

Growing and Mending Fences

As you grow in your social intelligence skills, you will develop a broader and more self-aware perspective on your past ways of managing conflicts. You may realize that you've fought with others in less than admirable ways. You may have been unkind, less empathic and caring than you wish you had been.

Sometimes, you even realize that your work relationships are still being affected by old feuds, maybe over things that aren't even live issues anymore.

While people are actually experts at rehearsing old grievances, perhaps it's time for a more mature approach. Maybe you've come to a point where you see you should seek out some old adversaries, bury the proverbial hatchet, and make peace. If you do, you'll not only reconnect with someone you may find useful or (less selfishly) a good friend, but you may also relieve yourself, and your overloaded social brain, of some of the burden of self-defense and self-righteous defensiveness that you've carried around with you for a long time.

Is there anyone in your life you need to reconnect with, to mend some fences? How long do you plan to take?

The Least You Need to Know

- There are few demilitarized zones in life—most human situations hold the potential for conflict!

- Conflicts can be destructive, but they can also energize people, motivate them to improve themselves and their work, and spur creativity.

◆ The key to productive conflict is to maximize your socially intelligent style of working with others: manage your emotions, tune in to them and why they feel and want what they want, and work together toward a more creative outcome.

◆ The best solutions to conflicts involve win-win solutions that may transcend the originally preferred solutions of the people involved.

◆ Old conflicts are a toxic burden on your soul. If you have some fences to mend, it's better to go out and do it than to carry the old fence on your back forever!

Appendix A

Recommended Reading

Social Intelligence–General Reading

Albrecht, Karl. *Social Intelligence: The New Science of Success.* San Francisco: Jossey-Bass, 2006.

Franklin, Benjamin. *Autobiography.* In *Franklin: Writings (Library of America).* New York: Literary Classics of the United States, 1987.

Goleman, Daniel. *Emotional Intelligence: 10th Anniversary Edition; Why It Can Matter More Than IQ.* New York: Bantam, 2006.

———. *Social Intelligence: The New Science of Human Relationships.* New York: Bantam, 2006.

Development of SI and Attachment

Bowlby, John. *A Secure Base: Parent-Child Attachment and Healthy Human Development.* New York: Basic Books, 1988.

Karen, Robert. *Becoming Attached: First Relationships and How They Shape Our Capacity to Love.* New York: Oxford University Press, 1994.

Siegel, Daniel. *The Developing Mind: How Relationships and the Brain Interact to Shape Who We Are.* New York: Guilford, 1999.

Stern, Daniel. *The Interpersonal World of the Infant.* New York: Basic Books, 1985.

———. *Diary of a Baby.* New York: Basic Books, 1990, 1998.

Introversion

Laney, Marti Olsen. *The Introvert Advantage: How to Thrive in an Extrovert World.* New York: Workman Books, 2002.

———. *The Hidden Gifts of the Introverted Child: Helping Your Child Thrive in an Extroverted World.* New York: Workman Books, 2005.

Wagele, Elizabeth. *The Happy Introvert: A Wild and Crazy Guide for Celebrating Your True Self.* Berkeley, CA: Ulysses Press, 2006.

Assertiveness

Alberti, Robert, and Michael Emmons. Your Perfect Right: Assertiveness and Equality in Your Life and Relationships. Atascadero, CA: Impact Publishers, 2001.

Peterson, Randy. *The Assertiveness Workbook: How to Express Your Ideas and Stand Up for Yourself at Work and in Relationships.* Oakland, CA: New Harbinger Publications, 2000.

Smith, Manuel. *When I Say No, I Feel Guilty.* New York: Bantam, 1975.

Shyness

Antony, Martin, and Richard Swinson. *The Shyness & Social Anxiety Workbook: Proven Techniques for Overcoming Your Fears.* Oakland, CA: New Harbinger Publications, 2000.

Burns, David. *Intimate Connections.* New York: New American Library, 1985.

Hilliard, Erika. *Living Fully with Shyness and Social Anxiety: A Comprehensive Guide to Gaining Social Confidence.* New York: Avalon, 2005.

Zimbardo, Philip. *Shyness: What It Is, What to Do About It.* Cambridge, MA: Da Capo, 1990.

Empathy

Ciaramicoli, Arthur, and Katherine Ketcham. *The Power of Empathy.* London: Piatkus Books, 2000.

Kohn, Alfie. *The Brighter Side of Human Nature: Altruism & Empathy in Everyday Life.* New York: Basic Books, 1990.

Rogers, Carl. *A Way of Being.* New York: Houghton Mifflin, 1980.

———. *On Becoming a Person.* New York: Houghton Mifflin, 1961, 1995.

Intimacy

Kelly, Matthew. *The Seven Levels of Intimacy: The Art of Loving and the Joy of Being Loved.* New York: Fireside, 2005.

Piorkowski, Geraldine. *Too Close for Comfort: Exploring the Risks of Intimacy.* Cambridge, MA: Perseus, 1994.

Toxic Relationships

Bernstein, Albert. *Emotional Vampires: Dealing with People Who Drain You Dry.* New York: McGraw-Hill, 2001.

Evans, Patricia. *Controlling People: How to Recognize, Understand, and Deal with People Who Try to Control You.* Avon, MA: Adams Media, 2002.

Forward, Susan. *Emotional Blackmail: When the People in Your Life Use Fear, Obligation, and Guilt to Manipulate You.* New York: HarperCollins, 1977.

———. *Toxic Parents: Overcoming Their Hurtful Legacy and Reclaiming Your Life.* New York: Bantam, 1989.

Friendship

Carnegie, Dale. *How to Win Friends and Influence People.* New York: Pocket Books, 1981.

Goodman, Ellen, and Patricia O'Brien. *I Know Just What You Mean: The Power of Friendship in Women's Lives.* New York: Simon & Schuster, 2000.

Yager, Jan. *Friendships: The Power of Friendship and How It Shapes Our Lives.* Stamford, CT: Hannacroix Creek Books, 1999.

Romance

Fenton, Bradley. *Stumbling Naked in the Dark: Overcoming Mistakes Men Make with Women.* Victoria, Canada: Trafford, 2003.

Valentis, Mary, and John Valentis. *Romantic Intelligence: How to Be as Smart in Love as You Are in Life*. Oakland, CA: New Harbinger Publications, 2003.

Sex and SI

Comfort, Alex. *The Joy of Sex: Fully Revised & Completely Updated for the 21st Century*. New York: Crown Publishers, 2002.

Locker, Sari. *The Complete Idiot's Guide to Amazing Sex, Second Edition*. New York: Alpha Books, 2003.

Schnarch, David. *Passionate Marriage: Keeping Love and Intimacy Alive in Committed Relationships*. New York: Holt Paperbacks, 1998.

Valentis, Mary, and John Valentis. *Romantic Intelligence: How to Be as Smart in Love as You Are in Life*. Oakland, CA: New Harbinger Publications, 2003.

Marriage/Commitment

Gottman, John. *Why Marriages Succeed or Fail: And How You Can Make Yours Last*. New York: Fireside, 1994.

Gottman, John, and Nan Silver. *The Seven Principles for Making Marriage Work*. New York: Three Rivers Press, 1999.

Wallerstein, Judith, and Sandra Blakeslee. *The Good Marriage: How and Why Love Lasts*. New York: Warner Books, 1995.

Parenting and Children

Elias, Maurice, Steven Tobias, and Brian Friedlander. *Emotionally Intelligent Parenting*. New York: Three Rivers Press, 2000.

Elkind, David. *The Hurried Child: 25th Anniversary Edition*. Cambridge, MA: Da Capo Lifelong Books, 2006.

Ginott, Hiam, Alice Ginott, and H. Wallace Goddard. *Between Parent and Child (Revised Edition)*. New York: Three Rivers Press, 1965, 2003.

Gottman, John, Joan Declaire, and Daniel Goleman. *Raising an Emotionally Intelligent Child*. New York: Fireside, 1997.

Siegel, Daniel, and Mary Hartzell. *Parenting from the Inside Out*. New York: Jeremy P. Tarcher/Penguin, 2003.

Workplace & Career Success

Covey, Stephen. *The 7 Habits of Highly Effective People*. New York: Simon and Schuster, 1989.

Cherniss, Cary, and Daniel Goleman (editors). *The Emotionally Intelligent Workplace: How to Select for, Measure and Improve Emotional Intelligence in Individuals, Groups and Organizations*. San Francisco: Jossey-Bass, 2001.

Goleman, Daniel. *Working with Emotional Intelligence*. New York: Bantam, 1998.

Networking

Ferrazzi, Keith, and Tahl Raz. *Never Eat Alone: And Other Secrets to Success, One Relationship at a Time*. New York: Random House, 2005.

Fisher, Donna, and Sandy Vilas. *Power Networking, 2nd Edition*. Austin, TX: Bard Press, 2000.

Mackay, Harvey. *Dig Your Well Before You're Thirsty: The Only Networking Book You'll Ever Need*. New York: Currency, 1997.

Managing

Boyatzis, Richard, and Annie McKee. *Resonant Leadership*. Boston: Harvard Business School, 2005.

Collins, Jim. *Good to Great: Why Some Companies Make the Leap... and Others Don't*. New York: HarperCollins, 2001.

George, Bill, David Gergen, and Peter Sims. *True North: Discover Your Authentic Leadership*. San Francisco: Wiley, 2007.

Goleman, Daniel, Annie McKee, and Richard Boyatzis. *Primal Leadership: Realizing the Power of Emotional Intelligence*. Boston: Harvard Business School, 2002.

Hughes, Marcia, Bonita Patterson, James Bradford Terrell, and Reuven Bar-On. *Emotional Intelligence in Action: Training and Coaching Activities for Leaders and Managers*. San Francisco: Pfeiffer, 2005.

Clients

Selby, John. *Listening with Empathy: Creating Genuine Connections with Customers and Colleagues*. Charlottesville, VA: Hampton Roads Publishing, 2007.

Politics

Reardon, Kathleen. *The Secret Handshake: Mastering the Politics of the Business Inner Circle*. New York: Doubleday, 2001.

————. *It's All Politics: Winning in a World Where Hard Work and Talent Aren't Enough*. New York: Doubleday, 2005.

Conflict

Cloke, Kenneth, and Joan Goldsmith. *Resolving Conflicts at Work: Eight Strategies for Everyone on the Job*. San Francisco: Jossey-Bass, 2000, 2005.

Maravelas, Anna. *How to Reduce Workplace Conflict and Stress: How Leaders and Their Employees Can Protect Their Sanity and Productivity from Tension and Turf Wars*. Franklin Lakes, NJ: Career Press, 2005.

Rosenberg, Marshall. *We Can Work It Out: Resolving Conflicts Peacefully and Powerfully*. Encinitas, CA: PuddleDancer Press, 2005.

Web Resources on Social and Emotional Intelligence

What follows is a grab-bag list of some cool links on SI and EI. Of course, web links change all the time, as do their content, but this is a good set of starting points.

For expert professional help:

American Psychological Association's "therapist locator" website: locator. apa.org

Psychology Today's "find a therapist" website—a gateway to thousands of therapists near you: therapists.psychologytoday.com/rms/prof_search.php

International Coach Federation—the best place to find an expert coach to help with workplace or personal life SI skills: www.coachfederation.org

For more info on social intelligence:

Emotions and emotional intelligence—an older website with lots of links: www.socialresearchmethods.net/Gallery/Young/emotion.htm#_jmp0_

The latest in emotional intelligence: www.eisource.com

Some more scholarly papers on SI: www.pubmedcentral.nih.gov/ articlerender.fcgi?artid=2042522#_jmp0_

Wikipedia article on SI (which will be updated on an ongoing basis): en.wikipedia.org/wiki/Social_intelligence

Daniel Goleman's info website—www.danielgoleman.info/social_intelligence/resources.html#_jmp0_

See also his blog site: www.danielgoleman.info/blog

"Is Social Intelligence More Useful Than IQ?" (October 23, 2006). *Talk of the Nation, NPR*: www.npr.org/templates/story/story.php?storyId=6368484

Social Intelligence, an online paper by John F. Kihlstron and Nancy Cantor (an edited version of this chapter was published in R.J. Sternberg (Ed.), *Handbook of Intelligence*, 2nd ed. (pp. 359–379). Cambridge, U.K.: Cambridge University Press, 2000): socrates.berkeley.edu/~kihlstrm/social_intelligence.htm

Open Directory Project, with many web resources on EI and SI: www.dmoz.org/Science/Social_Sciences/Psychology/Intelligence/Emotional_Intelligence/#_jmp0_

Consortium for Research on Emotional Intelligence in Organizations: www.eiconsortium.org

BNET—Resources on emotional intelligence in business: resources.bnet.com/topic/emotional+intelligence.html#_jmp0_

Emotions and emotional intelligence: www.socialresearchmethods.net/Gallery/Young/emotion.htm#_jmp0_

Themanager.org, a resource page on human resources management and EI: www.themanager.org/Knowledgebase/HR/EI.htm#_jmp0_

Info for teachers on enhancing children's emotional intelligence: www.edutopia.org/teacher-resources-social-emotional-learning#_jmp0_

More educational resources: www.bu.edu/sed/caec/

Developmental Studies Center, an educational programming with a SI focus: www.devstu.org/cdp/index.html

Collaborative for Academic, Social, and Emotional Learning: www.casel.org/

Columbia Business School's program on social intelligence: www4.gsb.columbia.edu/psi#_jmp0_

Index

D

V

W–X–Y–Z

Check out these BEST-SELLERS

READ BY MILLIONS!

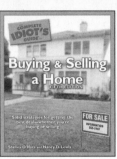

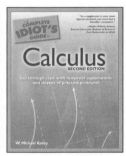

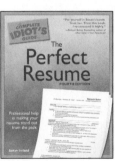
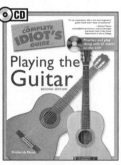